CHICANO EDUCATION
IN THE ERA
OF SEGREGATION

CHICANO EDUCATION
IN THE ERA
OF SEGREGATION

Gilbert G. Gonzalez

Number 7 in the Al Filo: Mexican American Studies Series
Robert R. Calderón, Series Editor

Denton, Texas

Preface to 2013 Edition Copyright by Gilbert G. Gonzalez

Permissions: University of North Texas Press
1155 Union Circle #311336
Denton, TX 769203-5017

10 9 8 7 6 5 4 3 2 1

The paper used in this publication meets the requirements of the
American National Standard for Permanence of Paper
for Printed Library Materials Z39.48-1984.

Library of Congress Cataloging-in-Publication Data

Gonzalez, Gilbert G. 1941–
Chicano Education in the Era of Segregation / Gilbert G. Gonzalez
p. cm.
Number 7 in the Al Filo: Mexican American
Studies Series; Robert R. Calderón, Series Editor
Includes bibliographical references and index
ISBN 978-1-57441-501-8 (alk. paper)
1. Mexican American children—Education—Southwestern States.
2. Mexicans—Education—Southwestern States. 3. Segregation in education
—Southwestern States. 4. Public schools—Southwestern States I. Title.

2683.3.G66 1990
371.97′6872073′079—dc20

*Dedicated to my Father
José Antonio Gonzalez*

Table of Contents

List of Figures

PREFACE

Much of the history addressed in this book has changed, and yet much remains the same. When historians first began to study the Chicano community, their emphasis was on the Southwest and often their home state and, of course, on the Mexican community. Things have changed enormously since then and the Latino population, including the Mexican community, is now spread across the nation. Chicano historians have moved onto new cultural landscapes to include migration from Puerto Rico and Central and South America and yet critical aspects of the social relations discussed in this book relative to the Mexican community have remained. Into the transition to the twenty-first century, segregation based largely on anti-immigrant politics has been combined with anti-undocumented politics and a neo-liberal ideology promoting privatization. To bring the educational experience up-to-date it is useful first to contextualize the educational experience of the Latino community.

Many studies of the Chicano, and now the Latino, community focus on domestic issues, as this book did when it was first published in 1990. However, the transnational conditions underlying migration, settlements and the social and political relations with the larger society are central to explaining this history. That is not to say that the domestic issues examined were not real or important. They are. However, domestic theories that indict an entire people and the educational practices that follow fall within a transnational context, particularly the economic and political relations of the U.S. with the sending countries. Let's examine that context in order to explain the educational history of the Latino peoples.

THE MEXICAN PROBLEM

In the early twentieth century a widespread alert warned of a "Mexican Problem" that was coming across the border and threatening to seriously infest the culture of the United States, particularly the Southwest. Nearly a million Mexican migrants entered over the first three decades of the twentieth century, forming the first phase of Mexican migration, a migration created by the economic expansion of U.S. investors, financiers and corporations into Mexico that uprooted Mexican peasantry on a massive scale. Mexican historian and demographer Moises Gonzalez Navarro estimated that 300,000 peasants were removed from traditional, self-subsistent agricultural villages due to railroad construction by U.S. corporations.[1] Uprooting sent the migrants on the migratory trail first in Mexico to work on U.S. economic investments; the same corporate investors then eventually recruited them into the U.S. Exclusion from the 1917 Literacy Act, which required migrants to be literate, and quotas from the national immigration policies of the early 1920s eased the entry of needed laborers into mines, railroads, agriculture and laundries. No sooner had migrants, documented or undocumented, set roots in *colonias* and *barrios* across the Southwest than word spread that the "Mexican Problem" had arrived. A statement by a U.S. citizen active in Protestant ministry in Mexico tells of the growing reaction to Mexican migration: " 'That Mexican' no longer lives in Mexico, he lives in the United States... The Mexican Problem... reaches from Gopher Prairie to Guatemala." [2] A swell of works in the media and academic and popular journals began to appear widely to address the newly coined phrase. The *Reader's Digest* listed fifty-one articles published between 1920 and 1930 on the "Mexican Problem" whereas only nineteen were published the decade earlier.[3]

And what was the "Mexican Problem"? A collection of distinguishing characteristics defined the "Problem": a culture and/or inherited characteristics predisposed Mexicans to laziness and poverty, to a "Manana syndrome," a proclivity to violence and heavy drinking, low intellectual abilities and more. Former U.S. Consul in Nogales, Frederick Simpich, put it this way:

> ...the undeniable fact that we do differ so widely from the Mexicans in race, in political and social habits and standards, and in history, traditions, and thinking processes, makes the settlement of the problem immensely difficult.[4]

Simpich described not only the migrants but also the whole of Mexico, a transnational definition viewing Mexico from a colonial mindset. Academics, political figures, the news media and public administrators took up the task and addressed the means for resolving a potential cultural infection that the "Mexican Problem" threatened.

The Santa Ana Board of Education in Southern California, for instance, met in March 1928, to discuss the rising number Mexican residents and related matters. A recommendation was made:

> Mr. Gardner objected to so much being spent on a Mexican school, especially when we do not have proper facilities for American school children. He advocated separate schools for Mexicans as has been the plan, which Superintendent Cranston explained was the only solution to the Mexican Problem.[5]

Most school administrators and academics studying the matter agreed. And what did the Mexican Schools emphasize? A former student at one of the Santa Ana schools described his experience:

> They didn't want us to speak Spanish. I remember they said, "You guys, I don't want to catch you speaking Spanish". We couldn't help it. That's all we knew at home... They kept warning us. They'd tell us "we're going to send you back to Mexico" because they wanted to scare us that way.[6]

Solving the "Mexican Problem" and all that it encompassed required the complete Americanization of the entire Mexican population, immigrant and future generations. Indeed, for the next several generations Mexican children were schooled in a segregated system with an emphasis on Americanization and industrial education. Even though desegregation court decisions eliminated de jure segregation, the remnants of the segregated era remained. Into the 1970s, Americanization was either the first order of education or a leading goal (along with an emphasis on industrial education). However, things moved forward in the 1960s and into the seventies with less emphasis on industrial education and increasing college preparation courses, enforcing affirmative action and rising attendance in higher education. However, into the late twentieth century the "Mexican Problem" was revived, this time defined as a social illness that no amount of Americanization could overcome.

THE "ILLEGAL ALIEN" PROBLEM

After the U.S. opened the door to Mexican labor in the first three decades of the twentieth century, the door closed as the Great Depression hit and a mass deportation drive returned nearly 500,000 to Mexico. Shortly after, with the installation of the Bracero Program in 1942, which implemented a controlled contract labor force to work primarily in agriculture, a large flow of undocumented laborers was attracted back into the same fields and was welcomed by growers. Over time the undocumented, labeled "wetbacks," grew to significant numbers and became a news story addressed widely by the *New York Times, Life* magazine and *Paramount* theatre newsreels among others. "Wetbacks" came to be addressed as a national problem. A remedy soon appeared. In 1954 Operation Wetback led by the Border Patrol deported 1,089,583 and the Bracero Program became the channel through which potential undocumented could enter for work. By the mid-1950s the Program grew to import nearly half a million men a year. However, what the Bracero Program did was to institutionalize working in the United States and when the Program came to an end in 1964 (after twenty-two years) the men contracted as braceros and accustomed to work in the U.S., continued to migrate but without papers, as undocumented. In the 1970s the undocumented again came to be seen as a national "problem," the "Mexican Problem," and over the next few decades came to be redefined as the "illegal alien problem." Few alarmist nativists (or defenders of the migrants) considered that the Bracero Program, the contract labor policy of the United States working on behalf of corporate growers, constructed the second phase of Mexican migration.

The question of assimilation into the dominant culture became a national political matter again, raising much discussion. The 1960s Chicano educational reform movement pushed against forced Americanization and the emphasis on vocational education and brought bilingual education into practice, which itself soon came under criticism. In 1983 a panel of educators from the Twentieth Century Fund led by Diane Ravitch, Professor at Teachers College at Columbia University, declared bilingual education a barrier to educational success. She stood with President Reagan who alleged bilingual education is "absolutely wrong."[7] The criticisms continued but with a new dimension added: the undocumented. In a 1986 article titled "Unassimilated Illegal Immigrants Imperil Society, Lamm Tells Panel," Richard D. Lamm, governor of Colorado, offered Americanization as the solution for the dangers posed by undocumented Mexican immigrants.[8] Note that the headline read "Illegal Immigrants," a new definition of undocumented migrants as "illegals." With the passing of the Immigration Reform and Control Act in 1986 the "illegal alien" problem was somewhat resolved for the time being. The matter of immigration moved onto heightened levels of concern, but Americanization remained an educational goal aimed across the U.S. Latino community, both documented and undocumented.

THE AGE OF NAFTA

By the end of the century and into the twenty-first century, Americanization as the main remedy was thrown overboard and discarded for border walls, border patrols, mass deportation drives and guest worker programs. Keeping Mexicans out became the principal means to resolve the late twentieth century "Mexican Problem." Nonetheless, immigration continued and even rose to new heights under the weight of NAFTA, the neoliberal trade agreement passed in 1994, which President Clinton promised would "lift all boats." Instead American imports drove Mexican peasants off their lands on a massive scale and onto the same migratory trails opened in the early twentieth century, followed by the braceros, to become the third wave of Mexican migration.[9] The undocumented as a percentage of Mexican migrants rose to new levels, believed to outnumber the documented during the first decade of the new century. An estimated 11.2 million undocumented migrants had come to make the United States their home by the first decade of the new century. Meanwhile, the newly coined term "illegal alien" came into common usage, the resuscitation of the early twentieth century "Mexican Problem." This version of the "Mexican Problem" defined undocumented immigrants (without evidence) as the principal cause of a spate of problems. Among the many claims were that they pay no taxes, that they take jobs away from residents, that they depend on welfare, that they increase criminality and that they undermine the culture and political institutions of the United States.

New organizations began to form to take up the political campaign to enforce laws to counter the "illegal aliens." The director of the newly founded Federation for American Immigration Reform, Ira Mehlman, wrote that "Illegal Immigrants alone cost California $3 billion" and that in New York the "net cost for all immigration to that state, legal and illegal, was $5.6 last year [1993]" (note that Mehlman did not distinguish between documented and undocumented).[10] A 1995 headline in the *Orange County Register* took up the story: "Study finds immigrants receive more welfare benefits."[11] Two years later an article headline in the *Los Angeles Times* read: "Immigration Study Urges New Curbs and Criteria... New Barriers to Immigration Urged." The Rand Corporation think tank that conducted the study declared that "the California economy cannot continue to absorb large flows of poorly educated immigrants..."[12] A spokesperson for then-Governor Pete Wilson added that "illegal immigrants represent an 'enormous' drain on the state treasury."

Those who charged Mexican immigrants with looting the state treasury, increasing crime or taking away jobs, ignored the news reports clearly demonstrating that peoples were uprooted from their towns and cities due to the massive imports channeled into Mexico via NAFTA. Migrants were escaping from an economic disaster as one headline testified: "Mexican farms go to seed under NAFTA."[13] A few years after NAFTA's passage 600 *campesinos* (peasants) were leaving the Mexican countryside daily unable to compete with imported agricultural and meat products. According to Victor Quintana, deputy in the Mexican Congress, eight years after the passage of NAFTA 1.6 million hectares of previously cultivated land was abandoned and 1.8 million people forced to leave the countryside.[14] More than agriculture suffered as 17,000 businesses went bankrupt and 36 percent of 1100 capital goods plants shut down. By 1995, unemployment reached 30 percent of workers, affecting 11 percent of the population and poverty increased such that the majority lived in poverty. According to the World Bank, "since the inauguration of NAFTA (1994–2000) the number of people living below the poverty line has risen to 36 million persons or 62 percent of the economically active population."[15] Earnings fell dramatically. Before NAFTA Mexican factory wages were 23 percent of U.S. wages; after NAFTA they fell to 12 percent. Meanwhile, Mexico has become one of the most economically polarized nations in the world, being home to the richest man in the world, Carlos Slim Helo, while migration became the means for millions to avoid hunger. The third phase of Mexican migration to the United States moved along the old routes, a social consequence of an imperial trade agreement fashioned in Washington D.C. Meanwhile, President Clinton implemented and George W. Bush continued Operation Gatekeeper, the newest version of Operation Wetback, which resulted in border walls forcing the undocumented into dangerous mountain and desert terrain with hundreds of deaths yearly, reaching 562 in 2007. Fifteen years after NAFTA was passed an estimated 5,600 migrants have lost their lives.[16]

THE ANTI-IMMIGRANT MOVEMENT

Into the twenty-first century undocumented migration surged forward dramatically and an old formula for resolving the matter was pulled out of the archives by President Bush: a new bracero program titled a "guest worker program" to resolve the undocumented migration by channeling them into a labor program. With Mexico's President Fox, Bush began a series of discussions for initiating negotiations for a new contract labor program, otherwise known as a cheap, highly controlled labor importation program. However, 9/11 pulled Bush away and into the Iraq and Afghanistan wars, while undocumented migrations continued and rose to new heights, as migrants escaped the economic disaster wrought by free trade.

Potentially violent private organizations had already formed around restricting immigration, particularly stopping undocumented migration. On the margins of a U.S. Marine Camp in Oceanside, California, in the summer of 1994, for instance, "six paramilitary style attackers posing as immigration officers stormed the migrant camp... wearing camouflage uniforms, guns, helmets, dog tags and combat boots" and proceeded to chase down agricultural workers and beat them.[17] Three years after that attack, six organizations from across the nation met in Schaum-

burg, Illinois, to initiate discussions to form a broad national organization.[18] Eventually fourteen members formed the National Grassroots
Alliance to support stronger border military presence to keep undocumented out. Armed paramilitary groups formed as well. The Civil Homeland Defense formed in Tombstone, Arizona, one of three groups organized by 2002 to patrol the border and detain and hold any suspected
undocumented migrant.[19] Vigilante groups joined in to run down the
migrants escaping from an economy hurtling downhill fast and moved
inland. The Minutemen moved from the border to a day laborer center in
Phoenix demonstrating with bullhorns shouting, "This is America, not
Mexico" and began taking photographs of the men waiting for a job offer,
forcing them into hiding.[20]

While paramilitaries patrolled the border, state legislatures proposed
measures that took up the cause of the grassroots organizations. California Governor Pete Wilson led the charge in 1994 with Proposition
187, named the "Save our State" initiative, aimed at denying the undocumented the right to public education, welfare and health care.[21] Fifty-
nine percent of California voters passed the measure, convinced that
"illegals" threatened their state. Although the proposition was contested
and declared unconstitutional, the ruling mattered little as more states
flexed their muscles to restrict immigration in a variety of similar ways.
The anti "illegal" agenda in California moved along a broad pathway
and three years later the state passed Proposition 209 which prohib-
ited affirmative action policies across the board. In keeping with Proposition 209, ten years later the Virginia legislature considered banning
"Illegal Immigrants" from attending state colleges and universities.[22]
Colorado Representative Tom Tancredo proposed legislation denying
birthright citizenship if parents are not citizens or permanent residents.[23]
In Colorado "activists pushing to curb illegal immigration," proposed an
initiative "barring all but emergency services to undocumented immigrants."[24] Meanwhile, Arizona voters approved Proposition 200 that
"requires proof of citizenship when registering to vote," and government

workers who fail to "report undocumented seeking benefits could face jail time and a fine."[25]

Towards the end of the first decade of the twenty-first century, the Tea Party movement took root and became the voice for anti-immigrant legislation across the nation.[26] Arizona provides a good example. Not content with Proposition 200, the most alarming anti-immigrant legislation in the nation emerged six years later. Arizona's SB 1070 came to symbolize the movement not only to restrict immigration but to force the undocumented to return to Mexico, Central America or wherever they came from (a consequence that Mitt Romney strongly favored during the campaign for the Republican presidential nomination). A new and broader "Operation Wetback" awaited implementation. The author of SB 1070, State Senator Russell Pearce, revealed his motives in a statement in which he claimed that "They [immigrants] create enclaves of separate groups that shall balkanize our nation into fractured nightmares of social unrest and poverty."[27] The law included provisions that required law officers to "reasonably determine the immigration status of a person only while in process of a lawful stop, detention or arrest." Provisions include arrests for anyone not carrying an Alien Registration Document, anyone transporting an undocumented, and employer sanctions for hiring undocumented. Legal challenges to the law reached the Supreme Court, which did not stymie the anti-immigrant politics. Shortly after Arizona passed SB 1070, a dozen states introduced bills that mirrored Arizona's.[28]

Georgia moved HB 87 forward, which was defended by State Senator Renee Unterman, who remarked in the legislature that "We don't mind taking care of our people; let's just take care of our own people," and added, "I don't want to take care of Mexico's people."[29] Perhaps the most notorious of the laws regulating the lives of undocumented migrants was Alabama's law that required schools to determine the legal status of students in public schools and for law officers to arrest or detain anyone "if they have a 'reasonable suspicion' they are in the country illegally."[30] The law bans renting housing to undocumented and makes certain contracts signed by undocumented unenforceable, which is why a water district refused to provide water for those unable to provide legal papers. While the law does not ban children from enrolling in elementary and high school it does ban the undocumented from enrolling in a state university or college.

According to Kevin Johnson, dean of the School of Law at the University of California, Davis, HB 87 comprises the "harshest provisions of anti-immigrant ordinances and state laws that have been passed in recent years."[31] One resident described the threatening effects on her *barrio*: "So many neighbors have left. Nobody goes out at night. Nobody is calm. Nothing is certain."[32]

Not surprisingly, a mass departure of Latino residents from Alabama followed upon that state's law's passing causing an agricultural labor shortage. When Alabama Congressman Mo Brooks was asked if this was the intended consequence he answered:

> Those are the intended consequences of Alabama's legislation with respect to illegal aliens. We don't have the money to keep paying for the education of everybody else's children from around the world."[33]

In the case of Arizona's SB1070, the Supreme Court struck down three parts of the law but left one that allows for police to detain anyone if there is a "reasonable suspicion" that they are undocumented. However, Homeland Security decided that it would terminate its agreements with Arizona and essentially not cooperate with police action in accordance with the Arizona "reasonable suspicion" ruling. Nevertheless, the *New York Times* headline made clear the significance of the ruling: "Immigration Ruling Leaves Issues Unresolved."[34] It is not whether federal courts or the Supreme Court uphold the racist laws or not; what is most concerning are the political forces that have moved the legislation forward. Membership and leadership from a variety of anti-immigrant organizations, not a few openly racist, have merged into the Tea Party to push for the legal measures regardless whether there is any evidence to support the charges.[35] The real question in their minds is that Latinos are becoming a significantly larger population, numbering 50.5 million in 2011, comprising 16 percent of the nation's population, and constituting the fastest growing community.[36]

As a supporter for a measure that would curb providing Spanish language materials in Colorado libraries said, "When you have a strong cultural identity and there aren't set incentives to become American, it creates a lot of tension and divides the community."[37] And this brings into the anti-immigrant discourse the central piece: American culture is undergoing deeply disturbing changes created by immigrants, whether undocumented or not. It is alleged that most of these changes originate from Latino immigrants who enter in overwhelming numbers and fail to separate from their national culture. For some, the Latino cultural spectrum is anathema to the very foundations of U.S. political, social and economic institutions. The "Mexican Problem" portends an end of the United States as the dominating world power as Pat Buchanan, a regular PBS news panelist and former congressman, would have us believe:

> This then is the Aztlan strategy: endless migration from Mexico north, the Hispanization of the American Southwest, and dual citizenship for all Mexican-Americans. The goals: erase the border. Grow the influence, through Mexican Americans, over how America disposes her wealth and power. Gradually, circumscribe the sovereignty of the United States. Lastly, economic and political merger of the nations in a binational union. And in the nuptial agreement, a commitment to share the wealth and power.[38]

Pat Buchanan may appear to some as a wacky, right-wing radical, but there are highly respected figures who feel similarly. Harvard University Professor Samuel P. Huntington writing in *Foreign Affairs* said the same in a more refined fashion in an article titled "The Hispanic Challenge."[39] Huntington argued that the United States is in danger of losing its global imperialist power. The decline of the unipolar world in which the United States serves as the supreme power is fading in the face of China, Russia, Europe and Japan. Meanwhile, Latin America, once under U.S. domain, is moving in an independent direction led by Cuba, Bolivia, Ecuador and Venezuela. And the biggest internal threat to maintaining and protecting that power is the rise in Hispanic culture, particularly bilingualism, which, Huntington claimed, poses a grave threat to the Western heritage upon which the United States was founded. He identified six factors leading to that condition. First, a common border divides a rich nation from a poor one; second, a rise in documented immigration; third, rising undocumented immigrants; fourth, immigrants' tendency to live in separate communities; fifth, continuing recent migration; and finally, a contention that the old Mexican territory is a target for repossession. Huntington minced no words:

> If over one million Mexican soldiers crossed the border Americans would treat it as a major threat to their national security and react accordingly. The invasion of one million civilians... would be a comparable threat to American societal security, and Americans should react against with vigor.[40]

Overall, Huntington argues that the culture south of the border is incompatible with key institutions of the United States, which are based on Western values. He contends that the culture of Latin America is incompatible with the culture of nations that have achieved the highest levels of development. For Huntington, the real "Mexican Problem" is that Latino immigrants threaten the imperial power of the United States by undermining its culture and therefore the governing institutional structures. A central point in his article is that Mexican culture generates a host of social problems including high secondary school drop-out rates, poverty and limited occupational opportunities. Huntington's solution: restrict Latino, particularly Mexican, immigration, deport the undocumented and enforce Americanization.

Not to be outflanked, the Obama Administration took up the cause and deported over a million undocumented during the first two years of his presidency and nearly 400,000 in 2011, a pace that will lead in four years to more than the 1.57 million that Bush deported during his two administrations. This occurred even though a more liberal policy to exclude those with minor offenses from deportation had been incorporated. Although the administration promised to focus on serious offenders, nearly 60 percent of all deportees are non-criminals. In the first six months of 2012, 46,000 parents of U.S. citizen children have been deported, described by one writer as "an exodus of parents who are leaving with their American sons and daughters." The U.S.-born children of undocumented parents have also been subjected to the mass drive. Between 2005 and 2010 about 300,000 U.S.-born children of Mexican parents moved to Mexico, reported the Mexican census bureau.[41] These find the bureaucratic paperwork requirements to register their children for school or healthcare to be a major barrier to becoming a resident. Hirokozu Yoshikawa, academic dean at the Harvard Graduate School of Education described it as a situation where "children... are kind of stateless in both countries."[42] Families are also being separated, many permanently. On the north side, many children are left parentless and the numbers are growing. In Los Angeles, parental deportation has resulted in one out of every sixteen children in foster care. One study has found that at least 5,100 children were left orphaned by the deportation drive.[43]

Young undocumented have also been subjected as individuals to deportation, a nightmarish threat that hangs over their shoulders every day, a threat that often strikes. An Associated Press journalist writing out of Tegucigalpa, Honduras, noted the large number of deported youth on street corners, found guilty of a minor offense and deported while in high school or college or working. Those deported were deeply frustrated, wounded, as these young deportees in Honduras and Guatemala said upon hearing of the temporary halt in deportations. One Honduran lived in the U.S. for eleven years and his primary language is English: "When I was watching the news today and heard [the Obama decision]

I couldn't believe it... I had to turn the TV off," he said and a second who was arrested while at work in a supermarket without being able to say goodbye to his family added: "I am a person who studied and I wish I could aspire to far greater things. I am sad." The journalist described young deportees as forming a new segment of Latin American society:

> ...one can spot the young and recently deported on Latin America's streets, where they sometimes fumble with their Spanish and have trouble fitting in.[44]

The massive drives to deport aroused millions from immigrant communities to protest anti-immigrant politics and demonstrate for amnesty in March 2006 from Los Angeles to Washington DC. This then is the political context within which the educational policies of the twenty-first century are shaped, implemented and drawing protests. No doubt the policy change enacted by the Obama administration in January 2013, to allow a softer approach for legalization, is a consequence of the growing political voice of the Latino population. Undocumented immigrants related to U.S. citizens will be allowed to remain, request a waiver, which costs $585.00, and apply for a visa before returning to their country to await the visa. However, while the liberal decree reduces the traditional long time period required to await the visa while in the home country and avoids long family separations, the time period remains an unknown.[45]

Anti-immigrant campaigners ignore or fail to recognize that it is the economic expansion of the U.S. into Mexico and Latin America that has created the conditions leading to migration to the U.S.[46] Pro-immigrant supporters also often fail to recognize the role of the U.S. Over the past century, U.S. immigration policy adjusted when necessary to ensure that the door was open to Latin American laborers who became integrated into the productive processes but remained socially segregated. Pat Buchanan and others exclaim that the U.S. is in decline because of immigration while no one complains that three out of every four agricultural workers are undocumented or that ICE raids are seldom conducted in the fields. Certainly no mention is made that for a hundred years the American economy has come to depend on Mexican labor.[47] Understandably, growers (really monopolistic agricultural corporations) oppose legal measures requiring that all new hires provide papers verified through a federal database operated by the Department of Homeland Security; at the same time growers support a new bracero program.[48] The anti-immigrant organizations welcome Mexican labor, but only if they are returned after the labor is performed.

THE UNDOCUMENTED AND THE DREAM

Nearly ten years after the DREAM act had come before Congress to legalize all undocumented if they are students or if they serve in the armed forces, headlines across the nation on June 16, 2012, boldly announced the Obama Administration's decision to change immigration policy with regards to undocumented immigrants. Rather than the mass deportation drive that the same administration imposed to drive out over 1.1 million undocumented in three years (a number that has not been reached since the Operation Wetback era) in which families were major victims of the massive campaign, a new measure was announced. With the election in sight and Latinos highly critical of the deportations, the Obama administration decided to take a step towards a "temporary... stop gap measure," in President Obama's words, and allow a two-year stay for those undocumented who arrived before reaching the age of sixteen, are under thirty-one years of age, are in school or are high school graduates, have no criminal record and pose no threat to safety or national security and had lived in the U.S. for five consecutive years before the announcement. They must apply and if granted a stay, they may work and apply for driver's license and they must reapply in two years. However, there is no guarantee that the request for delay will be granted; the permit will not grant legal papers or a green card, nor a pathway to citizenship; the only promise made is that the deportation is delayed, a "deferred action." If upon application the undocumented is found to not to meet the criteria, no deferral will be given and deportation proceedings will begin. Thus there is a potential risk and no guarantee that a deferral will be allowed in every case.

An estimated 1.4 million undocumented, 70 percent born in Mexico, might be eligible for the stay in deportation; the procedures are to begin two months after Obama made the announcement. Approximately 700,000 are under eighteen and enrolled in school according to the Pew Hispanic Center and they will no doubt be the primary beneficiaries of the measure. The remaining 700,000 between the ages of eighteen and thirty will also earn the right to remain. However, the mothers and fathers of those brought as children and those older than thirty are not eligible for the permit and their legal status remains the same. Moreover, what happens to those who have no high school diploma or GED? Approximately 65,000 undocumented high school students graduate each year, but how many drop out? One study estimated that 20 percent of the undocumented drop out, which means that a significant number will not qualify for a deferment. What is very clear is that this is not an amnesty, only a stop-gap measure. Those who qualify are very pleased and are celebrating but the reality is not lost on the undocumented. A student commented: "I might be able to get a work permit, but my parents can't... It's a victory but we need to keep on fighting for our families and everybody as a whole."[49] Families are once again divided, this time by a temporary legal definition distinguishing children from parents, high school graduates from dropouts, older brothers and sisters from their younger siblings. As one parent said whose oldest daughter will not qualify though her younger two will: "I will cry with her of sadness... And I will cry with my other two children of joy."[50]

The "stop gap" measure is not a complete resolution for an undocumented; it means that if they qualify the weight of being labeled "illegal" and subject to immediate deportation is *temporarily* removed, allowing them to pursue their educational goals or to work. However, they then enter a separate legal tier of the undocumented. Let us examine the educational conditions that will greet them.

THE ECONOMY AND EDUCATION AT K-12

Simultaneous with the anti-immigrant agenda and a three-decade drive toward the privatization of public education came the recession of 2008, which significantly impacted the Latino community. In 2008 the economy slid into a major recession caused by the failure of risky banking loans and immediately the unemployment and poverty rates soared. However, the rich remained rich, even more so. The Congressional Budget Office released figures reporting that between 1979 and 2007 the "richest 1% of Americans increased their after tax income by 275%... the bottom one-fifth saw their income grow by 18%."[51] In 1985 the upper 1 percent controlled 33 percent of the nation's wealth and took in around 12 percent of the income. By 2011 the upper 1 percent controlled 40 percent of the nation's wealth and took in around 25 percent of the income.[52] Most did not enjoy such good fortunes. In 2008 the unemployment rate stood at 6.5 percent; by 2010 it had risen to nearly 10 percent. In 2004 the poverty rate for Latinos stood at 21.8; by 2011 it had risen to 26.6percent, well above the national average of 15.1 percent, which in itself is a high figure.

Education continues to be a matter of critical concern, with many of the same problems faced by reformers throughout the twentieth century but with declining budget support, which exacerbates these problems. Given the relative youth of the Latino population (the average age is twenty-seven, while the median age is thirty-seven) and the number who are undocumented, education remains on the forefront within the context of a national anti-immigrant political movement. Attempts to restrict education to the documented or citizens must impact heavily on their emotions, the vast majority of whom crossed the border as young children and identify as Latinos reared in the United States.

While the anti-immigrant attack moves forward, the vast majority of Latinos remain integrated economically, that is, working for a wage. Along with increased migration the number of youth in schools has grown dramatically. Since 1970 the percentage of Latino fourth graders in the nation's schools has grown from 2 percent to 21 percent. There are four million Latinos in public schools whose primary language is Spanish; an estimated one million undocumented are under the age of sixteen.[53] Despite court decisions to block segregation, these children attend schools that have become more segregated and unequal over the past several decades, while a number of state legislatures have moved to deny public education to the undocumented. According to Jonathan Kozol "the inequalities are greater now [2011] than in '92. Some states have equalized per-pupil spending but they set the 'equal level' very low, so that wealthy districts simply raise money privately."[54] The most segregated schools are the charter schools, which Kozol contends "guarantees a swift and vicious deepening of class and racial separation." And given the poverty rate among Latinos, class segregation is the mode through which educational segregation takes place. The headline of an article on Alabama schools described the matter: "Legacy of School Segregation Endures, Separate but Legal."[55] In Texas and California, on average a Latino student attends a school that is nearly 70 percent Latino.

Not surprisingly, the education gap between rich and poor is growing and given the No Child Left Behind emphasis on continual testing (analogous in many ways to the old IQ testing), the gap merely reflects what testing measures more than anything else: family income. According to a study conducted by Julian Weinglass, University of California, Santa Barbara, "Testing leads teachers to focus on test scores rather than students as complex learners."[56] And Kozol adds that in wealthy districts the emphasis is on "joy... whim... charm... inquiry [while] the other class is trained to spit up predigested answers."[57] A study conducted by Sean A. Reardon at Stanford University found that "the gap in standardized test scores between affluent and low income students has grown by about 40 percent since the 1960s."[58] A good part of the difference is due to the privatization of education. In 2007 high income families were spending nine times as much on schooling for their children as did low income parents. The scores reflect the income distinctions dividing classes. Latino children in the fourth to the eighth grade scored twenty points lower in math and reading, equivalent to two grade levels, on the National Assessment of Educational Progress scale.[59] As the income gap widens the educational gap follows.

In addition to the long-standing gaps in learning experiences in segregated environments, budgets cuts in the national K-12 systems were $1.8 billion in 2011 and are expected to reach $2.5 billion in 2012. In Florida funding for a "school readiness program for low income families" that benefitted 15,000 students was cut by 15 percent while a similar program in Texas was eliminated completely. Texas' public school disparities between wealthy and poor districts are such that a per student funding gap of $1450 divides the wealthiest 100 school districts from the poorest. In California, 140 school districts are in serious financial difficulty and state funding since 2008 has dropped by at least $18 billion leading to a per pupil 20 percent decrease in funding compared to the 2007 level. This will disproportionately impact the 20 percent of California's 6.2 million school children who live in poverty. Wealthy districts can hold back cuts by private fund raising as the Wonderland Elementary School in the wealthy Los Angeles Laurel Canyon district did, which raised $450,000 in private donations to support six projects that would have either been reduced or eliminated.[60]

THE ECONOMY AND COLLEGE AND UNIVERSITIES

While K-12 budgets were being cut to Depression levels across the nation, higher education budgets followed course and were decreased by $1.2 billion in 2011 and expected to reach $5 billion in 2012. At the University of California's ten campuses the 2011 budget was cut by $750 million.[61] Michigan cut the budget for its university system by 15 percent and state funding now only covers 22 percent of costs whereas in 1987 the state covered 60 percent of the total budget. To cover costs, tuition (a term that was not used twenty-five years ago at public institutions) has come to be the means at public institutions. Since 1981, college costs including tuition have risen at an annual rate of 6.4 percent outstripping the annual income growth of 0.4 percent.[62] At the University of California campuses the tuition rose from under $4,000 in 2000 to $13,000 in 2011. In 2011 at the University of Michigan tuition went up 6.6 percent; at the University of California tuition went up by nearly 10 percent after a previous year's increase of 8 percent and more increases are envisioned.[63] With costs falling on students and primarily on families the debt loads are rising. The Federal Reserve Bank reported that student loans rose by $550 billion in the second quarter 2011, up dramatically over the 1999 level of $90 billion.

Clearly, the public higher educational system is becoming a private educational enterprise, a transition initiated by the neoliberal creed. The Director of Public Policy at the American Association of University Professors described higher education as more of "a market system rather than producing knowledge for the benefit of society."[64] While privatization removes the state as the main funding source, families and students themselves become the primary source for budget support. Two-thirds of 2012 college graduates assumed loans compared to less than half in 1993. There are an estimated 37 million with outstanding student loans, causing for many a lifetime burden.[65] The average loan in 2012 amounted to $24,301; the debt on college education in the U.S. totaled more than that owed on credit cards.[66] According to the National Center for Public Policy in Higher Education,

> ...college tuition fees increased 439% from 1982 to 2007, adjusted for inflation, while median family income rose 147%. Student borrowing has more than doubled in the past decade, and students from lower income families, on average, get smaller grants from

the colleges they attend than students from more affluent families.[67]

By 2008 rising tuition at public institutions across the nation amounted to 28 percent of median family income and 76 percent at private institutions, an increase of nearly 40 percent over the 2000 level. When we examine the median net worth of the households of Latino families, $6,325, we find that it is considerably below the $113,149 median for white families.[68] The median household worth for Latinos fell by 66 percent between 2005 and 2009, far more than that for Whites which fell by 16 percent. In addition, Latino families have traditionally larger families, increasing the economic barriers.

Given the financial pressures on working-class families, attending a community college is a choice made by 80 percent of Latino high school graduates. Community colleges, like four-year colleges and universities, are also moving from public to private institutions. Student tuition is increasingly becoming the main support for community colleges across the nation.[69] Budget cuts in 2008 at two-year institutions across the nation raised the costs to 49 percent of median family income of the poorest families, up from 40 percent in 1999. The average tuition rose 7.3 percent to reach $2,544 in 2009, which adds up when the costs for books, equipment, and computer and so on are included.[70] This of course, requires that students work to support themselves while in school adding to the weight on their shoulders. On top of that, cuts in budgets have affected the course offerings across the board. Arizona Governor Jan Brewer has proposed a 50 percent cut in community college funding while at California's 112 community colleges, declining state support often requires that students attend beyond the two years.[71] Since 2009 the California system has enrolled 300,000 fewer students and a 2011 projected funding cut of 10 percent amounting to $809 million will threaten to eliminate thousands of classes and lower attendance levels by 400,000.[72] City College of San Francisco, the largest in the state enrolling 90,000, sits on the brink of bankruptcy at the end of the 2011

academic year.[73] At my alma mater, East Los Angeles College, a traditional Latino-attended campus, "course offerings have plummeted to
their lowest levels in fifteen years," amounting to a near 30 percent
reduction.[74] Students were being turned back from enrolling in prerequisite courses in record numbers. Nearby colleges experienced the same
pains. An announcement by the Glendale Community College on their
website advised applicants that

> Due to the dramatic budget issues we all face in California, Glen-
> dale Community College will not receive funding to allow for a
> full range of classes and services. We will do our best, but be
> advised that many classes may be full and services may be limited.
> Contact your state representative to let them know education is
> important.[75]

There is no better example of placing the costs on the shoulders of
the students than the decision taken at Santa Monica College located
near Los Angeles. Due to budget cuts, more than 1,100 courses had
been eliminated since 2008 and the demand went far beyond enrollment
capacity. The College Board of Trustees decided to overcome the crisis by
implementing a two-tier tuition system for the upcoming 2012 summer
session. The college decided to charge $180 per credit unit for core
courses required for specific majors such as history, English, science and
math which are often the most demanded courses.[76] For the remainder of
courses the charge would be the normal $46 per unit (in 2009 the College
charged $26 per credit unit). According to the board, this was considered
a means to guarantee students a seat in the class. Students were outraged.
Student Government President Harrison Wills defined the measure as "a
two tiered system of wealthier students who can afford classes and struggling working class and low-income students competing for scraps of
what's left."[77] Students held a mass non-violent demonstration to address
the board meeting chanting "No cuts, no fees, education should be free."[78]
The Santa Monica police responded with tear gas into the crowd and
thirty were left choking and gasping; two were hospitalized. Actions by

the students and public outcry forced the board to cancel the two-tier proposal, but the budgetary crisis remains.

Another major consequence of the cut-backs is the increase in part-time and non-tenure-track faculty. According to the Coalition on Academic Workforce, these academics comprise 49.2 percent of all faculty members to constitute "the single largest category in the academic workforce." The average wage for a course taught by part-timers at the community college level was $2,700 in 2010, a wage far below that of a full-time academic.[79]

This has come to form the infrastructure of today's higher education, a sector of our educational system that is in a state of deepening depression and continuing to move toward privatization. Rather than the state governments raising taxes on the wealthiest corporations to overcome the downturn, public universities are forced to recruit out of state and foreign students as a fund-raising measure, which has resulted in 15 percent of all graduate students being foreign students.[80] Meanwhile, students living in the state find attending a college or university a difficult pathway that leads to long-time indebtedness, to say the least.

ETHNIC STUDIES AND TUCSON

However, there is another dimension to the educational gap. In addition to the Arizona legislature pioneering legislation allowing police to patrol the state and detain anyone suspected of being an undocumented, the Arizona State legislature passed HB 2281 in 2010 declaring that public school programs are illegal if they teach

> in a biased, political and emotionally charged manner...[or] promote the overthrow of the U.S. government, promote resentment toward a race or class of people, are designed primarily for pupils of a particular ethnic group or advocate solidarity instead of the treatment of students as individuals.[81]

The law would be applied simply in keeping with the ongoing anti-immigrant trend, since no evidence of such a problem ever existed. Its objective would be made known a year after its passage.

A very successful Mexican American Studies Program that had been operating in Tucson high schools for several years was eliminated. An independent audit of the Tucson High School Program, commissioned by Arizona Superintendent of Education John Huppenthal, gave it flying colors. The audit noted that the program promoted tolerance and that students performed better on standard tests and graduated at a 93 percent rate. No evidence of legal violations was found. Nonetheless, Huppenthal disregarded the audit and declared the Tucson High School District's Mexican American Studies Program to be in violation of the law and vowed to withdraw some $14 million in state aid unless the Tucson Board eliminated the program. His decision, supported by Governor Brewer and State Attorney General Tom Horne, moved the Tucson Board of Education to vote 4–1 to eliminate one of the more successful high school educational programs in the United States. The decision induced the district to remove dozens of books relating to Latino Studies from the eleven high school libraries, a form of book burning, of intellectual and cultural cleansing. According to the state, "Each book has been boxed and stored as part of the process of suspending the classes," and that the "books ... were cited in the ruling that found the classes out of compliance with state law"[82]

Not satisfied with destroying the successful educational program, the board fired Sean Arce, the instructor charged with administering the program. Arce notes that not all has been lost and that the community is in action:

> Another promising result of this anti-Mexican, this anti-Latino legislation has been that it's really organized our community. Our community is more assertive, politically active, organizing, getting out in the community.[83]

A 2012 Tucson Freedom Summer brought Latinos and supporters from across the nation to save Mexican American Studies and Ethnic Studies. Activities included demonstrations, classes, workshops on Mexican American Studies and community canvassing for board of education elections. The attempt to eliminate ethnic studies by government authorities is a learning experience for the Latino community of a repressive, reactionary political trend moving across the nation. This brings greater determination and political awareness and action from the Mexican community and beyond. The very condition that Huppenthal and his political cohorts sought to undermine in their quest to eliminate the latest version of the "Mexican Problem" has deepened the determination of the Latino community to defeat current and future anti-immigrant policies.

CONCLUSION

When we study Chicano-Latino history we are not merely studying the past; we are studying political processes and social conditions originating over a century ago, which continue today. Among the themes are migration, settlement patterns, economic integration, poverty and segregation. Many of the obstacles that faced Latinos in the first decades of the previous century remain. Into the twenty-first century we find obstacles imposed by deportation drives which implicitly deny the role of NAFTA in creating the mass migrations, the anti-immigrant movement under the deport all "illegal aliens" banner, neoliberal privatization of public education and the incorporation of class differences within instructional programs. A growing educational segregation over the past several decades is a major consequence of these policies, which have thwarted a truly democratic educational system. These conditions have set the contemporary political agenda for the Latino community. Latino political activities on reforming education began over a century ago fighting policies such as de jure segregation constructed under racist allegations of a "Mexican Problem." Significant changes in public education followed. Victories include the Lemon Grove Incident, the Mendez Case, the Delgado Case followed by student sit-ins, marches and the implementation of Chicano/Latino Studies and much more. Contemporary political action is one chapter in a history of struggle going back a century to make the U.S. educational system serve all equally. And that struggle includes the right of the undocumented, who were forced to leave their countries under the conditions imposed by U.S.-designed free trade policies, to remain, to work, study and live freely. The struggle continues as long as flagrant, discriminatory policies are in place such as the prohibition of Mexican American Studies denying the right of students to study the historical and contemporary Mexican American community and engage critical studies.

Acknowledgments

I would like to thank the following persons for their contributions to this study: my colleagues, Jose Ocampo and Raul Fernandez; for bibliographical assistance, Roger Berry of the University of California, Irvine, Special Collections; and for technical assistance, Edna Mejia. Finally, my thanks to my children, Ramon and Xochitl, for their support and constant interest in my research and writing. They inspired me to keep to my task.

A revised version of chapter 7, "The Rise and Fall of De Jure Segregation in the Southwest," first appeared as "Segregation of Mexican Children in a Southern California City: The Legacy of Expansionism in the American Southwest" in *The Western Historical Quarterly* 6, no. 1 (1985): 56–76, copyright by Western Historical Association and published with the permission of the Western Historical Association.

Chapter 6 is a revised version of "Inter-American and Intercultural Education," appearing in the *Journal of Ethnic Studies* 13, no. 3 (1985): 31–55, published with permission of the *Journal of Ethnic Studies*.

Chapter 2, "The Americanization of the Mexican Family," is a revised version of an article appearing in Sucheng Chan, ed., *Ethnic and Gender Boundaries in the United States: Studies of Asian, Black, Mexican, and*

Native Americans (Lewiston, N.Y.: Edwin Mellen Press, 1989), published with the permission of Edwin Mellen Press.

CHICANO EDUCATION
IN THE ERA
OF SEGREGATION

INTRODUCTION

BACKGROUND TO SEGREGATION

The American public school system has treated Mexican-Americans differently from other Americans; the consequences have contrasted markedly with the proposed objectives of dominant educational policies and practices. To understand the full nature of this contrast, we must first begin by acknowledging that historically, political domination and socioeconomic inequality have dictated the course of educational policy in America. As a result, we find that various factors and conditions external to the Chicano community have shaped the educational experience of that community. This appears evident in the Southwest, for example, where regional agricultural economies relied heavily upon migrant family labor and where the seasonal nature of this type of work affected the schooling process for members of the entire region and for Chicanos in particular. This does not mean, however, that regional factors dominated educational policy as applied to Chicanos. To be sure, that policy originated in national theoretical and practical constructions such as mass compulsory education, intelligence testing and tracking, curriculum differentiation, vocational education, Americanization, and segregation. In part, such international conditions as World War II and the cold war also influenced the development of this policy. This educational process has resulted in the inequality in educational achievement between Chicano and Anglo populations, and, as a result, it has impelled Chicano political action to overcome it.

The twentieth-century history of Chicano education may be divided into four periods. The first period, 1900–1950, represents the era of de jure segregation. Although there were no laws that mandated the practice of segregation, educators did invoke the state power granted to school administrations to adapt educational programs to the special needs of a linguistically and culturally distinct community. Thus, for example, as early as 1919, the superintendent of the Santa Ana, California, School District referred to a state attorney general's opinion upholding segregation as a legitimate educational policy for meeting the "special needs" of Mexican children. During the initial forty years of this period, educational policies for Chicanos involved the application of principles of biological determinism. Throughout the period, the Mexican community participated to a high degree in the agricultural economy, although many took up residence in cities and adapted to an urban industrial environment.

During the second period, 1950–65, the pattern of segregation remained, but without the deliberate official sanction of Mexican schools. For the most part, this period witnessed an educational policy that adhered to the culture concept: that is, Chicano culture was recognized as an impediment to Mexican-American adaptation to Anglo-American culture. In keeping with this perspective, educational programs tended to emphasize the acculturation of Chicanos to the dominant American culture, while at the same time Chicano laborers experienced an increasing shift away from agriculture and toward urban employment.

The third period, 1965–75, marked the militant and reformist era. Not surprisingly, education received much of the attention of the Chicano movement during this period, and the mass demonstration of discontent and demands for change forced substantial reforms of the schooling process. Programs such as bilingual and bicultural education, affirmative action, integration, curriculum reform, special admission to higher education, and financial aid, provided a substantially modified educational atmosphere. The reform phase, short-lived and quickly subverted by a conservative retrenchment, constitutes the fourth period beginning in 1975. Marked by a political conservatism emphasizing reliance upon traditional individualism and the marketplace and de-emphasizing and questioning the effectiveness of state-sponsored reforms, this period has witnessed at least a halt and, in some instances, a rollback of the reforms enacted during the previous period.[1]

A comprehensive study of the educational history of the Chicano community has yet to appear. I hope to provide the beginning of such a study in this book by examining the education of Mexicans in the Southwest during the era of de jure segregation covering the first half of the century. My intent includes an interpretation of the roots of inequality in education. The few texts examining the history of Chicano education somehow do not explain oppression. On the other hand, they are long on factual evidence. My analysis emphasizes the political economy (and not merely racial oppression as in most texts) as the key factor in shaping the social relations between the dominant and minority communities. Thus, I focus on an examination of that oppression by dissecting it and holding it up for analysis. In addition, I will look at one of the key efforts to overcome subordination in the 1947 case, *Mendez* v. *Westminster,* one of the major desegregation court cases in U.S. legal history.

The Chicano struggle to overcome segregation in schools has had a long history, and as Guadalupe San Miguel has recently shown, the League of United Latin American Citizens (LULAC) was at the forefront of that struggle. Because this organization remained limited to Texas until the 1940s, its efforts resulted in a number of court cases that unfortunately had no major effect on segregation until the 1960s and 1970s when the Chicano movement made its impact felt. A key consequence of the *Mendez* v. *Westminster* case was the inspiration it provided for a renewed campaign to terminate segregation, which resulted in more positive consequences than previous efforts. This study will focus upon *Mendez* v. *Westminster* as one example (and a major one, I might add) of a rather widespread movement in the Chicano community to overcome educational oppression.

Before proceeding, I must raise three points. First, the terms *Chicano* and *Mexican-American* had not yet become popular in the period under study; therefore, all persons of Mexican nationality or descent living in the United States are referred to as "Mexican." Second, I concentrate primarily on those areas of the Southwest that had a substantial Mexican population. I exclude the New Mexican Hispano population because these communities were isolated and historically distinct from those formed by Mexican immigrants of the twentieth century, and because the Hispano educational experience should be examined in light of the peculiar economic institutions shaping Hispano life. New Mexican villages are islands of traditional institutions and, during the de jure segregation period, stood outside of the educational developments taking place in the Southwest. Events since World War II have made it quite appropriate to include New Mexico in any analysis of southwestern Mexican communities today, but the immigration that has woven New Mexico into the Mexican Southwest was not a factor during the period under study. Third, I focus upon public education and exclude all religious and church-sponsored institutions of learning. In an effort to narrow my topic to manageable proportions and to identify the main currents in this historical period, I have concluded that an analysis of de jure segregation in public schools is comprehensive, logical, and significant.

Finally, in my research I utilize written documentation expressing those educational ideas predominate during the era under study. This does not negate the significance of classroom practice, however. This study will report upon that educational ideology that directed educational practice. There is sufficient reason to expect that the overwhelming pedagogical unanimity extant during the era of segregation would significantly impact upon classroom practice. Consequently, in the examples of classroom practice that I draw upon, the reader will readily note the unity between theory and practice.

An understanding of school segregation is contingent on an examination of two key factors that condition the educational process: the national political economy and the socioeconomic position of Mexicans within a class society.

POLITICAL ECONOMY AND EDUCATIONAL REFORM

Ironically, during the first half of this century, as the United States rose as a world power and as an industrial giant, its domestic social policy often proved to be oppressive and antidemocratic, especially toward minorities. Others have argued elsewhere that its supporters designed this broad social policy so as to insure the necessary internal social and political conditions for the realization of domestic and foreign policy objectives. Historian James Weinstein has concluded that Progressive "liberalism incorporated the concepts of social engineering and social efficiency that grew up alongside industrial engineering and efficiency."[2] Consequently, as Clarence Karier notes, a pervasive social engineering significantly affected the educational program of the United States, and as it did so, it maintained the existing socioeconomic and racial hierarchy in society. According to Karier, "The important theme which appears in the educational literature of the first three decades of the century was social efficiency and managed social order . . . the schools were used to standardize the future citizen as interchangeable parts for an intricate production and consumption system."[3]

The educational programs of the turn of the century fit the social conditions created by the growing corporate economy.[4] The reforms accomplished in the first few decades reflected new economic forces and social conflicts. An increasing concentration of production within large-scale enterprises and an industrial working class emerging on a national scale, were key factors leading to the rise of labor unions and labor-capital conflicts that threatened the social order.[5] Progressive reformism represented essentially the political face of the economic evolution of U.S. capitalism. By and large, schooling programs throughout the nation assumed the task of creating among minorities, the political conscious-ness and productive skills necessary for stability and growth in the economy.

The first item on the Progressives' agenda consisted of a critique of prevailing social theory and the presentation of alternatives that corre-sponded to new realities. It forecasted that as society became more industrialized and capital more concentrated, an "organic society" must be created. The organic society, the central concern of Progressivism, was posited in various theoretical ways by a number of social scien-tists and social philosophers, including the preeminent John Dewey.[6] The second item on the reformers' agenda expressed the need to incul-cate the Progressive ideology of political culture in the population espe-cially in the working class. Many reformers were academics and became leaders in the fields of sociology, psychology, anthropology, and polit-ical science, helping to organize research and instruction to fit the social, political, and economic needs of the emerging social order.

The general aim of reform (and the task to which scholarly research was put) involved the realization of the conditions for an integrated, effi-cient, and stable social order without altering the basic economic institu-tions and the class structure linked to them. If all classes shared a political culture, democratic capitalism could be preserved from political insta-bility. Influential reformers and adherents of organic theory including Dewey, William James, E. A. Ross, Teddy Roosevelt, Walter Lippmann, and Lewis Terman, considered many key traditional ideas and institu-tions to be out of touch with contemporary realities. They focused on competitive individualism, the labor theory of property and classes, and laissez-faire economics. These same reformers argued that in the absence of an effective socialization institution in the new urban industrial order, the state, through the local schools, had to intervene in the social process and guide its minions. The goal was stable, peaceful social relations based on the existing social division of labor. In the final analysis, schools became the key institution for socializing the individual to the emerging corporate industrial order. The movement to alter the ideological and institutional structures of society had a large-scale impact affecting policies nearly everywhere.

Progressive educational reforms operated on two levels. On the level of culture as shared information, Progressives aimed at inculcating a common culture that would bind together the various classes. On the level of the educational process, they sought effective training of the individual as a producer. The reforms instituted to these ends included testing, tracking, curriculum differentiation (i.e., vocational education vs. courses for the "gifted"), Americanization, and segregation. As they spread and took root, the mass migration from Mexico began its long historical course, and the immigrant community confronted not only the new large-scale economic enterprises, but also the reforms they had spawned.

THE SOCIOECONOMIC CHARACTER OF THE MEXICAN COMMUNITY

The economic integration of the Southwest into the national economy during the second half of the nineteenth century laid the foundations for its development in the twentieth. This process began as the capitalist political and economic system replaced the Mexican feudal system. The emergence of an incipient national democratic capitalism and the penetration of U.S. corporate enterprises into Mexico coincided with agricultural and extractive growth in the American Southwest. The increasing tempo of economic development in the agricultural economy of the Southwest—a labor intensive enterprise at the time—created a labor vacuum filled by a number of nationalities and native workers.

Immigration from Mexico became a crucial factor in the economy of the Southwest in the early 1900s and has continued to be so. Between 1910 and 1930, 661,538 Mexicans legally crossed the border, and it has been estimated that during the 1920s, at least 3 percent of the population of Mexico emigrated to the United States. The vast majority of the immigrants included small families (husband, wife, and unmarried children) whose able-bodied members sold their labor to corporate farmers, mining, commerce and industry, and transportation for construction and maintenance jobs.[7]

The sharp rise in Mexican residents during this period far outstripped the increase in the white American population. In the five southwestern states, the Mexican community grew from some 159,000 in 1910, to 1,283,000 by 1930, while the total non-Mexican population grew from 8,605,000 to 13,397,000 during that same period. In terms of percentages, Mexicans comprised 4.2 percent of the population in these five states in 1910, and nearly 10 percent by 1930. In one generation Mexicans had become much more visible and, in a rapidly changing environment, much more identifiable.[8]

The flow of Mexican immigrants into rural and urban areas where their labor was in demand, created a strained and unequal relationship between the Mexican communities and the more privileged sectors of the society. Poverty, segregation, and employment in low-skilled occupations, characterized the experiences of the Mexican community during the era of school segregation. A 1928 study in California showed that 35.7 percent of the first- and second-generation Mexicans were primarily employed as agricultural laborers, most often in the form of migrant family labor; 31.4 percent were employed in manufacturing, 12.2 percent in transportation (other than railroad) and trade, and 10 percent on the railroads.[9]

Mexican workers replaced Greek, Italian, Japanese, and Korean workers on the Southwest railroads between 1909 and 1929. For example, in 1909 Greek workers numbering 7,653, comprised nearly 22 percent of the total work force on nine western railroads. By 1929 only one tenth as many Greeks (767) were employed by these same nine railroads. In 1909, 5,972 Mexicans were employed on the same lines, comprising 17.1 percent of the force. In 1929 Mexican workers numbered 22,824 and constituted 59.5 percent of that force. In the same two decades, the Italian percentage fell from 17 to 3.5 percent, whereas the combined Japanese and Korean percentage fell from 11.2 to 1.0 percent.[10]

According to one study of agricultural workers in the Southwest, three fourths of the fruit and vegetable workers and half of the cotton workers were Mexican in 1922.[11] Seven years later three quarters of the 400,000 migratory cotton workers in Texas were Mexican. Because of a long-standing reliance upon foreigners for cheap labor, the southwestern labor force was largely segmented according to nationality. Because of concentration of Mexican labor in particular industries and their relegation to a limited range of unskilled and semiskilled occupations, Mexican labor became synonymous with unskilled, cheap manual labor. Differentials in living and wage standards between the United States and Mexico allowed employers to lower wage levels for Mexican labor, taking advantage of the lower expectations and often desperate situation of the immigrant. According to Victor Clark, a "Mexican wage" existed in agriculture as early as 1908. West Texas farmers, for example, paid Mexican workers $1.00 to $1.25 daily and native Anglo labor $1.75 to $2.00. Twenty years later Paul S. Taylor found that Dimmit County farmers paid Mexican workers $1.50 to $2.00 daily, while American workers received $2.50.[12] Such differences in wage rates also appeared in mining, railroads, and industry.

The rapid rise in immigration and the concentration of immigrants about their places of work created a "belt" of Mexican settlement approximately 150 miles wide extending from San Francisco south along the Pacific Coast, then inland along the Mexican border through Arizona, New Mexico, and Texas to the Gulf of Mexico. The cotton growers of the Rio Grande Valley, the Imperial and San Joaquin Valley farmers of California, the Salt River Valley enterprises of Arizona, and the great citrus and truck ranches of southern California, actively recruited a large force of Mexican families to work the fields. Mexican immigration was, moreover, not restricted to rural areas. Large numbers settled in or near cities as early as 1920. Indeed, 51 percent of the Mexican population was urban by 1930 (compared with 56 percent for the total population). In Mexico only 31 percent of the population was urban in 1930.[13]

Contemporary studies have documented the extreme precariousness and poverty of life in the barrios in the twenties, thirties, and forties. Dirt streets, makeshift shacks, dirt floors, and single-room habitations for entire families were common conditions in the hundreds of barrios in both the rural and urban centers of America. A higher incidence of disease and mortality prevailed in these communities than in the dominant community. The urban and rural *colonias,* labeled "spik-towns" and "Little Mexicos" by outsiders, existed neatly tucked away, often across a natural division such as a river or gulley or across the railroad tracks. Of course, the dominant society found this useful mainly for locating a necessary force of workers, even though its members classified Mexicans as "problems," "misfits," "welfare burdens," "carriers of disease," and "social deviants."[14]

Another salient feature of the Mexican population was its youthfulness. In 1930 the median age for Mexicans was twenty, in contrast to a median for the rest of the population of twenty-six.[15] Large numbers of preschool and school-aged Mexican children posed administrative and teaching problems for public educators. Fifteen percent of the Mexican population was of preschool age and 35 percent of school age;[16] for the total U.S. population, the corresponding figures were 9.3 and 30 percent. Forty-eight percent of all Mexicans were of working age, as compared with 56 percent for the total population. As compulsory education extended to all residents, disproportional numbers of the poorest sector in the society found themselves forced into the educational enterprise.

Mexicans became integrated into a dynamic economic process that conditioned their lives as capitalization in railroads, mining, agriculture, and industry created the basis for the incorporation of Mexicans into the nation. Almost without exception they became part of the working class —albeit a limited labor sector within that class. The status of Mexicans within the larger economic class structure without question influenced the educational experience of the Mexican community. The education of Mexicans reflected two emphases: political socialization shaped by the dominant economic forces at play, and training for horizontal movement on the hierarchical socioeconomic scale. Thus, public education of the Mexican community via segregation, tended to reproduce its class character from one generation to the next.

FRAMEWORK FOR SEGREGATION

As early as 1892, Mexican children were being denied entrance into "American" schools in Corpus Christi (Texas). Taylor found that "practically coincident with the entry of Mexican children to the city schools, a separate school was provided for them."[17] By the late 1890s, enrollment in the Corpus Christi Mexican school stood at 110, and thirty years later the same school enrolled 1,320.

While Mexicans integrated into the economy and as their numbers increased, school boards established a de jure segregationist policy that was to last until midcentury. A typical scenario across the Southwest was recorded in the Ontario, California, Board of Education minutes for 11 April 1921. "Mr. Hill made the recommendation that the board select two new school sites; one in the southeastern part of the town for a Mexican school; the other near the Central School. . . ."[18] His motion was seconded and passed unanimously. By 1920 most communities with sizable Mexican populations segregated Mexican children as a matter of course. In Texas, school districts often segregated Anglo, black, and Mexican children in a tripartite system.[19] Although Texas law mandated the segregation of only black children, Texas custom prevailed throughout as district officials assigned each black and Mexican minority to its own school. Thus, as the pattern of Mexican residential segregation into *colonias* developed, school segregation followed. Educational theory quickly assimilated the practice, and thus academics legitimized, strengthened, and otherwise assisted in the extension of the segregation of Mexican schoolchildren.

Rather than being shaped by local or regional pressures, as some scholars have suggested,[20] the education of Mexican children has always been an integral part of national educational theory and practice. Officials practiced segregation, for example, on a national scale in addition to widespread use of progressive educational techniques such as testing, tracking, curriculum differentiation, and Americanization. Moreover, U.S. foreign policy in the decade of the 1940s played a key role in an anti-segregation campaign orchestrated from Washington that affected social attitudes as well as the desegregation court decisions of the 1950s. The segregation of Mexican children attempted to extend an existing duality demarcating the colored minorities, including Mexicans from the Anglo communities. Thus, segregation reflected and recreated the social divisions within the larger society formed by residential segregation, labor and wage rate differentials, political inequality, socioeconomic disparities, and racial oppression. Public school segregation involved an extension of a prior condition to the socialization process—the psychological and socioeconomic reproduction of a social relationship dividing a dominant from a subordinate community. Education for the Mexican community therefore meant change as well as the preservation of their subordination. It brought the community into contact with new knowledge and skills, but at the same time prevented it from changing its economic and political relationship to the dominant society.

In the mid-1930s one study found that 85 percent of surveyed districts in the Southwest were segregated in one form or another, some through high school, others only through the fifth grade.[21] In some areas, such as in the south Rio Grande Valley of Texas, strict segregation existed through most of the grades. In others, as in some of the smaller districts of California, no such uniform pattern prevailed. Nevertheless, de jure segregation of Mexican children remained common throughout the Southwest until the late forties and early fifties when various court orders declared such segregation a violation of the Constitution's equal protection clause. According to educators favoring segregation, its general purpose was to "Americanize" the child in a controlled linguistic and cultural environment, and its specific purpose was to train Mexicans for occupations considered open to, and appropriate for, them.[22] Nevertheless, the "acculturated" Mexican child (one who had assumed the dominant society's language, dress, manners, and the like) experienced segregation as well. Although proponents justified segregation on grounds of language and culture, the essential factor involved the economic function of the Mexican community as cheap labor.[23] Popular as well as academic opinion held that Mexicans posed an "educational problem," a consequence of an alleged intellectual, social, economical, cultural, moral, and physical inferiority.[24] Whether U.S.-born or naturalized, many members of the dominant society commonly looked upon them as aliens or cultural outcasts whose principal function was to sell their productive human capacities, that is, their labor, in the lowest-paid occupations. Consequently, the American community perceived equal educational opportunities for Mexicans as a burden and of little value for the Mexican community. Segregation became, therefore, the ideal policy when legislators and other authorities enacted and enforced compulsory education laws. These laws created an inferior and separate education that reflected and reproduced the socioeconomic relations in the surrounding community and region.[25]

Inadequate resources, poor equipment, and unfit building construction made Mexican schools vastly inferior to Anglo schools. In addition, school districts generally paid teachers at Mexican schools less than teachers at Anglo schools, and many times a promotion for a teacher at a Mexican school meant moving to the Anglo school. Quite often, however, teachers in Mexican schools were either beginners or had been "banished" as incompetent. One investigator, a high school teacher in Sugarland, Texas, wrote that teachers placed in a Mexican school were resentful and that "most of the teachers in the Mexican schools hope to be transferred to the school for the other whites as soon as vacancies may occur."[26] They often realized their wishes because the frequent moving of teachers from Mexican to Anglo schools seems to have been the rule. Consequently, instruction was often left "in charge of teachers who are not specially prepared by training or experience for the particular work of teaching the Spanish-speaking pupils."[27] Pauline R. Kibbe noted that in 1943 in one six-room Mexican school in West Texas, which enrolled 357 pupils, the head teacher "changed three times," and that in several classes a new teacher arrived "every three weeks." One wonders what degree of Americanization could take place in such a setting. Officials in urban areas elaborated better-organized programs of segregation.

For the most part, instruction periods for Mexican schools in agricultural areas coincided with farm-labor demands. Thus, school officials shortened or modified semesters depending on the dominant agricultural products of the region in which the schools were located. Moreover, children of migrant farm workers usually had little or no access to public schooling.

If, however, Mexicans attended school, whether in a segregated school, in a specific Mexican room within a nonrestricted school, or in a mixed school, the transition from Spanish to English was expected to take place in the first and second grades. Consequently, in many school districts the bulk of the children enrolled in the first two grades, with a rapid decline in enrollment by the sixth and seventh. The policy requiring Mexican children to repeat the first and second grades, combined with the practice, in many districts, of modifying the academic year to allow for child labor, tended to retard school progress. In addition, the unwritten tradition of tracking Mexican children into vocational and slow learner classes became institutionalized almost everywhere.

By their sixteenth birthdays, many Mexican children had barely reached junior high, and the dropout problem, which subsequently became notorious, began to manifest itself. Since the schools strongly advocated manual vocations, and since most Mexican families lived in poverty, many expected the majority of Mexican children to leave their segregated schools before high school in order to enter the labor force.

The legal justification for segregating Mexican children generally rested upon educational, not racial grounds. Meyer Weinberg notes that, in a 1930 unofficial opinion, California State Attorney General U. S. Webb declared segregation justifiable on the basis that Mexicans were Indians and therefore subject to the state law allowing their segregation.[28] Webb's interpretation strained credulity as well as the law. Of course, it did not apply to *all* Mexicans in fact, but law and facts do not always converge. A 1935 revision of the California education code attempted to close Webb's loophole by legalizing the segregation of "Indians" (excepting descendants of U.S. Indians, who, after 1924, were citizens of the United States). Certainly, one could have interpreted the revised code in such a way as to justify the segregation of Mexicans given that they descended from Indians.[29] However, it seems that the code seldom if ever applied to the segregation of the Mexican community. It made no direct mention, however, of the Mexicans even though this group comprised the most commonly segregated community in the state. Therefore, where segregation existed, it did so mainly on the basis of educational argument. In the research of Dr. George I. Sanchez— professor of education at the University of Texas, Austin—and Virgil E. Strickland on segregation in Texas, a survey of ten school districts found that the "language handicap is the official reason [to justify segregation] found in the school board minutes."[30] However, most arguments went beyond language; a San Bernardino, California, teacher stated that segregation was the outcome of the deliberations of the Anglo community and "based largely on the theory that the Mexican is a menace to the health and morals of the rest of the community."[31] These opinions attached "a stigma to [the Mexicans'] very being," prompting one investigator of the segregation of Mexican children to write that Americans take for granted that, among other things, "Mexicans are dirty, lawless, disease spreaders, stupid, and lazy."[32] Not surprisingly, given the strength of such public and official opinions, the practice of an official though illegal segregation eventually anchored educational policy with regard to the Mexican community.

Not all opinions justifying segregation demonstrated such a vicious attitude toward the Mexican community. A number of prominent researchers and academics viewed segregation as the preferred method of meeting the educational needs of the Mexican community. They often considered this practice an educational asset for the Mexican community. Yet even here, these shallow arguments masked the same prejudices that motivated the overt racists. The Arizona State Department of Education, for example, concluded that segregation "gives opportunity for the inauguration of a special program to meet the bilingual group interests."[33] A superintendent of a southern California district alleged that experience had demonstrated the pedagogically sound nature of segregation by showing "that Mexican children advance more rapidly when grouped by themselves," and therefore profited "most by the instruction offered in such classes."[34]

Although 10 percent of the students in one South Texas Mexican school were tracked into the educationally mentally retarded group, one of its teachers argued that "the Mexican child is not discriminated against," and that "in the majority of cases, the [class] room is the child's best home. . . ."[35] In describing the impact on Mexican children, another teacher wrote of "a most impressive" change in them. "Their faces radiated joy, they had thrown off the repression that held them down when they were in the schools with the other children. . . . There was no one to laugh at any peculiarity they might possess, and they were free."[36]

These two arguments justifying segregation often intertwined. For example, the superintendent of the Garden Grove, California, elementary school district stated on the witness stand in the *Mendez* v. *Westmin-*

ster desegregation case, that integration would make Mexican children "feel inferior because of their clothing they have to wear."[37] This same superintendent had also written on the education of Mexican children in which he justified segregation with an opposite approach.

> Because of (1) social differences between the two races; (2) much higher percentage of contagious disease (among Mexican children); (3) much higher percentage of undesirable behavior characteristics; (4) much slower progress in school, and (5) much lower moral standards, it would seem best that . . . Mexican children be segregated. . . .[38]

Most districts that practiced segregation maintained a "Mexican" school, which admitted only Mexican children. Some districts, such as the Los Angeles City School District, segregated via districting boundaries (rather than a simple identification of nationality), because, according to one teacher, "One of the first demands from a community in which there is a large Mexican population is for a separate school."[39] In Los Angeles, the district did not refer to these separate institutions as "Mexican schools," as in many districts, but as "neighborhood schools" and sometimes as "foreign schools." One Los Angeles school administrator wrote that neighborhood (read "Mexican") schools existed as such "because the district gerrymandered schools [so] that they can be nothing but foreign schools and remain foreign schools."[40] The consequences of either policy were the same, although the Los Angeles system may have appeared to be a de facto system of segregation.

According to arguments raised by educators, one of the main aspects of the Mexican school was that it allowed a curriculum tailored to the needs of the student, thereby preparing him to transfer to an American elementary or junior high school. In the American school, educators expected Anglos and Americanized Mexicans to eventually compete in an integrated setting. Actually, that rarely happened. Mexicans seldom, if ever, Americanized to the extent that they no longer remained bilinguals. In fact, most retained their Mexican cultural heritage. Segregation seldom accomplished its objectives, then, and as Mexican children moved into integrated junior high, school officials tracked them into slow learner groups. This practice, wrote one teacher about a southern California school district, "appears to be a disadvantage to many of the Mexican boys and girls. With few exceptions these students are placed, as a result of the testing program, in the slower-moving classes. . . ."[41]

However, since many, if not most, students began dropping out at this point, such integration usually affected only a minority. Thus, a different type of segregation followed Mexican children when they graduated from their Mexican school to what was, for all practical purposes, an Anglo school that opened its doors to Mexican enrollment. In the late twenties at one Los Angeles junior high, Mexican children comprised sixty out of eighty entering lower-track students; the percentage of Mexican children in lower tracks at four other schools varied from 33 to 55 percent.[42] By the midforties the situation remained as such, prompting the superintendent of the Los Angeles County schools to comment that when the Mexican child entered the junior high, "he again finds himself segregated" into ability groups, and consequently, a "vicious cycle" of segregation was unbroken even in an "integrated" setting.[43]

A most significant aspect of the segregated program was that it not only applied to the education of children; it also included the adults of the community, especially women. In fact, in most districts where the segregation of schoolchildren appeared, a segregated adult education program generally accompanied it. In one southern California district, educators offered language instruction for both men and women. However, for women, these courses addressed "the care of infants, cleanliness, house sanitation, and economical house management, including sewing, cooking, and thrift"; for men these programs offered "courses in thrift, in gardening, and . . . principles of the American government."[44] Both adult and children's programs had similar objectives for substantially identical reasons, and through the same general method—the segregated school.

Segregated schools functioned not only as the center of the social-ization of the Mexican child, but also as laboratories for research into the "Mexican educational problem." In the early 1920s, the California State Department of Education assigned Grace C. Stanley, formerly of the Los Angeles School District, to undertake and supervise "an experi-ment in the education of the foreign child." Ten schools were selected throughout southern California "as centers for experimentation, with the "Mexican school" in Cucamonga as the principal station for experimen-tation, and it was from this project that teaching "methods were recom-mended throughout the State,"[45] including schools with "foreign" popu-lations other than Mexican. Many districts established special depart-ments entrusted with the design of the curriculum for the education of Mexican children. In the Southwest, various names identified such departments: the Department of Immigrant Education, the Department of Americanization, or simply the Department of Mexican Education. In one district in southern California, the superintendent, Merton Hill (who was soon to become the director of admissions for the University of California), ordered the Department of Mexican Education "to make a scientific study of the Mexican . . . the temperament of the race . . . those qualities and abilities that are recognized as peculiar to the Mexican people. . . ."[46] Furthermore, the "peculiar attitudes of these good-natured and kindly people" should be "developed along the best possible lines," and their "capacities to perform different types of service should be set forth [so] that their employers may utilize them to the best interests."[47] Such studies merely reinforced existing theories and practices subordi-nating the Mexican community in nearly every phase of their lives to the larger society.

Such schooling resulted in an education that recapitulated the migra-tion of Mexicans to the United States as a supply of flexible and cheap labor. Thus, segregation grew out of policy decisions corresponding to the economic interests of the Anglo community; it became a means of domination and control, the antithesis of equality and freedom; and it was intrinsically racist both in that it was based on racial social theories, and in that it led to educational practices that reinforced a pattern of social inequality based on nationality and race.

POLITICS OF DESEGREGATION

The Mexican community never accepted segregation. Indeed, records for the twenties and thirties demonstrate the fact that community organizations and representations voiced their opposition and struggled against segregation.[48] However, the big wave of protest occurred during and shortly after the Second World War, about the same time that anti-Mexican hysteria was sweeping Los Angeles and other urban centers. Ironically, the Mexican community resorted to the legal system to gain its democratic rights despite the violent attacks against Mexicans, the sympathetic defense of these attacks by police and courts, and the historical bulwark in defense of segregation by the courts.

The most significant court case affecting the de jure segregation of Mexican children in the Southwest was the *Mendez* v. *Westminster* decision of 1947 in California. The 1930 *Lemon Grove* case, also in California, the nation's first successful desegregation court decision, had had only local repercussions, and the Salvatierra, Texas, case of the same year, which enunciated the doctrine that Mexicans could not be legally segregated (as were blacks) on the basis of race, had simply underscored the widespread opinion that the only basis for separate schooling for Mexicans was educational (language, culture, etc.) and, in any case, it was struck down by the Delgado, Texas, decision of 1947. The plaintiffs in the *Mendez* case could not have known that their struggle would lead to an historic legal decision reaching far beyond their small community. It was the first federal court decision and the first use of the Fourteenth Amendment to overturn the widespread segregation of a minority group. That social scientists came forward to offer "expert" testimony in a court trial added to the case's significance. The anthropologist Ralph Beals, for example, successfully argued that segregation retards rather than helps the assimilation process. Robert Carter, one of the frontline attorneys for the NAACP (National Association for the Advancement of Colored People), was impressed by the utilization of social science knowledge to criticize segregation. Carter suggested to his friend Thurgood Marshall that the "social science approach would be the only way to overturn segregation in the United States."[49] Later, attorneys for the NAACP employed with success this particular strategy in the 1954 Supreme Court decision, *Brown* v. *Board of Education.* Carter, who later became a district court judge in New York, also felt that the *amicus curiae* that he and Marshall filed in the appellate court in support of the district court's *Mendez* decision was a "dry run for the future." Indeed, the attorney for the Mendez plaintiffs, David Marcus, provided Marshall with all of the briefs and notes compiled during the case. It is probably true, therefore, that Mendez was the first stage in the process of overturning the *Plessy* v. *Ferguson* doctrine of "separate but equal."

The *Mendez* case can be ranked as one of the key legal cases in U.S. history. Thus, one contemporary legal analyst wrote that the *Mendez* decision "must be ranked among the vanguard of those making a frontal attack upon the equal but separate canon of interpretation of the equal protection clause."[50]

The immediate effects of the Mendez case in the Southwest were widespread, and Mexican parents and civil rights organizations such as the LULAC and the GI Forum in Arizona, Colorado, New Mexico, and Texas, entered the campaign against school segregation shortly thereafter. Eventually, de jure segregation in schools ended throughout the Southwest,[51] but not before an educational policy reinforcing socioeconomic inequality severely victimized generations of Mexican children.

CHAPTER 1

CULTURE AND LANGUAGE

THE AMERICANIZATION OF MEXICAN CHILDREN

During the segregation period, Americanization was the prime objective of the education of Mexican children. Authorities reorganized schooling administration and practices whenever the Mexican population rose to significant numbers in a community and whenever Mexican children because increasingly visible on the school registers. This reorganization established special programs, including Americanization classes, and applied to both children and adults in urban and rural schools and communities. The desired effect was the political socialization and acculturation of the Mexican community, as well as, ironically, the maintenance of those social and economic relations existing between Anglos and Mexicans. Indeed, more than anything else, Americanization tended to preserve the political and economic subordination of the Mexican community. Moreover, Americanization merged smoothly with the general educational methodology developed to solve the "Mexican educational problem," as it went hand in hand with testing, tracking, and the emphasis upon vocational education.

SOCIAL THEORY AND AMERICANIZATION

Americanization was the practical form of the general sociological theory of assimilation, and assimilation was the specific application of the general theory of the organic society to the problem of immigrants and ethnicity in modern industrialized societies.[1] Consequently, Americanization corresponded in most respects with the dominant social theory at the turn of the century. Organic theory arose as a response to emerging social conditions of advanced capitalist countries in the late nineteenth century and focused upon problems of social order in a complex, urban industrial environment. It offered a critique of Social Darwinism and subsequently replaced it with a view of society as governed primarily by social, not uncontrollable natural or biological, forces. Society was perceived as a single entity, organic, that is, without critical internal contradictions, with a life of its own, composed of inter-related and interdependent parts, each functioning as part of a single whole. An early proponent of organic theory and pioneer in American sociology, Charles H. Cooley, defined society as "a complex of forms and processes each of which is living and growing by interaction with the others, the whole being so unified that what takes place in one part affects all the rest. It is a vast tissue of reciprocal activity."[2]

The forerunner of modern functionalism, the theory of the organic society, conformed to the ideological and institutional foundations of the existing social order. Consequently, the theory of assimilation that provided the practical basis for Americanization programs was designed to solve in "in-house" needs of a society governed by a dynamic capitalist system of production and characterized by a particular form of division of labor.

According to the organic theory of society, the maintenance of the modern social order is based upon a common "apperception mass" (experiential heritage) that subsequently forges a unified organization of individuals, although separated and differentiated by the economic roles corresponding to the complexity of a modern industrial society. The division of labor is highly complex; individuals are objectively inter-dependent, and individual roles cannot be separated from the whole.[3] However, individuals must have a subjective consciousness of interde-pendence and a commitment to engage cooperatively in the produc-tive process, and if not, the unity of society is seriously weakened. The absence of common norms undermines the social order; consequently, its survival is only as secure as the norms binding individuals together. The sociologist Florian Znaniecki, addressing the question of social order, summarized the prevailing views on the role of culture and social rela-tions in society.

> . . . uniformities of social systems, like those of cultural systems, are chiefly the result of a reflective or unreflective use of the same cultural patterns in many particular cases. There is obvi-ously a fundamental and universal, though unreflective, cultural pattern in accordance with which all kinds of lasting relationships between individuals and their social milieu are normatively orga-nized and which we denote by the term "social role."[4]

W. I. Thomas and Robert E. Park, major figures and collabora-tors in race relations and assimilation theory, strongly advocated the organic view of society. Fred Wacker writes that Park's race relations theory "emphasized organic solidarity of societies."[5] Consequently, the Thomas-Park conception of the integration of immigrants into society first and foremost concerned the functioning of the whole of society. The purpose of society, wrote Park, "is to organize, integrate, and direct the energies resident in the individuals of which it is composed."[6] Conse-quently, Morris Janowitz describes Thomas as a " 'functionalist' in the sense that he believed that hypothetical and value-oriented questions should be raised about the conditions under which optimum social rela-tions would occur."[7] Above all else, it was the "effort to establish and maintain a political order in a community that has no common culture."[8]

ASSIMILATION THEORY AND FOLK VERSUS MODERN SOCIETIES

The theory of assimilation derived directly from the very process of modernization that resulted in that sharp historical break distinguishing feudal, agrarian societies from capitalist-industrial, urban societies. In the late nineteenth century, European capitalist development wrought massive changes that accounted for the merging and eventual disappearance of small ethnic and linguistically diverse communities, initially scattered and separate, into a single dominant national institutional structure and culture.[9] Thus, according to European sociologists who initially analyzed this process and consequently constructed theories, the trend toward cultural amalgamation was not merely an American phenomenon, but the universal fate of all folk or peasant societies wherever they confronted an industrial bureaucratic social order. Moreover, they argued that the cultural composition of folk societies directly contradicted the culture of modern societies, thereby making traditional societies incompatible with industrial societies and a threat to their maintenance and development. Although social scientists espoused a deterministic view of the assimilation process—that is, that the peasant societies and their traditions will inevitably slip into worldwide oblivion —they also held the belief that an applied state-run program of assimilation can guide this evolutionary process. In the United States, this deliberate government-sponsored assimilation process was called simply, "Americanization."

Ethnic culture allegedly corresponded to a traditional society, justifiable and even necessary in a premodern context, but incompatible with the modern industrial setting.[10] Traditional societies manifested a spontaneous, but isolated, culture springing from a simple division of labor and, in turn, reinforcing that simple division of labor. Moreover, assimilation theory contended that traditional ethnic culture rejected external governmental methods to achieve normal social relations characteristic of modern societies. Social relations within folk societies sprang spontaneously from the very nature of the society. Thus, villages comprised self-contained social units having no need to relate in significant ways outside of their society. Theoretically, the ethnic village achieved a social harmony from its simple productive organization. In the modern context, the spontaneous and self-directed society characteristic of the traditional village conflicted with the need for the centralized state to intervene in the complex social process to create a consciousness that conformed to national policies and therefore impersonal exigencies. Theoretically, the traditional mind tended to respond to personalistic, familial, and communal ties and distrusted the impersonal, nonfamilial, and distant bureaucratic forces characteristic of modern societies.

Given that an evolutionary process was eliminating diverse ethnic cultures whose distinctiveness was that they were preindustrial or peasant societies, the majority culture that corresponded to the most modern stage of human societies inevitably became the embracing and dominant culture.[11] When ethnic diversity in a single society entailed peasant (or ethnic) cultures surrounded by an industrial culture, it constituted a formidable obstacle to modernization and posed serious threats to the exigencies of modern political life.

Within the assimilation process, language formed the core of transformation. The lack of a common language makes social cohesion impossible. In support of this view, Park and E. W. Burgess wrote that a common language becomes "indispensable" to the welfare of society and that "its absence is an insurmountable barrier to assimilation." On the basis of a common form of communication, "a gradual and unconscious modification of the attitudes and sentiments" occurs. Once a common language is established, a "unity of experience and of orientation" takes hold; a community with a unified sense of "purpose and action" develops.[12] Thus, from smaller social units a single large social unit emerges, but it can do so only upon the foundation of a common language.

Other issues remain, however. When coupled with class consciousness and political action, ethnicity poses even further problems for the realization of an organic society. Such occurred when the presence of large numbers of working people who descended from first- and second-generation immigrants from traditional societies and who formed the backbone of the union movement threatened the political and economic stability in the United States at the end of the nineteenth century. This was especially true in the industrial Northeast where first- or second-generation ethnics comprised 75 percent of the population.[13] The assimilative process consequently emphasized the ideological integration of these cultures into the dominant political ideology, entailing citizenship, patriotism, and allegiance to traditional American values and symbols. The integration of all social elements into a single unified and cohesive social order involved this process.

APPROACHES TO ASSIMILATION

At least three schools of thought engaged in the debate over assimilation. The first, the Neo-Lamarckian school, best exemplified in the sociology of E. A. Ross and the historiography of John R. Commons, rejects the possibility and desirability of assimilation on the ground that the "new" immigrants were biologically and culturally inferior to native American stock and therefore unassimilable.[14] This anti-immigrant wing of organic theory opted instead for severe immigration restriction as the key to social integration. In so doing it helped to shape negative stereotypes and whip up anti-immigrant sentiment that undoubtedly found its way into the Americanization practice.

The approach taken by Thomas and Park essentially argued that the dominant culture would eventually replace the immigrants' Old World consciousness through a process of a "natural" assimilation combined with Americanization classes. However, effective assimilation required immigrants to be allowed to fashion their own structures, organization, and nationalistic consciousness.[15] Following the corporate notions of Emile Durkheim, they contended that internally integrated immigrant structures were indispensable for the organic solidarity of society. As Joseph Hraba explains, eventually immigrant structures would disappear.

> The new order of Park is that of Durkheim. As individuals in industrial cities are freed from the bonds of the folk past and are diffused throughout a complex division of labor, vocational interests and the economic interdependence of vocational groups replace folk identity as the expression of solidarity in modern society. . . .[16]

Americanization must and would take place, but it could do so on the foundation of the language, heritage, "memories," and organization of the immigrant communities. Any other approach, argued Thomas and Park, would prove counterproductive. Yet, Thomas found serious faults with the heritage of some nationalities and races and, in so doing, undoubtedly contributed to the restrictionists' arguments.

> Every country has a certain amount of culturally undeveloped material. We have it, for instance, in the Negroes and Indians, the Southern mountaineers, the Mexicans and Spanish Americans, and the slums. There is a limit, however, to the amount of material of this kind that a country can incorporate without losing the character of its culture.[17]

Staunchly opposed by Thomas and Park, the third approach involves essentially the actual practice of Americanization programs. While they did agree that immigrant folk values could not permanently adapt to the American system, they opposed any form of Americanization that did not allow for the expression of ethnic consciousness and heritage as part of the Americanization process. The practice of Americanization by and large demanded the immediate and total cultural transformation of the immigrant community. Thomas quoted a statement made in 1918 by the superintendent of New York schools as an example of the approach undergirding Americanization programs across the United States. "Broadly speaking, we mean [by Americanization]

an appreciation of the institutions of this country, absolute forgetful-
ness of all obligations or connections with other countries because of
descent or birth."[18] Americanization early appeared as an "ordering and
forbidding" exercise—intolerant and more negative than positive in its
methods and objectives toward the communities being introduced into
the "welcoming" society.

Americanization teachers viewed immigrant communities as threats
to the well-being of society. The immigrants and their cultures became
the locus of destabilizing influences in society for supporters of Americanization. With such a negative frame of mind toward the immigrant
community, these practitioners launched Americanization programs
throughout the Southwest.

The historians Maxine Sellers,[19] Ricardo Romo,[20] and Mario Garcia[21]
have linked the Mexican Americanization experience with the national
Americanization effort, but our analysis stipulates that we highlight
the significant differences between European and Mexican experiences.
First, the Americanization of the Mexican community occurred in a
legally segregated system. Secondly, it was both rural and urban, as
contrasted with the European experience, which was overwhelmingly
urban. Thirdly, it was heavily influenced by the regional agricultural
economy, which retarded a "natural" assimilation process. Finally, immigrants from Mexico could not escape the effects of the economic and
political relationship between an advanced capitalist nation, the United
States, and a semicapitalist, semifeudal nation, Mexico, the latter increasingly under the political and economic sway of the United States. None
of the contributory European nations had such a relationship with the
United States, and thus, their national cultures tended to be judged more
on an equal footing with that of the United States. The Mexican case has
historically been one of a nation struggling to realize its national interests against the nationalism of a rising world power. This factor alone
would have made for a significant modification in the objectives and

manner in which Americanization was applied to the Mexican community.

THE AMERICANIZATION OF MEXICAN CHILDREN IN THE SCHOOL

In the first half of the twentieth century, when the Mexican community was more rural, separate, and identifiable than it is today, the schooling system constructed a cultural demarcation between a superior and an inferior culture. Assimilation, then, involved not just the elimination of linguistic and cultural differences, but of an entire culture that assimilation advocates deemed undesirable. Americanization programs assumed a single homogeneous ethnic culture in contact with a single homogeneous modern one, and the relationship between the two was not that of equals. Cultural differences explained in part the socioeconomic differences between the populations that bore these cultures. The dominant community, enjoying greater wealth and privileges, claimed its position by virtue of alleged cultural superiority. In one way or another, nearly every Mexican child, whether born in the United States or in Mexico, was treated as a "foreigner," as an alien, and as an intruder. The Los Angeles school superintendent voiced a common complaint in a 1923 address to district principals. "We have these [Mexican] immigrants to live with, and if we Americanize them, we can live with them. . . ."[22] The objective was to transform the Mexican community into an English-speaking and American-thinking community.

In addition, Americanization, wrote the superintendent of a southern California school district, "sets up those activities that will bring about the acceptance of aliens of American ideals, customs, methods of living, skills, and knowledge that will make them Americans in fact."[23] The Americanization program of a La Habra, California, labor camp (a project funded by a public school) entirely operated upon the assumption that Mexican "behavior patterns, the beliefs, the convictions . . . have . . . to

labor camp

be transformed in conformity with the new environment."[24] Americanization programs based upon academic and popular literature tended to
reinforce the stereotypes of Mexicans as dirty, shiftless, lazy, irrespon-
sible, unambitious, thriftless, fatalistic, selfish, promiscuous, and prone
to drinking, violence, and criminal behavior.[25] The La Habra Americanization teacher, Jessie Hayden, saw "Mexican apathy, . . . an infirmity of
the will, forever the promise of manana" as dragging "upon the wheels
of such progress as might exist" in the Mexican community,[26] but felt
that the "Mexican people are slowly struggling toward light," the light
of American culture that allows the Mexican community to "realize the
darkness with which they are surrounded."[27]

Sixteen years later, a Phoenix, Arizona, principal also offered his
diagnosis and prescription for the cultural illumination of the Mexican
community.

> Much more classroom time should be spent teaching the
> [Mexican] children clean habits and positive attitudes towards
> others, public property, and their community in general. . . . [The
> Mexican child] can be taught to repeat the Constitution forward
> and backward and still he will steal cars, break windows, wreck
> public recreational centers, etc., if he doesn't catch the idea of
> respect for human values and personalities.[28]

A statement concerning the sexual habits of Mexican children by the
assistant supervisor of the Compulsory Education Department of the
Los Angeles city schools, typified both the method of cultural analysis
and the fairly widespread stereotype of alleged Mexican promiscuity. He
wrote,

> Authorities on the Mexican mind agree that after the age of 12–
> 14 educational and higher ambitions turn to inclinations of sex
> impulse . . . the average [Mexican] boy and girl revert to the native
> instinct and throw up the sponge, where the more fortunate are

anxious to emulate their American classmates in an effort at resistance.[29]

Similarly, Professor E. E. Davis of the University of Texas, asserted in a 1923 publication:

> The American children and those of the Mexican children who are clean and high-minded do not like to go to school with the dirty "greaser" type of Mexican child. It is not right that they should have to. There is but one choice in the matter of educating these unfortunate children and that is to put the "dirty" ones into separate schools till they learn how to "clean-up" and become eligible to better society.[30]

These assertions, we presume, had some relation to classroom practice. Americanization, then, was an oppressive curriculum and objective enforced to acculturate the Mexican community. Educators may or may not have recognized the oppressive nature of school policies inasmuch as they were frequently rationalized in terms of the needs, interests, and welfare of the Mexican people. The Anglo image of the culture in Mexican communities appears to have instilled in educators an exaggerated sense of guardianship of the American way of life.

The Americanization literature, however, was not uniformly negative in intent. The intent seemed more often patronizing than negative, more insensitive than malicious. Administrators asked teachers to be "genuinely" interested in teaching the Mexican child. A principal of a San Antonio Mexican school suggested that teachers acquire a "knowledge of the characteristics of the Mexican children" and that it was "of first importance" for effective instruction to take place. To this end, special lessons were developed by the school district for the training of teachers in Mexican schools.[31] The supervisor of the K–8 schools in El Paso urged teachers in Mexican schools to "have a knowledge of Mexican history, and of the racial and cultural background of the Mexican people."[32] A common approach to the "Mexican educational problem" involved employing teachers who knew "something of the psychology of the Mexican." Consequently, many teaching colleges and universities created special courses for the effective instruction of Mexican children. The University of Southern California, the University of California, the University of Texas, and the Texas College of Arts and Industries, among others, offered courses for the preparation of teachers planning to work in areas with high Mexican enrollment. These institutions gave teachers ample opportunity to learn about current theories of Mexican culture and to translate them into classroom practice. School districts commonly adapted their Americanization methods to the presumed intelligence, personality, culture, and environment of the Mexican child.[33] Those teachers who became familiar with the social science literature concerning Mexicans were considered better able "to cope with the problems presented by their little Mexican pupils."[34]

Many school districts instituted in-service training for the teaching of Spanish-speaking children. Large districts with high Mexican enrollment, such as Los Angeles and San Antonio, organized courses to help their teachers understand the objectives of, and learn the methods for, the effective Americanization of Mexican children. Smaller districts at the time, such as Phoenix, El Paso, Santa Ana, Fresno, and San Diego, did likewise. California led the southwestern states in Americanization by establishing, in 1916, a Division of Immigrant Education within the Department of Education for the promotion, development, and improvement of Americanization programs. Out of this larger effort, many districts, such as Los Angeles, Long Beach, Santa Ana, and Oakland, established special Departments of Americanization (or sometimes Departments of Immigrant Education) and placed a supervisor in charge of these programs within the schools. When programs such as these were in operation, officials expected a much more effective Americanization curriculum. In Texas and Arizona, school administrators placed special emphasis upon the publication of bulletins and guidelines for the instruction of Spanish-speaking children.

Nothing short of total cultural transformation would satisfy many leaders in education. Vera A. Chase, an instructor in education at the Arizona State Teachers College (which later became known as Arizona State University), argued that the educational problems of Mexican children, in large part, grew out of the "cultural heritage" of the "non-English speaking child."[35] Furthermore, she stated:

> The immigrant child is different to the extent that he lives in a world of different standards and traditions. He comes more nearly to resemble the American group in his needs, interests, and achievements as his home environment becomes more like that of the American child. At some point in his advance he merges into the group for whom the other curriculum bulletins have been prepared.[36]

Chase did not offer her recommendations without acknowledging that Americanization had national political ramifications. She, like many educators, felt that for the benefit both of the larger society and of the immigrant, the immigrant child "must learn to live as nearly as possible in the way American people live [and] drop traditions and customs that conflict with American culture."[37] If the Mexican failed to assimilate, he remained "an isolated and ineffective element" and his relations with Americans were necessarily "distant and unsatisfactory, if not tinged with hostility."[38]

One researcher synthesized the teaching methods of thirty southern California schoolteachers working with Mexican children. The classroom served as a center where desirable traits slowly replaced "undesirable traits." Teachers urged Mexican children to "make fun of the lazy ones" in the classroom; to overcome uncleanliness by making a dirty child feel uncomfortable; to compare Mexican and American homes for the sake of imitation; and to overcome the "racial" desire to show off by ridicule.[39] One of the main weapons utilized by teachers in this process was imitation. "Since imitation is so dominant in the Mexican nature," she wrote, "opportunity should be provided for the Mexican to mingle with Americans worthy of imitation."[40] The state superintendent's office required California teachers to base Americanization upon this tendency to imitate. Since the homes of Mexican children were "so meager and simple," they hardly knew "what is normally done in a kitchen or a bedroom." Consequently, the state Department of Education recommended that course work include class visits to "an American home of four or five rooms" or examination of "carefully selected pictures."[41]

Even though teachers generally felt that Mexicans were endowed with a deficient or inferior cultural heritage, many held that this culture had some virtues that might perhaps be preserved. These virtuous traits, however, were but the flip side of the coin, for they placed the Mexican child in an inferior and paternalistic context. Observers often described Mexican culture as "gay, light-hearted," unaffected by the fast-paced materialistic American society, and passionately devoted to "color, music and dancing."[42] In essence, these paternalists credited Mexican children with having special talent in art and crafts. Annie S. Reynolds wrote, in her federally sponsored study, that "every opportunity to develop" artwork should be assigned to the Mexican child. "Here is a phase of education," she concluded, "in which Spanish-speaking pupils are certainly not handicapped." She added that "emphasis on book study is entirely inadequate to their needs."[43]

Very often teachers made attempts to stress Mexican traditions in the curriculum, for example, in music, dance, art, architecture, patriotic celebrations, history, and current events. While it may have seemed to some that the classroom actually preserved Mexican culture by displaying a Mexican flag on Cinco de Mayo (Mexico's second Independence Day, celebrating the expulsion of French forces in 1864) or a Diego Rivera reproduction, the purpose of these displays was to get the child to feel more secure. Gradually, however, class practice separated the child entirely from these symbolic representations. The practitioners would determine which Mexican virtues were proper for integration and which were to be eliminated. The cultural model, with its superior-to-inferior continuum, mirrored the political and economic relations between the Mexican and Anglo communities. Even in the attempt to assimilate, theory and practice at once reflected and strengthened the social relations of the community.

LANGUAGE AND ASSIMILATION

The essence of Americanization programs across the Southwest was language instruction. In fact, most of the literature on the education of Mexican children focused on language. This might be expected since English was the medium of instruction. Here again, theory also combined with practical questions since many southwestern school districts had large Spanish-speaking populations. In 1936 Los Angeles, for example, had forty-four thousand such children enrolled in its schools.[45] In San Antonio half of the school population was non-English-speaking, the vast majority Spanish-speaking. Moreover, 1930 estimates indicated that 90 percent of the Mexican children enrolled for the first time in Texas public schools could not speak or understand English.[46]

The language conflict, of course, presented a very real educational barrier. However, rather than addressing the problem as a practical one of overcoming the language gap in order to facilitate instruction, the school officials directed their energy to solving the larger problem, the Americanization of non-English-speaking children. The theoretical foundation for the emphasis on language came directly from contemporary interpretations of assimilation. This explains why the director of elementary education of the San Antonio public schools stated in the introduction to an article on the curriculum for Mexican children, that the "first step in making a unified nation is to teach English to the non-English speaking portion of the population."[47] Similar views appeared frequently in the literature on the education of Mexican children. For example, the assistant superintendent for Immigrant Education and Elementary Evening Schools in Los Angeles, bluntly stated that as to "the need of a common national language, there can be no debate," thus asserting that this task was as significant as any other in the public school system.[48] Thus, educators expected Americanization instruction to result in the termination of Spanish language usage in the community. A Grandfalls, Texas, schoolteacher wrote that in that system's Americanization program, "first place has been given to the substitution of English for Spanish in school life."[49]

Most educators who commented on the topic firmly believed that Spanish failed as a medium through which learning takes place. For example, in an educational manual published by the Arizona Department of Education, the author warned the teachers of Mexican children that language and culture were nearly identical. The failure of Mexican children "to learn English in their daily life" implied a retention of the "customs and traditions of their native land," which had a negative effect upon the educational problems of bilingual children.[50] "Bad habits," customs, and attitudes retarded learning; therefore, assimilation could not be realized until Spanish was eliminated.

The superintendent of Eagle Pass, Texas, schools followed conventional wisdom when he wrote that a Mexican child "is foreign in his thinking and attitudes" until he learns to "think and talk in English."[51] "The first great problem in Americanizing these children," he warned, was the teaching of English "to children whose vernacular is a foreign language." When the child has acquired English he has "already acquired much of the culture and outlook of the American." Presumably, the English-speaking child became an equal and full member of society, whereas the child who failed to learn English retained "the culture, ideals, customs, thought, and attitudes of another race and another people."[52]

School districts that segregated via spatial boundaries, followed the same language policies as districts that segregated on the basis of nationality or language. The Los Angeles School District utilized the former method when it created "neighborhood" schools or schools largely attended by first- and second-generation Mexican children. By the early 1920s, neighborhood schools functioned in the immigrant quarters and operated in much the same fashion as segregated or Mexican schools. The principal objective of the neighborhood school involved Americanizing Mexican children and educating them vocationally to the "level" of their abilities.[53] So-called foreign opportunity rooms also existed in schools whose student bodies were of mixed nationality. In 1924, Los Angeles operated forty-five such classes for non-English-speaking children as part of the overall Americanization effort. In the junior high schools, officials made provisions for the teaching of "American ideals of conduct, of education, and of home life" for non-English-speaking students. Lessons emphasized learning "the English language and the elements of American citizenship."[54]

A related and common assumption held that a diversity of languages in a single society predisposed that society to political antagonisms between language groups. Junius L. Meriam, a professor of education at the University of California, Los Angeles, engaged in pedagogical research on Mexican school children, warned that whenever distinct language-groups exist in a society, conflict is inevitable.

> Bilingualism becomes an acute problem when two languages spoken are of different families. . . . Here exists a situation, due to speech conflict, that usually cloaks, if it does not only express, a conflict of races. If those dwelling in the same land . . . can by sincere instruction in a second language, meet on common ground and . . . develop common interests, then springs into life the possibility of mental, spiritual, and artistic progress for all concerned.[55]

The Departments of Education of the southwestern states periodically published guidelines for the instruction of bilingual children. Their prescriptions generally followed a pattern of methodology and theory. While department officials permitted only English as the language for communication and instruction, Spanish was often allowed for the translation and definition of words. In general, as in Grandfalls, Texas, "All children were requested to speak English" in the classroom. In the early stages of the Grandfalls program, instructors followed a liberal policy; later on, they applied more stringent codes of conduct. For example, teachers forbade a child to leave the school grounds at noon "unless he asked permission in English."[56] The system of punishment seemed to work, as evidenced by this report on the Grandfalls Americanization classes. "Now in the third year of this effort in Americanization even the teachers are beginning to see some worth—with results. English is spoken in the [school] house and on the playground during school hours: nine until four."[57] In the Harlingen, Texas, Mexican schools, the principal instituted an English Club comprised of children who had not spoken Spanish in the previous six weeks. Membership fluctuated, and only members could participate in the quarterly picnics and other club activities held on a regular basis. Those who spoke Spanish during any of the activities were required "to remain in the room and study."[58] The English Club used the "honor system" to some extent, and according to the principal, teachers "checked each day by roll call, as to whether or not they [the children] have spoken English." Instead of answering "present," children responded with "English" or "Spanish." Students caught in a lie were "suspended from the club for the first offense" and expelled for the second. If their only transgression was to have spoken Spanish, they were allowed back in the club after a week of "nothing but English."[59]

The Arizona state superintendent's office advised teachers that "every phase of school life" of the Mexican child "should take part in promoting the meaningful use of English."[60] Without the English language, warned the superintendent, Mexican people would not realize "effective citizenship."[61] Indeed, in the schooling atmosphere based upon the forcible elimination of one language, by another, school authorities organized the system of rewards and punishments accordingly. The child achieved "success" when he learned English and became Americanized; a child "failed" when he remained a non-English-speaker. The Arizona State Course of Study for Bilingual Children arrived at a standard for successful behavior and learning on the part of the Mexican child when it posed the following questions: "Does he try to accommodate himself to American culture as represented by the school setting; does he try to learn to speak English?" If the child made an "honest effort" and if he "responded with genuine interest to the school situation," then the Course of Study concluded that the child had met minimal standards for Americanization. "He should feel pride," continued the Course of Study, "in making progress in the accepted task of learning a new language."[62]

Rural Americanization proceeded as facilities and curriculum developed. The goal, however, varied little from the pattern established in the Southwest. The 1945 logbook of a Ventura County, California, first-grade schoolteacher recorded a popular method of teaching English— peer pressure. The logbook read: "On Tuesday we reviewed our rules for walks and went to town to buy pumpkins for our jack-o-lanterns. The slogan shouted by the children as they started off was 'Talk in English.' And they did."[63]

School officials often combined English instruction with direct attempts to manipulate the "aliens'" cultural standards. For example, many segregated schools in the Southwest contained showering facilities where children were obliged, after a morning inspection, to shower. In the East Donna, Texas, Mexican school, a twelve-room building served five hundred students in which "morning inspections in each classroom [were] regularly conducted," and children who failed to pass inspection were "required to wash before they [were] permitted to begin the day's activities." If their clothes were dirty, they were required to change into clean clothes loaned by the school "in emergency cases."[64]

As illustrated by a teacher's guide issued by the state of California, English instruction complemented the cleanliness program. The method of instruction recommended must have been humiliating for the children. In one particular model classroom vignette, the teacher helps a child wash his hands and face and comb his hair. Upon completion of the assignment, the teacher brings "him before class and [comments] favorably upon his accomplishment and looks, as [in] 'Look at José. He is clean.'"[65]

The objective of the English instruction program for non-English-speaking children included creating a way of life characterized by initiative, cooperation, courtesy, cleanliness, and a desirable home life. "Help them to want to be clean," urged the California *Guide for Teaching Non-English-Speaking Children,* "and provide opportunities for making cleanliness possible."[66] The *Guide* also suggested a method of teaching "habits and attitudes that make home life clean, comfortable and happy."[67] Consequently, English drills incorporated practice in setting the dinner table and arranging bedrooms and living rooms. Such instruction also included "constant and careful work . . . to promote correct enunciation and pronunciation." Through the program, which combined language and culture, the state expected a cultural transformation.

> Constant contact with an environment that ministers to the love of the beautiful and orderly creates an abhorrence of anything that is not well-ordered and clean. Through this subtle, indirect influence the standards of foreign homes may be raised, for when these children grow up they will not be happy in an environment widely different from that to which they have been habituated.[68]

Through the program of Americanization, the Mexican child was taught that his family, community, and culture were obstacles to schooling success. The assumption that Mexican culture was meager and deficient implied that the child came into the classroom with meager and deficient tools with which to learn. This implication was quite consciously woven into the methodology and content of instruction.

Americanization, as a curricular activity, endured well into the late thirties, and even then, educators did not abandon the objective of assimilating Mexicans into the dominant culture; they merely changed the appearance of the program. Proponents of "Americanization" ceased referring to it as such, but the essential features of the program remained. Language and culture continued to be major educational concerns, and the identification of the Spanish language and Mexican culture as contradictory to educational success lost no ground in conventional theory and practice. Throughout the first half of the century, school policies treated the culture of the Mexican child as unworthy of equality with the dominant culture.

The segregated rural and urban Mexican communities contrasted markedly with the communities of the dominant society. Proponents of assimilation applied their policies to Mexicans with little effort because of the size, geographic isolation, cultural cohesion, and occupational homogeneity of Mexican communities. Consequently, educators generally approached the assimilation issue with single-mindedness. While integration was not quite the objective, eliminating the core of Mexican "folk culture" (i.e., replacing Spanish with English), certainly took precedence as an educational goal of assimilationists. To be sure, introducing new norms of health, nutrition, and child rearing were secondary to the education process.

In the educational decision-making process of the first half of the century, the Mexican community offered little political input. Moreover, few social scientists or educators found this lack of political involvement to be of major consequence. No lasting and significant changes could be realized, many thought, until Mexicans were Americanized.

CHAPTER 2

THE AMERICANIZATION
OF THE MEXICAN FAMILY

The target of Americanization extended beyond the Mexican child in the classroom to include the adults in the *colonia* or *barrio*. For example, in many communities of the Southwest, classes for women included English, nutrition, child rearing, hygiene, homemaking, and sewing. While the men also took courses in English, Americanization training for them also included various vocational subjects. Often public schools financed programs that provided teachers who taught English in factories and in agricultural labor camps, especially in the citrus-growing areas of California. In southern California, some teachers lived in the camps (performing a role not unlike today's Peace Corps volunteers). Others, called "Home Teachers," traveled into the urban *barrios* to offer classes.

The broad sweep of Americanization touched every member of many communities. The Los Angeles city schools' Americanization classes aimed no less than to offer Americanization "to the individual from birth to old age or death."[1] The Los Angeles program reached into nurseries, elementary, junior and senior high schools, adult evening schools, industrial work sites, day classes for mothers, and naturalization classes. Indeed, this was a comprehensive program designed to completely eliminate Mexican culture in the United States.

Although a significant chapter in the educational history of the Chicano community,[2] historians, hitherto, have overlooked the Americanization of the family. The insightful and important study by historian Richard Griswold del Castillo, for example, does not delve into the role of the public educational system in the evolution of the Mexican family,[3] and while Ricardo Romo's excellent history of eastern Los Angeles briefly discusses Americanization in the segregated schools, it does not recognize its impact on women.[4] Maxine Seller's essay on the education of immigrant women recognizes the Americanization emphasis of schooling and includes a discussion of Mexican women,[5] but, like Romo's account, does not link the two. The Americanization of Mexican children went beyond, however, the teaching of reading, writing, and arithmetic or allegiance to the country and its institutions. It involved separating children from home and family in such a way that they would come to desire a home and family of a different kind. Educators perceived the Mexican home as a source of Mexican culture and consequently as a reinforcer of the "Mexican educational problem." In its course of study for Mexican children, the Arizona Department of Education urged that the home be a "continuous topic through the school days," since "home life is the basis of custom and culture."[6] This body informed teachers that the measure of an effective educational program was whether or not it had "a lasting effect on home life." The superintendent of the Chaffey School District in southern California concluded that the learning "disability" of Mexican children (in his research, Mexican children were found to learn at 58 percent of the rate of normal American children) could be resolved only through an Americanization program that would "supply in some way what the home conditions lack."[7]

The focus upon the home had several aspects: the relations of boys and girls with the home; the young girl as a future wife, mother, and homemaker; and the woman as wife, mother, and homemaker. The Americanization program within the school addressed the first two aspects. Various contexts in the wider community provided forums for addressing the third aspect; for example, classes might be held in community centers, settlement houses, evening schools, cottages in the neighborhood, and the like.

The Americanization and homemaking instructor in the Covina California, elementary schools and author of a teacher's manual entitled *Americanization through Homemaking*, wrote that the "surest solution of the Americanization problem lies in the proper training of the parents of a future citizenry."[8] Homemaking focused on the future effect that the Mexican girl would have as a mother in creating an American-like home. The instructor cautioned teachers to be cognizant of the relationship between the home and political behavior. She wrote:

> The man with a home and family is more dependable and less revolutionary in his tendencies. . . . the influence of the home extends to labor problems and to many other problems in the social regime. The homemaker creates the atmosphere, whether it be one of harmony and cooperation or of dissatisfaction and revolt.[9]

THE MEXICAN GIRL

During an era when few questioned the future of all girls as mothers and homemakers, the practice of a near-universal training in home economics for Mexican girls in preparation for becoming mothers and wives seemed quite appropriate. Home economics for the Mexican girl had a wide range of objectives, including the political socialization of the Mexican community via the future mother.

Moreover, home economics was not to be taught uniformly to American and Mexican girls. An essential component of an Americanization program, home economics instruction for the Mexican girl commonly began earlier than for American girls because the former tended to drop out of school early. As part of their efforts, Americanization proponents identified the Mexican girls as a potential "carrier" of American culture, the social gene who upon her marriage and subsequent motherhood could create a type of home in which the next generation could be raised in an American cultural atmosphere. In assimilating the Mexican, wrote a home economics teacher, the "main hope lies with the rising genera-tion," and "since the girls are potential mothers and homemakers, they will control, in a large measure, the destinies of their future families."[10] An assumption prevailed that the Mexican girl needs education for her personal transformation, for the Americanization of her children, and, ultimately, for the Americanization of the Mexican community.

Across the Southwest, from Brownsville to Los Angeles, the Mexican girl learned the "practical arts," a "curriculum more suited to her needs."[11] "For [Mexican] girls," wrote the superintendent of the Needles, California, school district, "we have sewing, cooking, and general house-hold management, and we try to lay much stress upon ideas of sani-tation."[12] In one Rio Grande Valley Mexican school, a routine proce-dure separated girls for special course work in home economics, empha-sizing sewing and cooking.[13] At Belvedere Junior High School in Los Angeles, which was 50-percent Mexican, school authorities required only those girls in the "slow-learner" track to enroll in a demonstration home devoted to home economics instruction. According to the instruc-tors, "The . . . courses aim to teach the girls to do all work better which is required of them at home. . . ."[14]

Consequently, the Americanization of the Mexican community could theoretically be resolved within a generation through a program of home economics integrated with Americanization. Thus, throughout the Southwest, educators practiced the training of Mexican girls in a program geared to their presumed personalities, intelligence, apti-tudes, and culture. Therefore, in the segregated schools and in the inte-grated junior and senior highs, counselors, channeled Mexican girls into special home economics courses. However, the transformation of the girls required teachers to be educated about the peculiarities of Mexican girls compared with Anglo-Americans. Since the "needs of the Mexican home and community," argued a home economics teacher, differed "vastly . . . from those of our own people," the course of instruction in home economics should be shaped to "fit the needs of these people when they come to us."[15]

Along those same lines, another home economics teacher wrote that the effective education of Mexican girls required a knowledge of "the racial characteristics," because "many Mexican traits are exactly opposite of those of the Anglo-Saxon."[16] The Mexican girl, the same teacher continued, must be clearly "understood and appreciated" before a curriculum could be designed for her. The following includes a sample of the images of the Mexican girl as depicted in the literature:

> The Mexican girl develops emotionally at an early age. She becomes conscious of the opposite sex while she is still in the lower grades. This fact creates problems in the school which are difficult to cope with.[17]

> Mexican girls have inherited this remarkable aptness with the needle. We should strive to foster it in them. . . .[18]

> Mexican girls need a great deal of training in serving and table etiquette, as being a waitress may be their method of obtaining a livelihood.[19]

> Mexican girls frequently create very bad impressions with gaudy, inappropriate clothes, brilliant nails, cheeks, and lips, a mass of very oily curls, cheap dangling earrings, and heavily scented perfume.[20]

> Many of the [Mexican] girls will very likely find employment as house servants. They should be taught something about cleaning, table-setting, and serving.[21]

> . . . the background of the American and that of the Mexican
> girl differ. The former has learned the little courtesies of table
> etiquette in the home, but the latter, who may not have had a table
> in the home, must obtain her knowledge in the school room.[22]

> It is important that there is saving. . . . If we can get the [Mexican]
> girls to see the wisdom of doing this there will be . . . and fewer
> county charges.[23]

In the eyes of educators, the dual educational goals for Mexican girls—
to Americanize them while preparing them for the most menial service
occupations (e.g., laundry worker, domestic servant, waitress, or seamstress)—well suited their needs and aptitudes. At the same time, the girls
also received training in more appropriate standards of sex, appearance,
diet, personal hygiene, and child rearing.

TRACKING FOR AMERICANIZATION

A quite common educational experience for Mexican children took
place in slow-learner and educable-mentally retarded tracks. Often the
two curricula did not have a clear and definite demarcation. Consequently, the average Mexican girl, as well as the slow learner and
the educationally mentally retarded Mexican girl, had similar course
work. In Los Angeles an accepted practice tracked elementary and
junior high Mexican girls in home economics as their main course
work. This unwritten policy was especially well established in the case
of girls whose grades and scores on IQ and achievement tests were
low in comparison to the norm and who were judged intellectually
subnormal. In addition, since educators commonly assumed that the
"typical" Mexican girl would be an early dropout, home economics
training began in the elementary grades. The principal of the Delhi
Mexican Elementary School in Santa Ana altered the curriculum to
accommodate this pattern of early leaving. She found that a "need for a
simple, practical course in household economics is even more essential

to the girl from the Mexican home than to the average American girl and it is also essential that it be given at an earlier date."[24] Educators across the Southwest generally echoed her views.[25]

No matter their ability, instructors assigned the girls essentially the same course of study, with some differences in class materials and presentation. Oddly enough, the justification for this practice had its basis in the nature of the Mexican family, in which the woman's role was defined as child-bearer, nurturing mother, and faithful wife. Ironically, the home economics instruction in Mexican schools probably contributed more to maintaining the traditional Mexican family organization than to promoting changes that would have made it indistinguishable from the American. Thus, the schools opportunistically capitalized on an existing cultural pattern within the Mexican community although its objective was to reconstruct the family to conform to American standards.

An interesting aspect of this policy was that subnormal or intellectually deficient Anglo girls tended to be enrolled in the Mexican girl's curriculum. Amber Warburton, Helen Wood, and Marian Crane's report for the U.S. Department of Labor stated that the schools in the Rio Grande Valley had "special ungraded rooms in which home economics was emphasized for the girls" and that these "were sometimes provided for retarded children."[26] The California State Department of Education recommended that students categorized as "mentally retarded minors" be given special classes tailored to their abilities and future occupational potential, classes "equipped with tools and materials for appropriate forms of handwork, such as weaving, woodwork, sewing, cooking, and other manual activities of educational value."[27]

In most school districts Mexicans began dropping out in the junior high years. Those who moved from the segregated elementary school to the integrated junior high commonly found themselves in the slow-learner tracks, or in the mentally retarded classes. Another practice placed overage elementary pupils into junior highs regardless of what course work they had completed. In Los Angeles this policy affected Mexican children "more than it [did] any other group."[28] The special policy of transferring overage children to junior highs considerably enlarged the "low-mentality" track. In one San Fernando Valley, Los Angeles, school, "out of a group of thirty-six special girls, twenty-six of them [were] Mexican."[29] One observer commented that the "problems of the Mexican girl are learned and taken care of" through these classes.[30] In other words, the majority of Mexican girls enrolled in the low-mentality classes and the information regarding Mexican girls provided to teachers and administrators tended to emanate from these classes.

Although school administrators did not enroll all Mexican girls in special classes, an overwhelmingly large percentage of them did constitute such classes. In one valley junior high school "twenty-five percent of all Mexican girls enrolled" composed the "special group," and in another valley junior high the figure was 55 percent; in the remaining junior high of the valley, these special classes included one third of the Mexican girls in the school.[31] In each of these examples the traditional home economics classes provided the course work. However, in addition to home economics instruction they also experienced "hands-on" guidance by learning to cook and serve food in the school's cafeteria. In one case, school administrators assigned maintenance chores to Mexican girls as part of their training. The school with the highest Mexican enrollment routinely placed Mexican girls in "cafeteria work or janitor service."[32]

WOMEN AND THE FAMILY

California established the most ambitious and thorough adult program in the Southwest. The creation of the Commission of Immigration and Housing in 1913 placed California in the forefront of the Americanization effort. The commission mandated that it must "protect and deal with problems of foreign labor and of the communities in which they live." The act establishing the commission enabled the state to investigate "all things affecting immigrants, and for the care, protection, and welfare of immigrants."[33] The commission also empowered the state to cooperate with all other agencies in order "to bring to the immigrant the best opportunities for acquiring education and citizenship."

The commission could only make recommendations on the basis of its investigation. Upon the commission's founding, the lines of future Americanization programs had just begun to emerge. The law authorized the commission to design educational programs "for the proper instruction of adult and minor aliens in the English language and other subjects ... as soon after ... arrival as is practicable. The commission shall cooperate with authorities to extend this education, for both children and adults, to labor camps and other localities from which the regular schools are not easily accessible."[34]

In 1915 the commission succeeded in persuading the legislature to pass the Home Teacher Act, enabling the state, through local school systems, to enter immigrant communities and to Americanize them through the use of community-based teachers, or "home teachers." "It shall be the duty," read the act,

> of the home teacher to work in the homes of the pupils, instructing children and adults in matters relating to school attendance and preparation therefor; also in sanitation, in the English language, in household duties such as purchase, preparation and use of food and of clothing, and in the fundamental principles of the American system of government.[35]

The act then "recognized the family not only as the social, but as the educational unit"[36] and provided the right for local school systems to choose to incorporate home teachers into their program. Thus, the law did not mandate that all school districts employ home teachers but merely enabled them to do so. Given the nature of the act, the state elected to persuade school districts to employ home teachers by using Los Angeles as a demonstration of their efficacy. Several years after the Los Angeles experiment, and after home teachers had become a fixture in urban areas with large immigrant populations, Will C. Wood state superintendent of public instruction, reported that

> California was the first state to recognize the mother as the important factor in the home education, and to give her public school service, whether her child had shown any maladjustment or not. It is not because the child is undernourished or tardy or absent or dull or sleepy that the home teacher visits the foreign mother. It is because she is a foreign mother. If her child is doing well in school so much the better. It is still important that she learn English, have contact with American life and create for the child a home which will not be in conflict with his American education.[37]

If California did indeed lead the nation, then Los Angeles led California. By the close of the second decade, the home teacher held a prominent role in the schooling of the Los Angeles population. The purpose of such schooling included a plan to "devise means of placing within reach of all [immigrant] groups adequate facilities for becoming familiar with American social, economic and civic institutions and ideals."[38] One of the principal methods involved the use of "cottages" in the communities as Americanization centers. By 1928, 19 such centers existed with 280 classes teaching English at regularly scheduled meetings. "New World methods of housekeeping," whereby "a home may be made colorful and dainty and also may be kept clean and orderly," also found their way into the curriculum.[39] More than 70 home teachers worked in these centers, which were often refurbished and decorated so that they might represent "any attractive, modest American home."[40] Cottages usually had "a pleasant porch with flower boxes" and "fresh wallpaper, dainty window curtains, and . . . brightly painted furniture."[41] The district's assistant supervisor of Americanization stated that the home instruction emphasized English but that instruction in "cooking, sewing, millinery, budget making, thrift, home nursing, diet and nutrition" also took place on an ongoing basis.[42] While the neighborhood school provided the location for Americanizing the children, for the adult it was the neighborhood itself—which provided the use of a homelike structure that paralleled the state education institutional in identical purpose.

By the midtwenties, twenty-eight cities in California offered special courses to immigrant adults, with well over an enrollment of thirty thousand. In each of these centers, school administrators defined the foreign mother as "the important factor" in the task of the home teacher. In Los Angeles, teachers carried out their assignments in a variety of settings including the General Hospital, the Olive View Sanitarium, the Central and Lincoln Heights jails, railroad camps, and a number of industries (such as laundries) that employed large numbers of Mexican women.[43]

Los Angeles had reason to commit itself early to Americanization: 22 percent of its population were foreign-born as the third decade began, and 13 percent of the school population included people of Mexican descent as the decade closed. In that same period, half of its foreign-born children were Mexican. Throughout its history, Los Angeles has had a large Spanish-speaking population, and Americanization has had a significant effect upon the Mexican community. The alleged backward culture was challenged by the progressive culture. According to one home teacher, the Mexican's "tendency to wander and live in a shiftless way," which was "not checked by the economic conditions in which this type of family finds itself here," remained to be eliminated through the Americanization efforts of the schools and the home teachers.[44]

California established a statewide administrative bureaucracy that assumed centralized responsibility for Americanization work when it created the Department of Immigrant Education, which reported to the state superintendent's office. Other states chose to remain decentralized. Arizona and Texas, for example, did not create specific state-run adult immigrant programs, but they did recognize the importance of adult Americanization and sought to extend the influence of the classroom into the home. The *Course of Study for Elementary Schools of Arizona Instruction of Bilingual Children* (1939) emphasized the importance of "actual contact with the homes of the children" by their teacher. Through the extension of the school program to the home, the role of the Mexican mother would be changed to fit American standards. The *Course of Study* underscored the importance of home contact for the "marked improvement in standards of living" of the immigrant communities.[45] As a consequence of such programs, "many young immigrant mothers are now caring for their babies in a much better way than they themselves were cared for. . . . The use of English at home slowly gains ground. Receptivity to American culture slowly increases."[46]

In Texas, some authorities urged "Americanized" Mexicans, rather than the Anglo teachers, to be the main agents of cultural reformation. The state urged Texas schools to devise "new and original" methods for the Americanization of the Mexican community, including the employment of "capable English speaking Mexicans themselves." It suggested that

> the women's clubs, the Church societies, and all educational leaders interested in Mexican education should be ever on the alert for the enlistment of capable Mexican talent. . . . The work of Mexican education can best be done by the intelligent Americanized Mexicans themselves. No persons can understand the Mexican mind better than they.[47]

The governments of Texas and Arizona encouraged evening school programs for adults in Mexican schools and sponsored teacher-training programs in the normal schools.[48]

In California, the schools of Long Beach, Fullerton, Santa Ana, Riverside, La Habra, San Bernardino, Pasadena, and the Pomona Valley had adult programs that largely emphasized reforming the role of the Mexican mother in the home. Generally, Americanization represented a cooperative effort among various agencies, with the school district performing the key role. Often social work agencies, churches, and women's clubs joined together to offer classes. Some cities and localities offered evening classes on the school grounds, and one had a school bus refurbished as a classroom that traveled from labor camp to labor camp; in Fullerton and La Habra, an Americanization "teacher lived in one camp in a 'model' house which also functioned as a school and would travel by car to offer classes in model cottages in others camps"; Riverside and Pasadena employed a "settlement house" approach; Santa Ana offered classes in the county jail.

In Pasadena, the Edna P. Alter Mexican Settlement House promoted a program aimed at the Chihuahuita *colonia*. The articles of incorporation stated that its work was

> to maintain, conduct and operate one or more Settlement Houses for the use of said Mexican population; to conduct nurseries and kindergartens for the Mexican children and schools for the Americanization of said people, and for the teaching and inculcating of the essentials of good citizenship. . . .[49]

The settlement house sponsored "sewing classes for women and girls, English classes for men, women, boys and girls, . . . part-time classes for working girls, . . . [a] girls' club, [a] maternity hospital, rug weaving, [an] employment bureau," and other activities.[50] The Riverside Community Settlement Association sponsored Americanization in the Mexican community, but also offered separate classes for "colored women" with the support of the school district. The association offered classes in "sewing, weaving, cooking" as well as a "Boys' Club, and Girls' Club, Scout troop and various social activities."[51] In addition, it operated a maternity hospital where for "thirteen dollars, a Mexican or colored mother [could] . . . stay for ten days" and a bathhouse charging ten cents a shower.[52] Sewing classes were offered on a segregated basis for Mexican and black women, and a store in the building sold used clothing and the weavings made by the women.

Santa Ana had two home teachers, a nurse, and five evening-school teachers under the direction of the supervisor of the school district's Department of Americanization. The department classes offered "English, sewing, cooking, naturalization, orchestra, typing, and

athletics at the various centers" located in the three Mexican communities.[53] Courses held in the jail devoted time to English instruction and
intended to teach "some of the men why they are there."[54] According
to the warden, the courses had done much to raise the morale of the
inmates. One Americanization teacher reported that each of the localities' programs offered courses in "health, domestic science, recreation,
and training in English [and] everyone is organized with the ideal of
making the [Mexican] immigrant a valuable factor in the life of his
community."[55]

Americanization programs in agricultural areas generally differed
from the urban ones. In El Centro, California, the school board and the
local women's club cooperated to hire a "director of immigrant education" who spent "most of her time in the homes and in the teaching of
the Mexicans."[56] In the neighboring town of Calipatria, the school board
employed a "spirited young Mexican woman with an American education" to carry out its Americanization program. Santa Paula, in Ventura
County, employed a director of Americanization who organized "schools
for the workers in the various little foreign communities" located near
the large ranches that hired Mexican laborers.[57] The biggest effort at
rural Americanization took place in the citrus areas of southern California, where the Mexican communities consisted of more or less permanent residents. Citrus growers often had "company towns" or labor
camps where Mexican workers either rented or purchased homes at
minimal prices. Finally, the citrus industry had discovered that language,
work habits, and labor-management relations proved important to the
welfare of the industry. The Industrial Relations Bureau of the California
Fruit Growers Exchange realized that it had an interest in Americanization and thus actively promoted it among their affiliates. For example,
George B. Hodgkin, one of its officials, noted that the "sole object of
building a labor camp is to provide a satisfactory supply of labor to
do good work at the lowest possible cost."[58] Often, he continued, the
cost of upkeep of the camp proved "unexpectedly high" because of the
"ungentlemanly manners of some of the tenants."[59] Officials claimed that

camps left unsupervised, allegedly had a high incidence of gambling, unemployment, brawls, and disease and were marked by an "undependable and disappointing" supply of labor.[60] "In order to make the labor camp pay, to make it produce the desired workers," he said,

> it is necessary to create an atmosphere that will attract and hold such workers. The Mexican is reached most easily through his home and friends. If his family is well and happy, if his house is good and clean, and his meals good—and above all if his yard is full of vegetables and flowers which he has planted—he will be pretty certain to think twice before uprooting himself. Moreover, if he becomes a member of a local society, or baseball team or band, or if he joins an English class and finds pleasant companionship in the Camp he will probably think even three times before leaving.[61]

Furthermore, a definite relationship, he argued, existed "between picking costs and teaching the Mexican women to sing 'Open the Window' in English."[62] Not content with merely advocating Americanization, the Growers Exchange published its own "textbook of lessons in industrial English," which also functioned as a "compact description of the several processes using foreign laborers."[63] Used in English classes for men, the book taught them "not only the English vernacular" of their jobs, but also the skills of the "related processes of growing, cultivating, pruning, picking, and irrigating."[64] Here Americanization teachers devoted themselves mainly "to the labor camp, paying special attention to the housemother and her problems," as well as the hired laborer, who also attracted attention.

Every adult program had its graduation exercises, and at La Habra they consisted of well-orchestrated rites of cultural passage. At the 1921 graduation ceremonies, the few women who had completed their English classes assembled before a "large group of growers, directors of the La Habra Citrus Association, merchants, educators, and camp dwellers to receive their diplomas."[65] With the cottage "decorated with streamers and gay paper flowers," and the graduates "attired in white graduation dresses . . . bedecked with multi-colored paper flowers,"[66] the women stood before a table, displaying "miniature beds, wash pans, brooms, dolls and other household paraphernalia."[67] As proof of her expertise as English-speakers, each graduate came to the table, picked up an object, and in English described the particular activity she engaged in, such as "making a bed, dressing the doll or sweeping the floor."[68] Then, in unison, "they sang songs in English about opening the windows, washing the baby and learning English."[69] Graduation certified that the students had learned desirable cultural traditions. Americanization teachers, said Hodgkin, created "a desire for higher, healthier standards of living" and became "more likely to achieve lasting results than the supervisor who attempts to force the tenant to walk the chalk line."[70]

Thus, through Americanization, program proponents expected the laborer to become self-directed, rather than externally directed, manifesting such qualities as thrift, good health, homeowning, clean living, and sobriety—in short, all those things that he was not because of their Mexican culture.

By the end of the twenties, "industrial" Americanization had grown to encompass more than citrus belts as laundries, sugar mills, and "industries of all sorts having special vocabularies such as vineyards, canneries, railroads, and factories" began to hire or sponsor Americanization teachers and programs for their workers.[71] Given the demand, the state normal schools began early developing special Americanization curricula, teaching methods, and teacher training. Indeed, by 1920 the state offered a special Americanization Teaching Certificate for the credentialed teacher. At middecade, nearly three thousand teachers had "taken the required training courses," and over half of them were employed in Americanization education.[72]

When the Americanization program emanated from a cooperative arrangement between the school board and a business, industry, or grower, generally the teacher organized the course work along the lines desired by the employer. Thus, for example, employers and school board officials expected teachers like Arietta Kelly, who taught at the La Habra camp, to not only teach courses, but also to keep "closer track of them" [Mexicans] than would normally be the case without the program.[73] (Similarly, the Riverside school administrators required a "home visitor" to report "all unsanitary conditions to the city health department," to "keep a careful check on domestic affairs, and cooperate with the district attorney if need arise," and to work with the county welfare organizations.)[74] Thus, Americanization programs extended a system of surveillance into the Mexican community that went largely unnoticed. A significant example of this surveillance occurred in the great citrus strike in Orange County in 1936. Nearly three thousand citrus pickers struck for higher wages and union recognition, and after a six-week strike, masked by wholesale vigilante and official violence against the workers, management soundly defeated and destroyed the union. The Americanization teacher, Kelly, sided with the growers and translated antistrike literature into Spanish. In a 1970 interview she recalled that the manager of the Placentia Mutual Orange Growers "sent over a lot of material for me to translate for him into Spanish so he could disseminate it through the groups that were working for him, telling them what they (management) would promise them (nonstrikers) and so forth, and trying to explain that this agitation was coming in from the outside."[75]

The opportunity for activities exceeding the scope of Americanization existed with widespread availability. Consequently, many employers saw value (meaning profits) in Americanization, especially the citrus growers, and did not hesitate to offer their support. A statement from the 1933 Biennial Report of the Department of Education encapsulated their motives. "The Mexicans who are regular attendants at school are taught to *think,* the employers say, and are consequently better workmen."[76]

Generally, before school district officials offered Americanization courses, they would consult with local employers for their input on the program design. "The employers of alien labor," stated the superintendent of the Chaffey Union High School District, "should be consulted about the matter [Americanization]."[77] The officials of the Lucas Co., Inc., a ranch of some four thousand acres in the Pomona area, gave their approval to remodel a "bunk house" at high school expense for Americanization instruction. In neighboring Upland, the growers' associations built labor camps for their workers, "three-roomed houses . . . rented . . . at ten dollars per month."[78] The Upland camps, called "Sonora Town," and populated by several hundred families, resembled towns found "in practically every citrus section."[79] After consultations between the growers' association and the Chaffey Union High School, "it was arranged that a . . . house in Sonora Town . . . should be fitted up as a school and a community center" for the exclusive use of the workers and their families. The superintendent maintained that cooperation "between school authorities and employers of labor is absolutely necessary in the development of a successful plan of Americanization."[80]

Americanization teachers felt impressed not only with the power of their employer, the school district, and their students' employers, but also with the deep sense of professional importance that greatly influenced their jobs. The Americanization teacher at La Habra, Jessie Hayden, stated that her colleagues "have been the sources of the greatest improvement in human living" in instructing Mexicans in the camps. Their responsibilities as Americanization teachers, she added, not only

> set forth to the Mexicans the rules of health, but also [brought] them indirect contact with a deep, overflowing, sympathetic source of human action where American ideals, ambitions, attitudes and aspirations for clean, pure, healthful thinking and living are born.[81]

In spite of the successful extension of Americanization, the depression had an adverse effect upon the adult programs. Whereas Americanization work would continue in the segregated elementary schools until the termination of segregation, adult Americanization began to wane in the late 1930s. By the end of the decade the community and adult Americanization among Mexicans had reached a high tide and a slow decline followed. In part, massive repatriation drives lead to such a decline as they reduced both the number of Mexicans in the United States, and the influx of new immigrants. In addition, the financial costs of special Americanization teachers and curriculum must have had a decided impact on any extension or cutting back of adult Americanization work. Thus, the chief of the State Division of Adult and Continuation Education (within which Immigrant Education was administered) reported in 1933 that Americanization would increasingly "concern itself with the children of foreign-born parents. . . ."[82]

In spite of the chauvinistic character of Americanization, the curriculum for Mexican adults undoubtedly had some benefits. Within the Mexican community, there did exist a need for courses in English, sanitation, hygiene, and sewing, given the problems created by the high rate of illiteracy among Mexicans and the traditional methods of health care. Without their Americanization objectives, the instruction offered in these programs could have benefited the Mexican community in addressing these problems. It is highly probable that many people did gain from learning English, or new methods of child care, or nutrition. But herein did not lie the essence of Americanization. Essentially, Americanization programs functioned to maintain the Mexican community at its socioeconomic level by ensuring that the learning process coincide with dominant political and economic interests.

English courses first met the needs of employers, and then those of the workers. Thus, English instruction aimed at making Mexicans more efficient and reliable workers and seldom concerned itself with changing their socioeconomic status. Americanization for mothers and housewives proposed to make them more effective reproducers and training agents of future labor. Although a particular form of assimilation, Americanization however did not mean social change. Instead, it provided a state institutional structure for strengthening the social relations between Mexican labor and their employers, between Mexican and

Anglo communities. Furthermore, the theoretical basis for Americanization—the alleged cultural inferiority of the Mexican community—represented an academic sociological racism that could have never provided a foundation for a democratic educational experience. Consequently, the theoretical argument that Mexican culture proved antithetical to the continued economic development of the United States was not consistently upheld in practice. For example, the Mexican patriarchal family easily integrated within capitalist agriculture and proved profitable and productive. Moreover, employers highly valued the attributes of cheap and mobile labor, two conditions that emanated from Mexicans' status as immigrants from peasant villages.

A schizophrenic Americanization policy emerged in the Southwest: on the one hand, there was an opportunistic incorporation of Mexican labor valued because of their peasant background, especially in modern agriculture capitalist production; and on the other, there existed an aggressive policy of de-culturalization aimed at eliminating the ethnicity of the Mexican community. The former practice informally preserved key elements of Mexican culture, especially the traditional family and language; the latter deliberately sought the elimination of Mexican culture. Often both practices applied to the very same community—what one hand gave, the other took away—within a single institution, public education. Furthermore, Americanization occurred in a segregated setting, an environment that contributed to separation rather than assimilation.

While in the United States, Mexican immigrants absorbed themselves in the culture of their homeland. However, those who argued that ethnicity hindered economic progress never fully demonstrated this, and it is more likely that the justification for Americanization stemmed from the chauvinism that found its way into the popular sociological concepts of the period. American culture was nationalistic, racist, chauvinistic, and prone to that arrogance characteristic of a rising world power. Consequently, social theory, too, would inevitably contain those

elements that promoted antidemocracy, inequality, and the subordination of ethnic minorities.[83]

CHAPTER 3

INTELLIGENCE TESTING
AND THE MEXICAN CHILD

Studies of the intellectual abilities and educational achievement of Mexicans in relation to other races and nationalities in the United States between 1915 and 1950 showed the Mexican child scoring consistently lower than the normal range and the average for the Anglo population. The authors of no fewer than sixteen studies, most dating to the twenties and early thirties, concluded that heredity intellectually handicapped the Mexican. Another seventeen articles attributed the low average scores mainly to environmental, cultural, or language factors. Some studies straddled both positions, and a few argued for neither. Nevertheless, whether the research leaned toward nature or nurture, the findings revealed that Mexican children consistently failed to do as well as Anglo children on one of the key educational tools of the twentieth century: the intelligence test.

Although the concept of intelligence developed apart from the concept of the organic society, testing psychologists and proponents of organic social theory had much in common. Both sought to maintain the social order as an efficient, harmonious, and cooperative organization. One might even say that the theory of the organic society laid out the long-range objectives and the concept of intelligence in its practical form, the IQ test, facilitated the realization of those objectives. Thus, a principal contribution gained from the extensive application of IQ testing among minorities, Mexicans in particular, involved the efficient social, political, and economic organization of society. The public school provided the main arena for the testing of individuals and for the changing of various cultural acts, beliefs, and sentiments.

The adherents of testing, whether proponents of nature or of nurture, generally agreed that the educational process could be centered upon the concept intelligence. Thus, in the case of research and debate on the nature of the intelligence of Mexican people the question of education became the overriding concern.

The Development of the Concept of Intelligence and Nature versus Nurture

The concept of intelligence, a late nineteenth-century theoretical departure from classical mental theory, became the core of twentieth-century educational practice. According to the classical thought emanating from the Enlightenment, the mind of each individual consisted of abilities or faculties that were similar if not identical within any given population. The zeal, industriousness, labor, or education of the individuals accounted for the differentiation within the population in terms of productivity, talents, abilities, or social standing. Thus, the mind did not determine the range of abilities or social distinctions; the class order developed as a consequence of the nature of the interaction between the individual and the environment. Thus, the classical methods for "getting ahead" included hard work and education, the key elements in the progress of the individual.

In the late nineteenth century William James, James McKeen Cattell, and Alfred Binet, among others, theorized that each individual was endowed with distinctive mental abilities that predetermined his social existence. Theoreticians of intelligence proposed the novel idea that the ability to think determined the life of the individual and therefore became the central force in the organization of society. They further postulated that (1) socioeconomic distinctions reflected the range of the ability to think abstractly, and (2) individual mental ability was an innate trait. Genetics, then, was introduced into social theory.

The concept of intelligence strongly implied that a biological factor determined the ability to perform mental processes. Nevertheless, two positions, "nature" and "nurture," emerged among researchers developing intelligence theory and its practical application, the IQ test. The nature theorists emphasized an immutable genetically based intelligence; the nurture theorists emphasized the environmental factors (language, culture, and socioeconomic milieu) that may influence innate intelligence and its manifestation. The two sides agreed about the utility and importance of the concept but emphasized differing determinants of the level of intelligence for an individual.

In their most controversial conclusion, the adherents of the "nature" position argued that intelligence distinguished the various races and nationalities of the world. Thus, many influential intelligence experimenters concluded that socioeconomic differences naturally reflected the biological trait "intelligence" and that humanity is divided in terms of innate intelligence into superior and inferior races and nationalities. Between 1900 and the 1930s, researchers in support of the nature argument conducted literally hundreds of comparative racial studies with the aim of discovering the precise biological, physical, or intellectual distinctions among the diverse races, nationalities, and cultures of the world. Thereafter, the culture concept eclipsed, but not entirely defeated the hereditarian position.

The implications of the nature and nurture intelligence theories proved crucial to postulates about the organization of society, class structure, the distribution of wealth, the production of wealth, and the evolution of society. These theories explained aspects of society and political economy not just in terms of the social context, that is, capitalist democracy, but rather in terms of nonsocially determined biological factors. Compare this with classical social theory of a century earlier. Whereas classical political theory held that the social context liberated the individual to fulfill his potential in society, social scientists like Lewis Terman and even his opponent Franz Boas argued that genetics determined, in varying degrees, the social context.

The concept of intelligence also had major implications for political theory, since it identified a small percentage of the population as superior. Terman claimed that only 2½ percent comprised the gifted, while 65 percent consisted of those deemed average. Moreover, Terman upheld the politically radical notion that, in addition to bestowing intellectual superiority on this 2½ percent, nature had also endowed this group to govern the remaining 97½ percent. Thus, IQ theory was elitist and, in essence, antidemocratic, for it upheld the right of a minority to govern the majority not by virtue of free choice and elections, but by virtue of natural selection.

Consequently, the concept of intelligence radically altered and reshaped political theory as government of, for, and by the people became government by a minority in the name of the people. Furthermore, since the intellectual superiors generally came from the wealthy propertied classes, then government by intellectual superiors also meant government by the wealthiest class. This radical departure from nineteenth-century political thought lent support to one major twentieth-century political theory—the theory of elite rule.

Terman spoke for a great many followers of intelligence theory when he enunciated the new social theory.

> It can not be disputed, however, that in the long run it is the races which excel in abstract thinking that eat while others starve, survive epidemics, master new continents, conquer time and

space, and substitute religion for magic, science for taboos and justice for revenge. The races which excel in conceptual thinking could, if they wished, quickly exterminate or enslave all the races notably their inferiors in this respect. Any given society is ruled, led, or at least molded by the five or ten percent of its members whose behavior is governed by ideas. The typical pick-and-shovel man does his thinking chiefly on the sensor motor and perceptual levels. Add a little more ability to think on the representative level and he may be able to repair your automobile, build a house according to an architect's specifications, or nurse you in illness. Add a large measure of ability to associate abstract ideas into complex systems and he can design a new type of engine, draft the plans for a skyscraper, or discover a curative serum.[1]

Terman, extrapolating from a general psychological theory, explicitly divided mental from physical labor and placed it at the center of the social universe. The theory also implied that no amount of education could change a person of "low intelligence"; knowledge should not be equally accessible to everyone but apportioned in relation to mental ability. Thus, the poet's warning, "A little learning is a dangerous thing," did not apply to those peoples, races, and nationalities whose mental abilities were judged to be mediocre or inferior; a little learning was beneficial for many.

Terman urged the use of testing to discover "native abilities," to adjust curriculum accordingly, and to group children according to "ability" levels. He wrote that industry or hard work was not a good measure of ability and an apparently "lazy" child might be mentally gifted.[2] Consequently, hard work, the nineteenth-century predictor of success, did not fit into the measuring scheme of the proponents of IQ testing. Industriousness, argued Terman, did not of itself spell success. Instead, intelligence—an inherent biological trait immune to human control—provided the real basis for success. Thus, the theory of naturally endowed intelligence highlighted the inability of the individual to control the essential factor conditioning his life. All that one could do was apply oneself within the limitations of his preordained intelligence.

Schooling the child to believe in the determination of social existence by inborn intelligence served an important function in the operation of modern corporate society.[3] Intelligence theorists assigned the responsibility for the existence of disparities in wealth, political power, privileges, education, and the like, to an immutable, universal, predetermined trait —the alleged ability to think abstractly. In adults, belief in the concept of intelligence led to a politically acquiescent population, more easily controlled and less interested in radical political activity.

In terms of the social relationships between minorities and the dominant culture and society, IQ theory tended to maintain and strengthen those relations. Intelligence theory contained the potential to argue that the social status quo also derived from national intellectual character. Given the national and racial hierarchy that to varying degrees corresponded to the class structure in the United States, Terman and his followers went relatively unchallenged when they linked IQ with nationality, race, and social standing. When officials administered IQ tests to the Mexican community, theory led to oppressive practice. Well over seven thousand Mexican children provided raw material for the testing of "native ability" and for the comparison of nationalities in terms of intelligence. Of course, the middle-class Anglo child (that mythical being who was generally expected to score 1.00 on the IQ measure) provided the standard for comparative purposes. Those who scored higher were generally of the same nationality; those who scored lower quite often included the foreign-born, or blacks. Thus, the wealthier Anglos "demonstrated" superiority in intelligence while the poor, as strongly represented by various nationalities, proved inferior. Consequently, access to education corresponded to the social hierarchy created by the distribution of intelligence.

Throughout the Southwest in the first half of this century, the school system defined Mexican children as intellectually inferior and placed them in segregated and inferior facilities where instructors schooled them primarily on vocational subjects. When economic conditions demanded, authorities simply excluded them from school. Because concern for the economic well-being of agriculture made family labor indispensable, children were denied the state-mandated right to education. IQ theory placed the Mexican community at a particular disadvantage in that it barred its educational advancement, justified its segregation, legitimized its political domination by boards of education, and contributed in no small measure to an education that stressed preparation for semiskilled and unskilled labor.

During the period 1900–1930, racist political domination characterized the experience of minorities and of various immigrant nationalities. For the most part, the social scientists who discussed and studied the importance of nature versus nurture were white males, all middle-class by profession, some upper-class by ascription. They did not represent the interests—political, educational, or social—of the groups considered intellectually inferior, whether by nature or nurture. By and large, the social sciences expressed the thinking of the privileged classes, and their research instruments and methods corresponded to the prevailing political, economic, and social organization of society. In essence, the social order fashioned social science research and ultimately determined its findings and conclusions. Although social scientists claimed scientific neutrality, the theories that they propounded mirrored the social order as they thought it should be.

Clearly, not all social scientists who adopted the intelligence concept accepted the hereditarian doctrine. Many argued that while intelligence was innate or inherited, no one particular race or nationality possessed it as a heralded genetic feature. These "environmentalists," while admitting that intelligence played a significant role in shaping the social order, argued that factors such as language, culturally determined values, or social milieu could impede the full development or manifestation of the natural intelligence of individuals. Dr. George I. Sanchez summed up the nurture position well when, as an official of the New Mexico Department of Education, he wrote, "Environment . . . is largely responsible for 'intelligence' as measured by tests. *It at least conditions innate ability, and intelligence tests are in part measures of environmental effects*"[4] (emphasis mine). Furthermore, these social scientists concluded that in any race or nationality there exists a similar range of mental abilities, from genius to dullard. Some races might score consistently lower on IQ tests, but this was due mainly to "nurture" factors that limited the manifestation of innate intelligence. The proponents of the nonracial position concluded that the optimal society would allow for the unimpeded positioning of individuals in the social order according to their intellectual abilities. Those in support of this position included Boas, Walter Lippmann (who had an ongoing debate with Terman in the twenties), and the pioneers in intelligence research, Alfred Binet and Thomas Simon. Simon wrote:

> Of what use is a measure of intelligence? Without doubt one could conceive many possible applications of the process, in dreaming of a future where the social sphere would be better organized than ours; where everyone would work according to his own aptitudes in such a way that no particle of psychic force shall be lost for society. That would be the ideal city.[5]

This division between hereditarians and those who underscored nurture would inevitably affect research on the intelligence and educational achievement of the Mexican community. Consequently, studies of Mexican intelligence divided into two main types: those that followed the racial hereditarian path, and those that considered nonracial factors (and therefore nonsocially determined) factors as the key to the persistence of low scores on intelligence tests. In either case, the problem of education of the Mexican child gave the studies their practical value. Environmentalists such as Sanchez, Herschel Manuel, and L. S. Tireman led the countercharge against the racial hereditarians. Their research spearheaded the successful rebuttals of racial intelligence doctrines by working within the theoretical and practical parameters of the concept of intelligence rather than by criticizing its utility.

A few die-hard hereditarians continued to pursue their course of demonstrating racial distinctions, but the trend in comparative studies after 1930 shifted away from blanket indictments of entire races and nationalities toward analyses and comparisons of a cultural nature. Research on the intelligence of Mexican children certainly did not cease, but its explanatory basis swung toward environment, language, and culture and away from racial or genetic inheritance.

RACIAL INTELLIGENCE RESEARCH AND THE MEXICAN COMMUNITY

The "tendency among educators and psychologists," wrote an official of the Orange County, California, Health Department in 1934, "is to assume that children of Mexican parentage are mentally inferior to white children."[6] Not only did a mental differentiation manifest, but this difference provided the key to the "low social status" and educational level of the Mexican child.[7] In one study of Mexican intelligence, the authors found "social status and educational level to be of the same order as intelligence,"[8] and this conclusion was in keeping with the general theoretical structure of the concept intelligence. The pioneers in the concept intelligence, William James, Terman, Edward Thorndike, and others, had causally related intellectual abilities and education with social structure. That research performed upon the Mexican community merely kept pace with some unquestioned theoretical principles. Those who "are bound to get ahead," wrote Kimball Young in his study of San Jose, California, "Latins" (Italians and Mexicans), included members of races and nationalities of "better than average ability."[9]

Throughout the de jure segregation period, the controversy over "nature versus nurture," in relation to studies of Mexican intelligence, became integral to the analysis. Not a few of the studies began their reports with a reference to the controversy.[10] Some straddled the fence.[11] Consequently, experimenters divided into two currents: (1)

those who assumed racial distinctions existed and could be proved by the experimental method; and (2) those who felt that racial distinctions possibly existed but needed verification through the experimental method. Terman emerged as the theoretical leader of the former position and, in relation to research on Mexican children, Young most clearly expressed it.

> Whatever be the individual nature of the carriers of [intelligence] in human beings, we must accept the facts that intellectual traits are to a considerable if not complete degree transmissible by and subsumable to the laws of heredity. . . . The same laws must hold for the crossing of family strains of various racial or sub-racial strains.[12]

Representing the latter position, Thomas Garth argued that research needed to verify possible racial distinctions. Perhaps no other psychologist proved as influential as he in broadcasting the finding that Mexicans consistently scored lower than Anglos on mental tests, but he exercised extreme caution by not assuming that racial distinctions were already proven.[13]

Nevertheless, even the cautious Garth candidly admitted in 1931 that his investigations "in the field of race psychology were accompanied by a silent conviction that he would find clear-cut racial differences in mental processes."[14] He further concluded that "this conviction was shared by many and still prevails to be true."[15]

O. K. Garretson's study on the causes of retardation among Mexican children in a small public school system in Arizona assumed mental inferiority among Mexicans and applied the scientific method to the factors that allegedly produced it: "(1) irregular school attendance, (2) transientness of the Mexican family, (3) native capacity, or intelligence of the Mexican people. . . ."[16] The first two factors measured the same phenomenon inasmuch as family migration caused irregular attendance. Garretson, however, did not assess the causes of migration. Families migrated because agricultural production required cheap, mobile, and subordinated labor. Garretson ignored the consequences for Mexican families of low wages, seasonal labor, and public and private policies that discriminated against migrants. He appears to have been unaware that labor contractors and agents sought laborers and transported them to distant fields.[17] He blamed the victim: the Mexican people were responsible for the form of agricultural labor.

Garretson's causal theory proved ideologically sound, however, because it essentially justified the social and economic processes as they appeared. Mexicans experienced meager material gains, and in a society that stressed a highly individualistic social theory, that is, the intelligence concept, Mexicans should bear responsibility for their own poverty. At the root of this social problem was the intelligence of the Mexican people. "Probably the principal factor governing retardation of the Mexican child," concluded Garretson, "is his mental ability as measured by the group test."[18]

The labor processes in the Southwest and Midwest figured significantly in bringing the Mexican to the United States. Yet, many social scientists focused on the Mexican community as if it existed in a vacuum. Garth, in a study of Mexican "industrial psychology," concluded that the responsibility for bringing "sickness and diseases of contagious sort, and of causing poverty and lawlessness rested with Mexicans."[19] A corollary opinion identified Mexican children as "problems" within the educational system. Had the steady development of mass compulsory education not occurred, the assessment of Mexican children might never have been carried out. Mexican children attended school only in relationship to the social development of corporate capitalism, which Mexican labor, ironically, helped to develop.

In every intelligence study conducted on Mexicans, researchers, in effect, focused on the members of the very poorest of the working class. The burdens of the unskilled work force created large enough problems for the community, and now, in addition to their inferior social standing, Mexicans found themselves penalized for their culture. The results of psychological testing conducted in English seldom took into account the very real language barrier.[20]

"It is unusual for a Mexican child to be able to speak English when he enters kindergarten or first grade," acknowledged Garretson, but he administered the test nevertheless. According to him, "normal children" should acquire language by the third grade, and even though language was a factor in grades one and two, it did not figure significantly in grades three through eight. He never acknowledged how he arrived at this conclusion, but he added to his analysis by saying that "regardless of the method of accounting" the same results would inevitably obtain.[21] The scientific method was quickly dispatched.

In their studies, Franklin C. Paschal and Louis R. Sullivan, B. F. Haught, and Florence L. Goodenough, devised definite methods in order to cancel out language as a factor. They administered tests considered "completely independent of language."[22] Paschal and Sullivan designed "a test or scale that can be applied by an American to the Mexican child or adult and despite his limited use of English obtain results as free from personal error as the theory of mental tests demands."[23] However, these scientists refused to make such an adjustment in their method. In their preliminary statements, they accused Mexicans of not adapting themselves "to our form of life" and of refusing to "use English or encourage their children to use it."[24] Nevertheless, they administered their "nonlanguage" mental tests in the most unscientific of methods. For example, one test composed of a battery of six questions, asked individual children to arrange numbered blocks into their proper sequence after the examiner scrambled them. "The child was given no other instructions than 'Put these back as quickly as you can,' which was accompanied by motions indicating the task so that in case the words were not understood the child would nevertheless understand what she wanted."[25] After three trials, the rearrangements of blocks varied. "It was customary to warn the child to go faster on the second trial, but no additional instruction or encouragement was given except to call 'pronto' before each trial got well under way."[26] One can imagine what the Anglicized "pronto" sounded like to the Mexican child; moreover, the emphasis on speed on all six of the tests must have certainly unnerved the children. One can only speculate what those 410 children felt as the examiner subjected them to such a hostile exercise or what the many hundreds of other children felt as subjects of the social sciences.

B. F. Haught demonstrated even more hostility toward the children in his study, since his research intended to dispel the notion of language as a factor.

> When intelligence tests are administered to both groups, the children of Spanish descent fall considerably below the standards obtained by those of Anglo descent. There is an inclination to assume that this does not mean an inferiority but a language difficulty encountered in taking tests.[27]

Haught concluded that Mexicans were truly inferior arguing that "since the older children are handicapped as much as the younger there seems to be no justification for assigning the difficulty to inability to use or understand English. . . ."[28] Thus, like Paschal and Sullivan, Haught appeared frustrated because the subjects were not assimilating quickly enough. He concluded that their intelligence presented a barrier to the learning of English: nonuse of English gave Haught sufficient reason to assume that language did not cause low scores, and that failure to learn English resulted from low intelligence! Thus, knowledge of English became the objective standard for intelligence, and even though he had stated that his investigation intended to clarify the importance of language in psychological tests, he concluded that the command of the English language proved as much the indicator of intelligence as the intelligence test itself.

Goodenough also sought to define the role of language in intelligence tests by developing a nonverbal experiment. Goodenough, a psychologist for the Institute of Child Welfare at the University of Minnesota, tested 2,457 school children in 1928, of whom 367 included Mexican children from Los Angeles. Her results coincided with those of her colleagues who administered verbal tests. The non-language scale test, said Goodenough, "is completely independent of language" and that furthermore, "the rank order of the various nationality groups corresponds very closely to that found by means of other intelligence tests."[29]

In reality, the biases of the researchers made knowledge of English and at least a middle-class background, a prerequisite for objective consideration. Thus, according to their perspective, the inability to speak the "correct" language posed a "problem" not only for the researcher, but for society as a whole.

The research described the average Mexican child as subnormal in intelligence and concluded that therefore schools should adjust their educational "treatment" of Mexicans to meet their particular level of intelligence. Haught, in 1931, found that the "average Spanish child has an intelligence quotient of .79 compared with 1.00 for the average Anglo child."[30] However, the liberal side of Haught quickly advised the reader that "there are some Spanish children as bright as the very superior children."[31] Garretson found that "retardation of the Mexican child . . . is from three to eight times as great as that of the American child. . . ."[32] Don C. Delmet concluded "that the Mexican children studied show, on the whole, greater school retardation and less acceleration, and are on the whole much older for a given grade than are white children."[33]

Leo M. Gamble's study found "the average intelligence quotient for the Mexican was 78.75." Furthermore, he stated, "This quotient is . . . approximately the same as that found by Garth."[34] Helen L. Koch and Rietta Simmons, W. H. Sheldon, Kimball Young, Ellen A. McAnulty, F. C. Paschal and C. R. Sullivan, Florence L. Goodenough, and O. K. Garretson reached similar if not identical conclusions. Mexican children were inferior to "American" children on the most scientific of instruments, and were still as inferior when the language factor was "controlled." However, these "facts" did not arise out of abstract theoretical conclusions, for it was always the intention of the investigators that their conclusions have practical application in the socialization programs of the state's educational institutions.

Nurture and Mental Measurement of Mexican Children

A number of scholars who generally utilized the culture concept as their research weapon, challenged the biological determinists who underscored racial and national variation in genetically determined intellectual abilities. By the late thirties, leading authorities had demonstrated that the field of "racial intelligence" could not withstand rigorous evaluation. Moreover, the common assumption held that cross-cultural comparisons proved impossible on "a test standardized on one racial or national group . . . of differing culture and background."[35] The adherents of experience and learning as affecting innate intelligence and therefore the measurement of IQ, usually argued that the language variable arbitrarily lowered the scores of non-English-speaking and bilingual children. In order that a test be valid, argued Sanchez, it must be based on norms founded upon the experience of all children undergoing testing. "A test is valid only to the extent that the items of the test are as common to each child tested as they were to the children upon whom the norms were based."[36]

Nevertheless, the culture concept did not exclude the concept of intelligence. The "nurture" position separated itself from the hereditarian approach but did not reject the significance of differentiated levels of innate intelligence. The culture concept and the intelligence concept had much in common. Both essentially posited the centrality of ideas, the patterning of ideas into behavioral norms, and the consequent organization of individuals into social beings. The nurturists leaned toward the effects of experience in affecting innate intelligence; the hereditarians leaned toward emphasizing the effects of innate intelligence upon experience.

Consequently, the major figure in the development of the culture concept, Boas, while critical of the racist biological determinists, could nevertheless accept the role of intelligence in constructing social inequality. "Every race," he counseled, "has its mentally strong and weak individuals, its great intellects and its idiots, its men and women of strong and weak will power."[37] Moreover, Boas, well-known for his relativistic culture theory, embraced a modified hereditarian and eugenicist point of view.

> Eugenics, therefore, cannot have any possible meaning with regard to whole races. It can have a meaning only with regard to strains. If the task of the eugenicist were the selection of that third of humanity representing the best strains, he would find his material among all European and Asiatic types, and very probably among all races of man; and all would contribute to the less valuable two-thirds. . . .

> . . . . the task of eugenics cannot be to devise means to suppress some races and to favor the development of others. It must rather be directed to the discovery of methods which favor the development of the desirable strains in every race.[38]

Nevertheless, Boas urged great caution in the interpretation of intelligence tests, arguing that testing devices could be effective only if they fit the experience and background of the person being tested. Psychology, argued Boas, has not achieved success in controlling "the factor of social milieu."[39] Boas, however, did not rule out the possibility of estimating the intelligence of an individual; he only asked that "we . . . base our tests on situations with which he is familiar."[40]

Within that body of research on the Mexican child, the anti-hereditarians led by Sanchez heeded Boas's warning and made it key to their research. They aimed to dispel the idea of Mexicans' intellectual inferiority and sought to construct theory and amass data that demonstrated language and cultural experience as the critical factors in the low scores reported in the literature. They did not argue against the role of intelligence and of the innate inequality in the distribution of intelligence. Their position held that the range of abilities of the Mexican population did not differ in any significant respects from the Anglo population. Therefore, the solution to arbitrarily low IQ scores was a test that did not penalize for environmental, language, or cultural factors. Such a goal inspired efforts to create a test that could accurately measure the intelligence of Mexican children. Rather than critique the concept intelligence, the nurturists accepted its premises and attempted to modify them to the cultural and environmental milieu of the Mexican community.

From such a point of departure, the scholars H. T. Manuel, Sanchez, and Tireman sought to construct measuring devices such as nonverbal tests and Spanish translations of the Stanford-Binet. A survey of the literature reported that

> the general findings have been that bilinguists are penalized when their intelligence is measured on verbal tests of intelligence but that there is no indication of the inferiority of bilingual subjects when their performance on non-language tests of intelligence is measured against that of monolingual subjects.[41]

Sanchez pioneered a version of the culture concept, the cultural deprivation thesis, in his early critiques of the biological determinists. Sanchez suggested, but did not consistently adhere to the idea of intelligence tests as tools for the measurement of learning (and not of the potential to learn). It would have been very worthwhile indeed had a school of thought appeared that sponsored that approach for the use of tests (then, of course, they would have ceased to be IQ tests). Unfortunately, intelligence theories and practices marched forward, although subject to modification. Sanchez, however, urged compensatory education as a solution to the problem of measuring the abilities of the Mexican child.

> The school has the responsibility of supplying those experiences to the child which will make the experiences sampled by standard measures as common to him as they were to those on whom the norms of the measures were based. When the school has met

the language, cultural, disciplinary, and informational lacks of the child and the child has reached the saturation point of his capacity in the assimilation of fundamental experiences and activities—then failure on his part to respond to tests of such experiences and activities may be considered his failure.[42]

Given then the acquiescence by the leading figure in anti-hereditarian research on the education of Mexican children to the assumption of the necessity of mental tests, it appeared inevitable that he would write in an article on bilingualism and mental measures that "it would be short-sighted to propose the abandonment of mental tests in the bilingual problem, and nothing herein should so be interpreted, a note of caution in their use is in order."[43] Thus, through the first half of the twentieth century, IQ tests became integral to the education of the Mexican child and as significant as segregation, the arbitrary exclusion of migrant children, and vocational education. And in spite of the strong warnings against the uncritical acceptance of intelligence test scores for bilingual children by many scholars, their voices seemed to disappear in the wilderness. At the end of the first half of the century mental testing held fast as a pedagogical tool with the same oppressive consequences obtained as in the 1920s. A pair of southern California academics, in summarizing their research published in 1950 on the intellectual ability of Mexican children as "contrasted" with "American children" wrote that their

finding raises the question of the appropriateness of the common practice of recording for predictive purposes an index of intellectual brightness for a child who is not a member of the cultural group upon which the test was standardized.[44]

Thus, in spite of compelling arguments to the contrary, researchers consistently tested Mexican children on instruments that penalized them on a variety of factors. Even if there had existed a scientific measure of abilities, a number of factors including learning, language, social environment, and culture made the Mexican child so different that it would have made it impossible to accurately measure his abilities. Not a few old-line hereditarians, including Raymond B. Cattell, Terman, and Edward L. Thorndike, now raised the ante and embarked upon a search for a psychological device adequate for the study of comparative and cross-cultural, cross-racial, and cross-national intelligence. In a response to a critique of the hereditarian position, Cattell warned the profession not to join "absurdly in the current panic stampede" despairing of the possibility of making comparisons of intelligence across cultures. When such universally applicable tests became available, claimed Cattell, racial studies could then rest upon sounder footing. As the nature-nurture debate moved forward, many of the lines, props, and postures remained.[45]

However, in spite of the nature-nurture polemic, the environmental question should not have emerged as the fundamental issue. The real issue actually involved the concept of intelligence itself, that central idea that tied the educational process to an uncritical acceptance of the use of tests for purposes of prediction, tracking, grouping, and other forms of differentiation that arbitrarily selected children for a slot in a hierarchy of educational privileges. It should come as no surprise, however, that in a class society the educational hierarchy would conform to the socioeconomic hierarchy. And thus, by midcentury the social science concept of intelligence and its practical application, intelligence testing, had helped fashion a well-established pattern of education for the Mexican community. Its effects are well-known; the educational experience for disproportionate numbers of Mexican children meant forced enrollment into slow-learner, educationally mentally retarded, and vocational education courses.

Chapter 4

Training for
Occupational Efficiency

Vocational Education

The educational program of the segregated school featured vocational education as the curricular track suited to the particular needs of the Mexican community. Teachers, administrators, researchers, and boards of education functioned as a single mind when it came to planning such educational programs for Mexican children. These programs placed such a pronounced emphasis on vocational, non-academic education that quite often the Mexican school became known as the industrial or vocational school of the district.

Vocational education not only applied to the Mexican community, but in theory and practice its proponents specified its usage for students of inferior mental ability as well. A strong tendency of academics and the general public emphasized vocational training for the working classes as a means out of poverty and as a move up the social scale. However, the theory behind vocational education stipulated that, in the main, those identified as the intellectually slower student should be so placed so that in a "normal" population only about 20 percent would be labeled slow to mentally retarded. Thus, vocational education included both Anglo and Mexican children; however, the disproportional enrollment of Mexican children determines the issue here. For practically all Mexican children found themselves performing vocational course work in the schools.

As in the case of the research upon the intelligence of Mexican children, an examination of the emphasis upon vocational education must begin with the national economic and social changes occurring in the late nineteenth century.

The School as Industrial Training Agency

As mass compulsory education gradually expanded at the turn of the century, schools incorporated the productive training functions formerly reserved for the family, community, or apprentice system.[1] This earlier training system corresponded to that era of capitalist production when the owners of capital were also, by and large, the direct producers of commodities. Gradually, technology developed that separated the owners from direct production, so that two social categories emerged: (1) the owners of capital, or the employing class, and (2) the nonpropertied labor, or direct producers. The later nineteenth century also witnessed the economy emerge as a system of corporate industrial production based largely upon socialized labor. This meant that the producers of commodities were not, as was the case in the early nineteenth century, owners of the means of production.

Adolescent youths also emerged as an identifiable social entity principally because that age group, no longer needed in the labor force as in the earlier epoch, became increasingly superfluous to production (except in the case of family migrant labor, as we shall see in chapter 5). Consequently, schools took over as holding institutions and as socialization agents in the era when entirely new forms of productive processes and social classes became permanent elements of the twentieth-century social order. Public schools were assigned the responsibility of integrating all youths into the objective social, economic, and political conditions of the period. Thus, schools had the task of training for a class society, for a complex industrialized form of a division of labor, and for the particular types of political ideals necessary to maintain the unity of society in spite of the socioeconomic divisions that separated its citizens into a hierarchical social order.[2] This naturally meant that not everyone could receive the same level of education even if all demonstrated equal capability or preparation for it. Some received training destined to place them in the higher more powerful echelons of the division of labor, and therefore the social order; the type of training introduced to others inevitably prepared them to fill in the slots at the lower echelons. The course work for this latter group emphasized vocational education, or training suited for industrial wage-labor.

Vocational education had two aspects. The first consisted of the adaptation of the individual to the general economic activities within the larger society. The second emphasized technical, trade, or industrial training. Thus, vocational education prepared the individual to find his place in a skilled, semiskilled, or unskilled manually oriented occupations. Vocational education provided a direct linkup between the school, the student, and the economy. In fact, its adherents designed all vocational education to serve the existing labor needs in business and industry. Thus, according to a 1945 state of California Department of Education publication, vocational education existed for "the preparation of workers for jobs that do or will exist."[3]

Defining the precise current and future needs of employers became one of the key functions of the schooling system. This proved no small task, and in many of the larger school districts, school board officials instituted a bureaucratic entity to constantly survey the labor needs in the region in relation to the curricular program of the schools. The California Department of Education superintendents' office regularly urged the local school districts to "canvas . . . local employers" to discover employment opportunities.[4] In addition, districts also conducted surveys of students' interests to see whether labor needs and student interests corresponded. If the two did not, then, of course, the employer's needs would not be satisfied. A specific goal of the schools, then, involved bending, if necessary, the students' interests to meet the available occupational opportunities.[5]

Lastly, not the least of the responsibilities of the schools in this training process involved the matching of the individual's abilities and interests with the intellectual demands of the employment possibilities. Thus, California superintendents informed teachers that their vocational education students "must understand the opportunities which are open to him, must understand his own abilities, interests, and needs, and must plan according with these facts."[6] The match between abilities and level of difficulty of the training involved became one of the critical concerns of guidance programs. "Within each of these fields there . . . is variation in terms of the levels of each kind of required abilities. Wise vocational planning . . . requires that he harmonize these two sets of data."[7] Consequently, districts instituted guidance programs; counselors were responsible for matching the individual with the curriculum, and for placing students into the appropriate educational levels. In general, the program consisted of at least three tracks, the superior, normal, and slow. The first track emphasized academic course work, the preparation for the professions, while the "slow" track usually emphasized nonacademic course work, the preparation for the manual occupations, or vocationally oriented education.

Thus, as the school systems of the Southwest gradually modernized, incorporating the most recent schooling theories and practices, counseling, tracking, and curriculum differentiation became standard procedure. Such modern practices, however, centered around the testing program of the school—the process of selecting and placing students into the track system. The Los Angeles school district incorporated a guidance program in the early 1920s, the Division of Psychology and Educational Research. According to the division, the policy stated,

"It is chiefly on the basis of test scores that pupils are classified into equal ability groups."[8] This division set the process of counseling in motion and monitored it with a fierce determination so that the whole district operated on a common set of principles and would not veer from it.[9] However, placement into the various curricular levels considered more than just IQs; counselors also considered nationality, parents' occupation, teacher evaluations, grades, school progress, and behavior. However, IQs provided the key to placement.

ABILITY GROUPING AND VOCATIONAL EDUCATION

In practice, education involved "a process [of] enabling young people to move themselves from where they are to where they ought to be."[10] For this educational process to occur, the teacher needed to know precisely where the student "ought to be." As a part of its duties and responsibilities, the school administration needed to "coordinate the work of a school with reference to the capacity of the student."[11] The educational objective consisted of both general and particular features: (1) the political and cultural socialization of each pupil into the larger society, together with certain minimal training necessary for social and economic functioning; and (2) the specific objectives determined by the particular "abilities" of each individual pupil. Within the general educational orientation, modified according to a hierarchical ordering of intellectual abilities, a multi-tiered curriculum reflecting this hierarchy became standard. Based upon the theoretical and practical recommendations of those social scientists involved in intelligence research related to education, this education procedure placed disproportionate numbers of Mexican children into vocational education. In his study, "Mental Differences of Certain Immigrant Groups," Kimball Young (a former graduate student of Lewis Terman at Stanford) presents the best examples of this type of research.[12]

Young's study exemplifies the classic practical scientific investigation, for his whole purpose in research was to solve social problems. Like many educators in the Southwest, Young felt that large numbers of overage Latin children clogged "the school machinery," and that the teaching objectives of the schools had become insurmountable by the presence of large numbers of "failures." After concluding on the basis of his own research that "Latins" were inferior to "Americans," Young then suggested a reorganization within the educational system recognizing above all, this range of mental abilities. He proposed a tracking on the basis of intelligence since, he argued, "The problem of teaching the American children in terms of ability, is far easier than with Latins who in on case rise but a few points above the standard average intelligence...."[13] Educators, warned Young, must take into account the mental abilities of the children who come from these racial groups."

This formed the core of Young's proposals for the solution of the education of alleged social misfits. Rather than placing these students into mental asylums, Young proposed that schools care for them by "educating" them according to their capacity. Toward this end he recommended four basic reforms involving: (1) school policy, (2) administrative and supervisional changes, (3) curriculum changes accompanied by changes in teaching practice, and (4) "a public conscience of cooperation with the schools." Under "school policy" Young essentially suggested that a new policy must grow from a careful sociological-educational survey of the localities, the economic life of the inhabitants, what the children of the present will be doing in later life in industry and agriculture or in business.[14] Essentially, in order to carry out this suggestion, each school needed to develop and adjust its curriculum according to the community's level of "intelligence."

Second, Young suggested changes in school administration and supervision, which he described as the application of "standardized intelligence tests which should be applied throughout the elementary schools." This was "only suggested from the side of the schools predominantly foreign because it is there that the largest numbers of the backward are found."[15]

Third, after testing, Young proposed that a reorganization of teaching units must be made that took into account "at least for three classes of pupils, the mentally retarded, the normal, and the superior."[16] Finally, Young urged that a program in Americanization with English classes as the central core of instruction, be instituted in each city with a significant enrollment of foreign children.

The practical effect of such proposals resulted in the development of a state institution with enormous power over individual lives. As far-reaching as these proposals appear, they only proved significant when linked with the proposed curriculum that Young developed upon the following grounds:

> Given the range of abilities measuring from those represented by the lowest 25 percent of the Latins to those found in the upper 25 percent of the non-Latins, what must be done to make the content of education more commensurate with the abilities of these pupils?[17]

The curriculum content consisted of (1) "training for occupational efficiency," (2) "habits and attitudes as make for social cooperation," and (3) "training for appreciation . . . of the arts and sciences for satisfaction and happiness." Each of these curriculum guides held special meaning for the social classes of society—the poor, or "less intelligent," received training for a "commensurate" task in society: ". . . For those who do not possess the capacities of the average school child, the curriculum must provide vocational training, and skills which will allow their best abilities to express themselves."[18] Not only would those of "backward mentality" receive training to fill a manual vocation, but they also had access to courses given in "science, literature, art and music" geared to their intellectual level, for there always existed the possibility of "considerable appreciation of these cultural forms."[19] Ultimately, a paternalistic education system developed as a near absolute power over the destiny of the individual, and for Young (as for Ross, Terman, and Edward Thorndike) functioned as a necessary form of governmental intervention in order to salvage the "American system" through identification and training of the "innately" more intelligent races and nationalities of the population. "Let our segregation be along the lines of ability, never race as such, and with the proper opportunities for all, especially for those capable of leadership, the future of culture itself is secured."

By the 1930s, the educational systems of major cities across the United States generally incorporated programs nearly identical to Young's proposals. A federally sponsored study published in 1933, cited vocational courses as the commonly applied curriculum program for Mexican schoolchildren throughout the Southwest.[20] In the program of the Los Angeles educational system, which had schools with large Mexican populations, Young's proposals resembled the practices of that particular school system.[21] In Los Angeles, approximately 55 percent of Mexican children scored below 90 on the IQ test. This fact provided a justification for channeling these children into the slow-learner classrooms. Twelve percent had IQs that qualified them for mentally retarded classes. Only one third of Mexican children qualified for normal and superior classes.

THE MEXICAN SCHOOL AS INDUSTRIAL SCHOOL

Under the administration of its superintendent, Susan B. Dorsey, Los Angeles adopted a "scientific" educational philosophy. Dorsey, a strong advocate of testing—the hereditarian doctrine on intelligence, curriculum differentiation, and tracking—considered the large presence of Mexican children a heavy burden upon the school system. By the early twenties Los Angeles had incorporated one of the most influential research, counseling, and psychological programs in any school system with significant numbers of Mexican children. The advent of the large-scale immigration of Mexican workers and their families into the region corresponded with the integration of the state-of-the-art educational theories based largely upon prevalent theories of intelligence.

The critical viewpoint adopted and incorporated into the educational program maintained that intellectual abilities vary according to the individual, that inheritance principally determined this variation, and that a normal distributive curve was to be expected of any given population, except those with biologically or culturally determined low intelligence levels. The variation in intellectual abilities ranged from the very superior to the educable "feeble-minded," with the majority clustering within the normal range. Administrators adapted the schooling program to this alleged social and biological reality, and consequently devised procedures that determined the educational needs of the pupil according to their intellectual abilities. In the first half of this century, Los Angeles adopted the most significant administrative units in the form of the Division of Psychology and Educational Research. This unit served as the nerve center of the school system as it largely shaped the philosophy, curriculum, objectives, and consequences of the district's program. In fact, it may be said that this division laid the foundation for the district that lasted well into the sixties. In essence, this division adopted a hard-line on the question of intelligence and its effect upon learning potential. The director of the division, Willis W. Clark, wrote a rather lengthy analysis of the elementary school program for 1922–23 in which he stated that the data had demonstrated that "intelligence level or mental ability is . . . [of] fundamental importance in indicating the capacity of a child to progress in his studies."[22] Furthermore, he continued, the policy objectives of the district was that each "pupil attain an accomplishment in school subjects commensurate with his capacity."[23]

In general, educators designed the course work to adapt to at least four levels of "native capacity": the very superior, the normal, the dull-normal or slow, and the mentally retarded. By the midtwenties a four-tiered tracking system, each with its specific teaching methods, curriculum, and educational objectives and consequences was in full swing. The largest distinction occurred between the two poles, the very superior and the mentally retarded, but clear distinctions also existed between the curriculum designed for the intellectual superiors and for those labeled "dull" or "slow." The curriculum designed for the students with the highest IQ emphasized intellectual pursuits: academic subject matter, creative activities, and scientific projects. The curriculum for the "bottom of the line" emphasized manual training. In between, the curriculum was distinguished by subtle shading, with the "normal" student receiving course work more similar to the "very superior," and the "slow" student receiving course work resembling but not identical to the program for the mentally retarded. The assistant supervisor of the Department of Psychology and Educational Research aptly summarized the district's general approach.

> It is useless to try to push a child beyond his native capacity into activities which he cannot comprehend and for which he will never . . . rise [in]; but it is quite possible and very much worthwhile to enrich his experiences and to train to the limit of development all the useful habits and skills which the child's capacity enables him to possess.[24]

While the general assumption held that the average Mexican child exemplified either innate or cultural inferiority, most upheld the conviction that Mexicans were superior, or at least equal, in terms of artistic, craft, or manual activities. "Judging from . . . indications of the mental characteristics of the Mexicans," wrote Grace Stanley in 1920, "emphasis on book study . . . is entirely inadequate to their needs . . . they are in need . . . of being trained in the skilled occupations for which they may be fitted."[25] Such a program, the author continued, should be based upon "the culture and crafts of the Mexican people in order that it [occupational training] may be a development of their race. . . ."[26]

Perhaps the most common justification for the emphasis upon vocational training (apart from the prevalent assumption that Mexicans excelled in manual labor) held that such training would be the first step in the process of socioeconomic advancement. Such reasoning fit well the liberal attitude of helping the downtrodden to move up the social ladder. The boot strap philosophy, reminiscent of Booker T Washington, provided much of the rationale for promoting vocational education among those who did not particularly adhere to racial or hereditarian doctrines. The assistant superintendent of the Los Angeles city schools pointed to the close ties between Washington's philosophy and the Los Angeles schools. In recent years there has been a greater acceptance, he wrote,

> of the principles taught by the former head of the Tuskegee Institute. The foreign people are feeling this influence and impulse. In Los Angeles they realize that the best training for an individual is that which fits him to be most useful to the community . . . the influence of vocational work, and the training of people for other than what are known as "white collar jobs" are bringing a change in the life conditions of the foreign born.[27]

Through this influence, continued the assistant superintendent, the foreign community integrated and connected itself "more closely with American life and tending away from . . . segregation."[28]

Consequently, both sides on the question of intelligence agreed that vocational education was the ideal program for the Mexican child. Nevertheless, significant differences remained. The biological/racial determinists foresaw vocational education as a permanent educational program; the environmentalists (those underscoring nurture) chose to emphasize vocational education because they considered it to be the first step in the process of assimilation and upward mobility. Both positions converged and formed a nearly unanimous choice for the course work emphasized in Mexican schools. Many also believed that since Mexican children would drop out early and enter into industrial occupations, providing vocational education merely accommodated an inevitable situation. In fact, such a widespread practice of manual/ vocational training existed, that teachers and administrators in Mexican schools commonly thought of their institution as an industrial school. The principal at the Grant School in Phoenix, Arizona, accordingly wrote:

> The vocational school, such as now located at Lowell [Mexican] School, is a step forward toward meeting the needs of those boys who cannot continue their education. The manual training and home economics departments at Lowell are also striving to give the children training directly applicable to their own life situations. What we need is more such vocational schools with varied activities for both boys and girls to train them to do better the things they will very likely do any way out of life. Very few of them will reach the white-collared job. . . .[29]

The case of the San Fernando, Los Angeles, elementary school provides an extraordinary example of the vocational emphasis for Mexican children. In 1923 the principal requested that the school, "attended entirely by Mexicans" and totaling 600 students, be officially transformed into "a Mexican Industrial School." The superintendent of schools and the Board of Education were favorably disposed to such a change, which they thought would "better fit the boys and girls to meet their problems of life in future years." School administrators considered regular schoolwork sufficient for the lower grades, "but the older children will have a longer time to finish their academic work and will have more vocational training. Such training involved the following:

> The girls will have more extensive sewing, knitting, crocheting, drawn work, rug weaving, and pottery. They will be taught personal hygiene, homemaking, care of the sick. With the aid of a nursery they will learn the care of little children. The boys will be given more advanced agriculture and shop work of various kinds.[30]

Such a philosophy of vocational education would have contributed toward the greater isolation, segregation, and socioeconomic distinctiveness of the Mexican from the Anglo communities. Once segregated, each aspect of the lives of the segregated community continued to experience the impact of that segregation. Educators did not limit their pursuit of the objectives to Los Angeles; these educational goals gained currency in programs throughout the Southwest, as well.

In the late 1940s, at Los Angeles' Roosevelt High School, largely attended by Mexican students, the principal, Frances Daugherty, appealed to the local school administrators for support in order to reformulate the curriculum to meet the needs of the student body. Daugherty called a meeting attended by "principals and vocational teachers in various Eastside high schools and junior high schools on the matter of the new vocational building to be constructed at Roosevelt." According to Fred W. Ross, an Eastside community organizer in attendance:

> The meeting was opened by an explanation of the anticipated ethnic composition of the Roosevelt student-body. It was estimated that in the immediate future 70% of Roosevelt's students would be of Mexican ancestry, 30% Negro, and the remainder would come from "Anglo-American" and Jewish communities. Mr. Daugherty stated that in light of such an ethnic composition Roosevelt High School would unquestionably become a completely vocationalized school in the immediate future. He substantiated by saying that at present less than 2% of the Spanish speaking students go on to college and that at least 50% drop out. . . .[31]

While Daugherty defended vocational training on the basis of a low rate of college entrance and a high dropout rate at the high school level, many others defended vocational training at the elementary level because of early departure. Thus, the Mexican child began to receive earlier exposure to vocational training in the elementary and junior high levels to accommodate the high dropout rates, so that by the time he graduated from high school, his education might have consisted of twelve years of vocational training. One researcher found that the "sentiment of many teachers of Mexican children was known to favor an earlier introduction in the grades of these subjects [vocational training] for Mexicans."[32] He went on to clarify his statement further.

> The introduction of manual and domestic arts at a lower level than is now practiced is the wish of a large majority [of teachers] who want to have the Mexican children to have the advantage of these courses before the early drop-out prevents them from receiving this important instruction.[33]

The introduction of manual training by the fourth grade seemed not unusual, but more common practice introduced it between the fifth and seventh grades. The principal of the Montebello Elementary School in southern California found vocational education as early as the fifth grade necessary in light of the educational problems affecting Mexican children, citing several factors, such as limited cultural experiences, a lack of "a need for learning," and an early dropout rate. Girls learned cooking, while boys received lessons on "the uses of tools and how to operate and care for them."[34]

One of the most instructive examples of the practice of defining and molding Mexican schools as Mexican industrial schools involved the case of the Miami, Arizona, school system. With a town population of ten thousand, mostly miners, many of whom included Mexicans, the school board decided in 1923 "to equip the new Mexican building with a view to emphasizing industrial and homemaking courses for these children."[35] The Miami school program of 1923 resembled that of the Zavala Mexican school in Austin, Texas, of 1949. The latter represented the "only elementary school in Austin . . . equipped with an industrial arts shop and a home economics laboratory," and although the school was located only three blocks away from the Anglo school, it was far distant in terms of educational objectives.[36]

One teacher's example cited in Texas' *Course in English for Non-English-Speaking Pupils* (1932) reflected the general practice of using the occupational level of the Mexican community as the starting point for schooling. In her English instruction she placed "special emphasis upon the words the child will use in his work-a-day life as a tiller of the soil."[37] A combination of factors including intelligence, retardation, dropping out, socioeconomic level, and cultural and/or innate non-academic propensities (e.g., handwork) usually appeared in discussions of the justification for vocational education as *the* course of study for Mexican children.

The pattern, then, throughout the Southwest consisted of an emphasis upon vocational subjects in the Mexican schools. Educators considered such a curricular model to be especially adapted to the particular innate or cultural characteristics of the Mexican student, to the expressed needs of industry, and to the ideological prescriptions for socioeconomic advancement.

The soon-to-be superintendent of the Chaffey School District in southern California, Merton Hill, strongly advocated vocational training for Mexican children, since, he argued, Mexican children work at only about half the normal capacity of white children. "In communities where there is sufficient Mexican population," wrote Hill, "there should be developed industrial high schools for Mexican pupils. . . ."[38] He also proudly pointed out that the Chaffey Board of Education passed a resolution on 6 February 1927 that was "looking forward to the development of an industrial high school for Mexican pupils of the Chaffey district and other portions of San Bernardino County. . . ."[39]

Generally, schools taught the type of occupational training that addressed the labor needs in industry and the types of occupations open to Mexicans. Thus, by the late twenties, counselors in the Los Angeles area carried out "surveys of the occupations suitable to and firms employing Negro, Mexican, and Jewish help."[40] Moreover, the vocational program designed by the California State Department of Education in the 1940s, integrated the special occupational needs of minorities, apart from those of the majority, into its overall program guide. Consequently, the highest levels of educational administration also segregated the voca-

Planning on them dropping out is like always taking their chance at sucess

tional program, reinforcing the practice of allocating specific curriculum to Mexican students. In reference to minorities and vocational education, the California State Department of Education Bulletin of 1937 stated that the trends in the population of minorities "would seem to present a problem of which educators must take cognizance, that a minority group . . . may receive appropriate instruction, *especially in reference to their probable vocations* (emphasis mine).[41]

With the incorporation of the testing and vocational education, many school districts in the Southwest chose to establish a close cooperation with local business and industry as the procedure to select the most effective and efficient educational program. The managers of the Los Angeles Chamber of Commerce's Industrial Department described this cooperative effort.

> The interest of the businessman in the schools of Los Angeles is naturally keen. Employees of his concern are the products of the public schools and their efficiency depends in large measure upon the methods employed in the schools.[42]

The director of vocational education for the Los Angeles city schools concurred. "Los Angeles was fortunate in bringing about [a] most wholesome cooperation in the schools . . . from business and industry."[43] Consequently, the vocational education program reflected to a significant degree the wishes and interests of employers, not the interests of the Mexican community.

The policy of the Arizona State Department of Education toward the education of bilingual children also emphasized planned outcomes. Since it was a foregone conclusion that "under present conditions," most bilinguals would enter the unskilled or semiskilled ranks of labor, their vocational education was "to be introduced early and homemaking should be an important part of the elementary course for both boys and girls."[44]

Like many urban school districts in the Southwest, San Antonio's Mexican schools underscored vocational course work to a greater degree than it did its academic subjects. The Sidney Lanier Junior School, for example, had the largest and most complete shop building in the city. According to the *Bulletin* of the San Antonio Public Schools, "the most distinguishing feature of the Sidney Lanier Junior School, is the elaborate shops."[45] The Texas Educational Survey Commission strongly recommended that "special curricula should be constructed for Negro schools, and for Mexican schools. The degree of differentiation should in each case be determined by a careful study of the situation."[46] The value of industrial schools for Mexicans, stated the Texas Commission *Report* on "Vocational Education," evidenced when these schools placed them in occupations where their "ability and opportunity" permitted them.[47]

The San Antonio administration concluded that since most Mexican children entered the industrial occupations upon either graduating or dropping out, a vocational education served in their best interests. In addition, stated the district's *Bulletin,* "motor minded ability seems to be a social characteristic with all the Latin peoples."[48] Consequently, when constructing the Lanier Junior School, the architects included plans for a school that differed from all other junior schools in the district, being conscious of the need to include additional space for shop activities. Lanier emphasized "special courses, flexible programs, home making, and industrial activities."[49] Courses offered included "sewing, cooking and art work for girls; machine shop practice, auto repair, auto painting, top making, sheet metal work, plain bench and cabinet work in wood and a department in which type-setting and job printing are taught for boys."[50]

The educational programs, then, during the de jure segregation period, placed emphasis on vocational education, and this was the case whether or not the school was integrated. Moreover, because of the low average test scores obtained in Mexican schools or in schools with high Mexican enrollment, the curriculum tended to be modified as a whole to reflect the school's level of intelligence. Thus, the categories, or tracks for superior, normal, or slow in the Mexican school did not measure up to the general definition of those tracks. A slow track in a Mexican school would very probably have been given a more vocationally oriented program than that same track would have received in an Anglo school. There prevailed then, two separate standards for judging the quality of the pupils and two different types of curriculum differentiation.

SLOW AND MENTALLY RETARDED PUPILS

By the close of the fifth decade, most school districts throughout the Southwest had adopted testing, tracking, and curriculum differentiation as the best method for tailoring education to fit the child. It should come as no surprise then that the very same scheme for segregating the mentally retarded in 1919 in Los Angeles became the state of California's general policy in the 1940s. Any child who scored below 70 on the IQ test qualified for admission to either a development room, or a development center, thereby designating each child as incapable of normal educational development. The provisions of the Los Angeles city schools denied that the mentally retarded could profit from an academic emphasis, but that his education should consist primarily of vocational training. "Generally speaking," stated the district's policy manual on high school development pupils, "these students are programmed in the regular non-academic or vocational classes indicated by their special interests or abilities."[51] The same fare was doled out for elementary development children: "for girls cooking, sewing, laundering, and personal hygiene. There are also classes in music, art, dancing, and weaving for both boys and girls. The garden is large and colorful with flowers. Vegetables are also raised for the cafeteria."[52]

In 1941 schools assigned nearly five thousand children to the thirty-three development classes, and ten schools at the elementary level. Their educational horizons did not extend beyond the level of manual training, since, in general, educators never expected these children to move to a higher level. Their status was fixed.

> These children are capable of learning the simple mechanical phases of the academic curriculum but they are unable to master the secondary or more abstract accomplishments of the higher levels. They usually find their greatest efficiency and usefulness in work of a vocational or pre-vocational nature.[53]

Adherents to this view argued, then, that these students would never "enter the professional ranks" and that it was inevitable that they would "learn to do fairly good work with their hands." Consequently, their training prepared them to "find their places in the unskilled or semi-skilled trades."[54]

By way of contrast, the superior students stood at the opposite pole. Los Angeles, as did most school districts, provided an "enriched curricula, creative work, and training for leadership" specifically for children of "superior" intelligence.[55] The schools gathered together the "gifted few" who allegedly possessed the "rare ability for organization ... leadership ... scientific discoveries and inventions." Moreover, according to district policy, they alone had the potential to "revolutionize and enrich life for the many . . . a most valuable asset to the nation."[56] With such a program for the top 2 percent, it seemed logical that Los Angeles, as did many districts, placed "superior" teachers in the gifted classes.[57] Thus, the segregation of children according to IQ, also represented a segregation of nationalities, curriculum, and teachers.

Generally speaking, Mexican children fell victim to significant over-representation in the slow-learner and developmental classes and under-representation in superior classes. By 1931 Los Angeles maintained twelve development centers, at least ten were located in the poorer or working-class sections of the city. The Mexican children enrolled in six of these schools, comprised the entire enrollment in the Eugene Street School, one third of the Gorman Avenue School, and varying portions of the four remaining schools. In the school attended entirely by Mexican "mentally retarded" youngsters, the majority of the parents of the children were "employed in the seasonal occupations."[58] In all of the schools, a disproportional number of students were minorities.

One Los Angeles school administrator wrote that "the subnormal child is rather apt to come from a low type home—financially, socially, or emotionally. Often he comes from a foreign home where the parents have not yet adjusted themselves to American standards."[59] During the years 1926, 1927, and 1928, that same administrator conducted a survey of the distribution of intelligence in the district's schools and found that those populated largely by "foreign students" stood much lower intellectually than Anglo children. Los Angeles categorized its schools as neighborhood or foreign, semineighborhood, normal or Anglo, and rural. Nearly 12 percent of neighborhood school sixth-grade children scored below .70, or development room material; only 1.3 percent of Anglo children scored below .70. Nearly 43 percent of neighborhood school sixth-grade children scored between .70 and .89, sufficient to earn them the title of slow learner, or "dull-normal"; only 14.4 percent of Anglo children scored in that category. About 1 of every 3 neighborhood children scored between .90 and .109, whereas 47.9 percent of Anglo children scored in that range.

Perhaps the most interesting statistic in the survey showed that 9.7 percent of neighborhood children fell within the superior range, as compared to 36.5 percent for Anglo children. Fifty-five percent of neighborhood schoolchildren qualified for either the slow learner or mentally retarded classes. On the other hand, only 15.7 percent of Anglo children scored accordingly. By way of summary, that researcher wrote:

> The percentage of mentally retarded children is greatest for the neighborhood type of school, and least for the normal type of school. The reverse is true of the children of superior mentality who are found most frequently in the normal type school.[60]

Consequently, minority children largely populated development centers as evidenced by this brief description of one development center.

The Gorman Avenue School is located in the small town of
Watts. . . . The population of this school is approximately one-
third colored, one-third Mexican, and one-third white. The social
and economic conditions in this district are very much below
average.[61]

In 1931, 2,460 children enrolled in the twelve centers, but the total
enrollment varied according to "seasonal employment in the country,
where the children and their parents [were] employed picking fruits
and nuts." According to the district publications, enrollment reached its
maximum in the spring "when many Centers and Rooms have to maintain waiting lists." However, by the month of June there occurred an
"appreciable exodus" to go "into harvest the onion crop."[62] Given this
characterization of the enrollment patterns, it can be deduced that high
numbers of Mexican children appeared on the development registers,
perhaps one third to one half, at a time when they constituted only 13
percent of the entire school population. Their school experience typified
the layout found at the Norfolk Street School, a school populated by a
"mixed" student body.

Each building is equipped with a home economics unit, consisting
of a cooking room, cafeteria, sewing room, and laundry; a manual
education unit, consisting of the main workroom, a lumber room,
a paint room, and a tool room; a hand-work unit, with provision
for loom weaving, clay work, basketry and miscellaneous types
of craft work.[63]

Such an educational program held terminal status, that is, it did extend
to students beyond the eighth grade. Overage development children
attended a special center, the Coronel School, even though they could
graduate to junior high and high schools where a program "fitted to
their needs" and educational experience awaited them. However, most
children finished their schooling either upon reaching their sixteenth
birthday, or upon finishing the elementary level curriculum. According

to one district administrator, employers often prized these graduates. He wrote that the development centers resulted in a boon in industry.

> Several employers have told us that a dull girl makes a very much better operator on a mangle than a normal girl. The job is purely routine and is irksome to persons of average intelligence, while the sub-normal seems to get actual satisfaction out of such a task. Fitting the person to the job reduces the "turnover" in industry and is, of course, desirable from an economic point of view.[64]

On the eve of the Second World War the principal of a Phoenix Mexican vocational school urged school districts throughout the state to establish "more such vocational schools" for Mexican children. Each boy should be "taught to read at his own level" as well as enroll in course work in "writing, spelling, and some arithmetic." However, the afternoon should "be given to art work, handicraft and gardening."[65] Such a prescription was not unusual, nor out of line, with the general course of study in the Mexican schools of the Southwest. As early as 1915 most educators considered vocational education as the ideal course work for Mexican children; by the 1940s, that belief and practice had become firmly entrenched. In school after school, the pattern of vocational training for Mexican children became just as visible as the pattern of academic training in the middle- and upper-class Anglo schools. The segregation of nationalities included a segregation of the curriculum and tended to reproduce the social relationships between Mexican and Anglo communities.

Figure 1. Mexican School less than two blocks away from Anglo American school

Herschell Manuel Photographs, Nettie Benson Latin American Collection, University of Texas Libraries, University of Texas at Austin.

Figure 2. Mexican School in a small Texas City

Figure 2 Herschell Manuel Photographs, Nettie Benson Latin American Collection, University of Texas Libraries, University of Texas at Austin.

Figure 3. Mexican School in small former church building. Other children in district are transported to city schools.

Figure 3 Dr. Hector P. Garcia Papers, Special Collections & Archives, Texas A&M University-Corpus Christi Bell Library

Figure 4. Shows the typical, dilapidated, inadequate, rotting old shack, which is one of the mainstays of the "Mexican Ward School" of Mathis. Notice the rooting [*sic*] lumber. No screens on windows. No screen doors. Improper lighting. No fly-proofing or rat-proofing. Inside it is dark, crowded and generally an uninviting appearance.

Figure 4 Dr. Hector P. Garcia Papers, Special Collections & Archives, Texas A&M University-Corpus Christi Bell Library.

Figure 5. School for White children in Edcouch-Elsa, Texas, school district.

Figure 5 Carlos I. Calderon, "The Education of Spanish-Speaking Children in Edcouch-Elsa, Texas," Master's Thesis, University of Texas, 1950.

Figure 6. A Part-time Class of Mexican Girls (Industrial Education in a Southern California Mexican School)

Figure 6 Chaffey Unified High School District and the Chaffey Junior College, 1928.

Figure 7. Industrial shops at Sidney Lanier Junior School

INDUSTRIAL SHOPS AT SIDNEY LANIER JUNIOR SCHOOL

Figure 7 "The Junior Schools Organization and Administration," *The San Antonio Public School Bulletin* 1, no. 1 (February 1924): 59.

Figure 8. Uneducated Mothers are bad for the country (Americanization program in a Southern California City)

Figure 8 Merton Earle Hill, "The Development of an Americanization Program," Master's Thesis, University of California, Berkeley, 1928.

Figure 9. Southgate School District, Texas

Figure 9 E. E. Mireles & Jovita G. Mireles, Special Collections & Archives, Texas A&M University-Corpus Christi, Bell Library.

Figure 10. Parents petition the Westminster School District calling the Board
to end school segregation

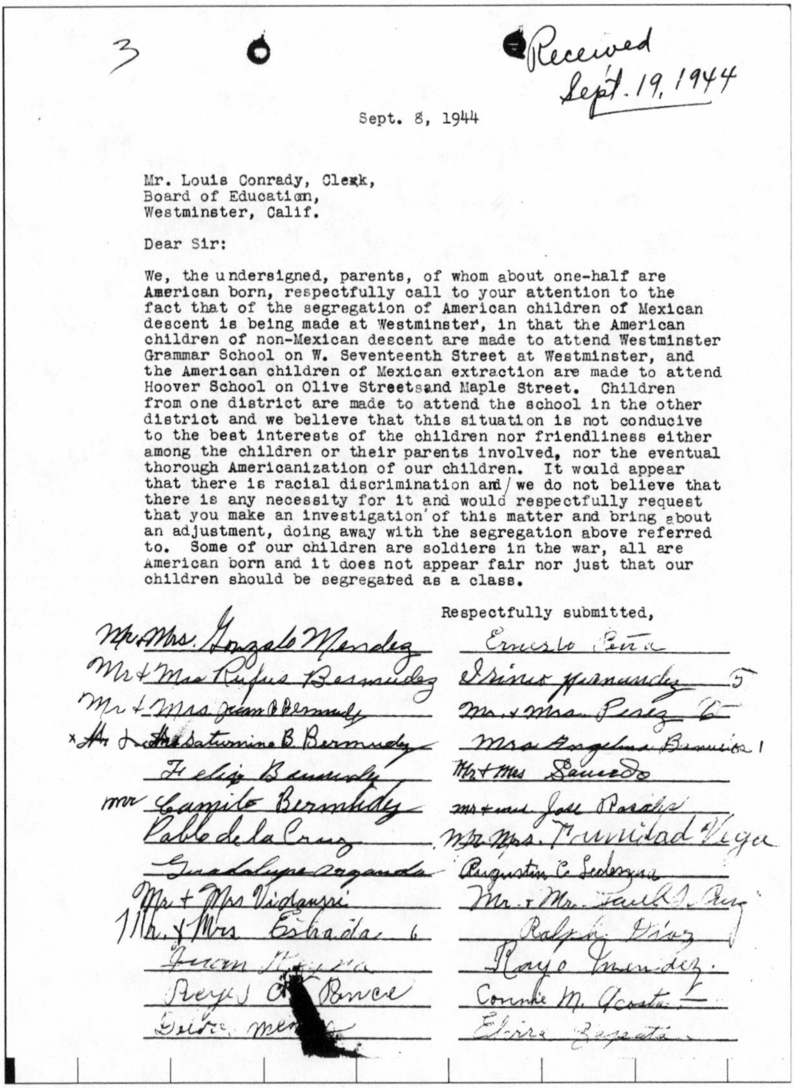

Figure 10 Courtesy of the Chapman University Mount Pleasant Library,
Special Collections & Archives

CHAPTER 5

THE EDUCATION OF
MIGRANT CHILDREN

This chapter explores and analyzes an ignored yet crucial topic: the education of Mexican migrant children. In general, most educational historiography has lumped the education of the urban resident child · with that of the migrant child.[1] It is important to recognize the variation within the educational experience of the Mexican community. We will provide a comprehensive view of the education of Mexican migrant children based upon materials published during the segregation period.

Within the educational history of the Mexican community at least three main patterns emerge and take shape according to the regional economy patterns in which educational services are rendered: the urban working class, the occasional migrant class, and the truly migratory class. The first includes the urban working class child whose family integrates him into an industrial, manufacturing, or service economy. This pattern, found in the larger urban centers such as Los Angeles, Chicago, and El Paso, was characterized by a permanency of residence. At the opposite extreme, the migratory pattern involved family integration into a seasonal agricultural economy, and permanency or impermanency of residence. Within these two poles lived a semiurban, largely permanent but occasionally migrant community. Although this community existed within an agricultural area, its members also participated in light industrial, manufacturing, or service enterprises. Within these three patterns (each instance influenced by the regional economy), are three noticeably distinct educational experiences. By and large, the urban, permanent resident child experienced segregation in neighborhood schools. Moreover, authorities enforced compulsory education laws as well as policies allowing open entry of Mexican children into secondary schooling.

By contrast, the migrant child very often faced exclusion from schooling, both by the policy of Boards of Education and by survival needs emanating from their participation in agricultural production organized on the basis of family labor. The migrant child generally attended an inferior and segregated school with emphasis on Americanization and vocational education. Rarely did the migrant child progress as far as the fifth grade.

The contrast appears when comparing the urban and rural migrant child. However, even these patterns did not hold consistently for the entire educational experience for both populations since many children entered into both experiences. Many residents of urban centers, Los Angeles and San Antonio as examples, entered into agricultural *and* industrial labor markets. A principal of a San Antonio, Texas, school noted the interrelationship between the Mexican community and the surrounding agricultural economy, especially in its effect upon education. "Strangely enough enrollment of the pupils in a Mexican school, even though it is in one of the State's largest cities, is influenced more by the economic conditions over the farming areas than by the conditions in the city itself."[2] Thus, employers frequently recruited families in urban centers to perform seasonal agricultural labor. Finally, permanent residents in agricultural communities migrated within their counties of residence also to perform agricultural labor.

In areas such as southern California, many Mexican settlements arose to serve local farms. These children normally attended local schools. However, if they migrated from the country they became subject to that educational experience reserved for the "true" migrants. Children of migratory settlements usually attended a segregated school, or a Mexican room, in an otherwise Anglo school. Like the migrant children, true migrants also encountered Americanization and vocational education courses. However, unlike migrant children, permanent residents in agricultural communities had far greater opportunity for participating in the educational process, although this depended upon the child labor demands in the locality.

Schooling facilities in agricultural communities adapted to grower demands for child labor and consequently adjusted their schedule to picking seasons. Such schools usually started at 7:00 a.m. or 7:30 a.m. and continued until noon, so that children could join parents in the groves and fields.[3] Children seldom attended beyond the fourth or fifth grades and rarely entered high school. Thus, these three variations greatly affected the educational experiences of Mexican children.

In order to understand more clearly these variations, let us focus upon those children whose lives and education took shape in accordance with the migration of family labor in agriculture. During the 1900–1950 period a large percentage of the Mexican population either resided in rural villages and towns, or lived in urban centers while working in a rural economy. In 1930, about half of the Mexican population resided in rural, or semirural regions; by 1950 that figure decreases to only one third. The changes in occupational structure reflected this demographic shift. In 1930, 35 percent of the Spanish-surnamed labor force of the five southwestern states worked as farm laborers; by 1950, that number had declined to nearly 25 percent. The concentration in agriculture continued to decline, so that by 1960, only 17 percent listed farm laborer as their occupation, and by 1970, only 8 percent. However, for purposes of this analysis of migrant education, the history clearly shows the close ties between the Mexican community and the rural agricultural economy for the first half of the twentieth century. The migrant experience played a significant part in the lives of hundreds of thousands of Mexican children, and this feature of the educational history of the Mexican people certainly deserves our attention.

The Migrant and the Agricultural Economy

Basic to the education of migrant children is the economic context shaping the organization and type of labor force. Migrant children appear only in an economy based on migrant family labor, a creation of a particular type of capitalist agriculture. The history of agriculture in the United States has demonstrated at least six variations in the form of labor power—we see the use of family and hired-hand labor on family-owned farms; tenant and sharecropping family labor on large-scale farms; migratory single men (or "tramps") on large-scale farms; and migratory family labor, also on large-scale farms. In the earlier period of agriculture, which lasted most of the nineteenth century, family and hired labor on individually owned small-scale farms predominated. However, in the Southwest, since the rise of capitalist agriculture from the 1870s, to roughly the 1920s, migratory single men, tenant, and share-cropping, prevailed as the predominant forms of labor.

The land tenure pattern in the Southwest has consisted predominantly of large-scale farming, with small-scale farming subject to economic and political domination of their larger class partners. Ever since the integration of the Southwest into the United States, land has come under the direct or indirect control of relatively few giants. This fact, along with the geographic and climatic conditions as well as technological adaptations, and protective legislation, has led directly to the extensive use of migrant family labor.[4]

Seasonal production enhanced by such technology as large-scale irrigation works, refrigerated railroad cars, tractors; protective legislation such as the Dingley Tariff of 1896, which placed a high duty on sugar imports "and stimulated the development of the sugar industry,"[5] and various immigration laws, depended upon the importation of cheap foreign labor. Thus, family labor moved to the center stage but only after certain conditions were met for the integration of the family as a single laboring unit (as contrasted to a single person in industry) into production.

The most significant factor leading to the extensive use of migrant family labor involved the concentration of land among a few large farming enterprises. The second condition represented the application of industrial concepts to agriculture, that is, the factory system as applied to agriculture and the technological adaptations that made "factories in the fields" (as Carey McWilliams referred to farms) inevitable. Consequently, socialized production process emerged as it demanded a large mass of constantly moving landless workers, an inescapable social product of the most successful capitalist agricultural area the world has ever known.

In Texas, this migratory family pattern evolved from a tenant and sharecropping system due initially to land speculation, later accelerating upon the introduction of the gas-engine tractor that eliminated most preharvest labor needs. This fact also made the small-scale, family-run tenant farms unproductive and introduced the utilization of large-scale operations based on seasonal harvesting-labor. Landowners came to rely not only upon the dispossessed tenant families, but upon a "new" labor supply—the Mexican immigrant family. From about 1910 on, Mexican families increasingly picked cotton in Texas, and by 1925, they comprised the main labor supply numbering about 300,000 out of 400,000 migrant cotton workers.[6] By and large, Mexican migratory workers worked in several agricultural enterprises, such as cotton and vegetable truck farming and beet work, the latter especially in Colorado and Michigan.

Mexican migratory cotton workers operated through the contract system whereby an agent of the employer supplied a specified number of workers for a specific period of time. The contractor hired the laborers, transported them to the fields, and in turn paid them out of deducted wages by the employer.

In the case of Texas migrant labor, Mexican families became the most preferred form of labor because of their large size and susceptibility to domination by a single male. Thus, under the conditions of an industrialized form of agriculture, migratory family labor came into existence. McWilliams summed up the profitability of family labor.

> Family ties remain exceptionally strong among Mexicans. It is not surprising, therefore, to find that the contractor system is largely based upon the family unit. The contractor may be the general, but the Mexican patriarch is the major. He has his own family organization, consisting not merely of the members of his immediate family, but of collateral relatives. Embraced within the family unit may be twelve, fifteen, or twenty workers. They stick together; they work and camp and move as a unit. This, in turn, helps to organize the labor market and it also gives the contractor a closely knit working organization.[7]

More importantly, under the migratory system the employer had little responsibility for the welfare of his employees outside of the contractual relationship. Migratory families traveling from the valleys of south Texas (a traditional center, or home base, for Texas migrants), California, or Colorado survived as best they could, although subjected to the vagaries of the labor market and production, as well as the racial and social oppression that they encountered by virtue of their status as outcasts.[8]

Migrants followed an agricultural production pattern determined by growing and maturing seasons. In one analysis of Texas migrants, the following pattern emerged: cotton was picked in the Rio Grande Valley in early summer; in late summer in the Coastal Bend area near Corpus Christi; and in October, November, and December in central and north Texas and the Plains. In between, migrants tended to the citrus and bean harvests in the Rio Grande Valley, and afterward they moved on to Raymondville, Texas and Robstown to gather onions and vegetables.[9]

In spite of the continuous flow, uniform employment patterns did not exist in all areas. For example, unlike the cotton-growing areas, migrants faced extremely variable employment during produce harvests. In vegetables, workers could be employed by several contractors in a single day, and during that one day they may work all day or only one hour depending entirely upon the orders received for that day. Thus, only the immediate labor of the picker was organized. However, the pay-scale, hours of employment (no matter whether all members of a single family worked or not), the number of laborers needed, and the working conditions were not subject to control, review, or regulation. The process consistently met the needs of the employer, and this necessitated the extremely variable and oppressive conditions in terms of wages, living quarters, and welfare of workers.[10]

The advantage of family labor was that the wages earned by all members was considered sufficient for the entire family to subsist. The family wage was thus roughly on the same economic plane as the individual wage of a factory worker—both wages were considered necessary to sustain a worker's family. However, in the former the entire family worked to sustain itself, and, for the vast majority, it could only barely exist above starvation levels.

The landowner, thus, had the advantage of hiring many more workers than he remunerated; in essence, unpaid labor supported the agricultural economy. Consequently, women and children worked as virtual slaves in an economic enterprise vital to the health and nutrition of millions of people. Children provided employers with free labor and by their status as such were victimized in many other ways. Migratory children were commonly denied the basic right to education, not merely because their poverty often prevented them from attending, but also because their status as migratory laborer placed them outside of the protection of educational rights mandated by the states. In essence, they did not enjoy the constitutional guarantee of equal protection of the laws.[11]

The educational experience of migratory children represented the social aspect of the economic system, which established the migrant family as the foundation for its productivity. The Mexican family proved integral to the economies of Texas, Arizona, California, and Colorado, but such a preindustrial labor form hearkened back to the feudal village. Once the Mexican family formed into the basic unit of migratory agricultural labor, a host of consequent social conditions inevitably arose. These conditions condemned generations of Mexican children to poor nutrition, poor health, poor housing, and virtually no education. The educational pattern of migrant children was characterized by exclusion, segregation, irregular (or seasonal) attendance, and very early dropout rates.

General Features of the Education of Migrant Children in the Southwest

For migrant children schooling was a privilege since most had their admission denied through board policy; they could not attend due to their economic function as cheap labor, or could attend sporadically or irregularly due to seasonal labor. A policy of the deliberate exclusion of migrant children from schooling either through a denial of admission or because of the deliberate failure to enforce compulsory education laws, stood out as a common feature of the education of migrant children. "Probably at no time during the [1930] school year," wrote Paul S. Taylor, concerning Dimmet County, Texas, "are more than 25 percent of the Mexican scholastics, i.e., children aged 7 to 17 inclusive, in school; the average number in attendance undoubtedly less."[12] Seldon C. Menefee's 1938 study of Crystal City in Zavala County, Texas, found that only "about 17 percent of the children aged 7 to 10 years and about 40 percent of those 11 to 13 attended school for the full year." On the other hand, 53 percent of the 7- to 10-year-olds did not attend school at all during the 1938 school year.[13] Gilbert Ennis Hall cited the "tabulated reports of [Texas] school superintendents for the fiscal year 1942–1943 [which] revealed that only 53 percent, or approximately 138,000 Spanish-speaking children, were enrolled in the public schools for that year."[14] Amber A. Warburton, Helen Wood, and Marian M. Crane in their study on "The Work and Welfare of Children of Agricultural Laborers in Hidalgo County, Texas," analyzed the fundamental reason for this low attendance figure.[15]

> Little if any attempt was made by the school districts studied to account for all the children listed in the annual school census to determine why many of them were not in school, to compel enrollment of all those of compulsory-attendance age, or to require regular attendance of the total group enrolled. The procedure for obtaining permission to remain away from school, as set forth in the laws, was generally dispensed with, regardless of the age of the child or the grade he had completed. In consequence, large numbers of school-age children did not enroll, and many of those who were enrolled attended irregularly. A school principal stated for example, that of the 2,600 children between 6 and 18 years of age in the school census for his district only about 1,600 had enrolled during the current school year.

The authors reported a widespread "attitude that school attendance should not be allowed to interfere with the supply of cheap farm labor."[16] Not only did officials fail to enforce laws, but deliberate loopholes in the laws themselves made lax enforcement legal. Moreover, when attendance by Mexican children was imminent, school authorities merely refused admission. Herschel T. Manuel quoted a west Texas county superintendent who said:[17]

> I have just recently learned that there are Mexicans in two or three districts who really wanted to send their children to school, but the "whites" scare them out of it. They tell them if they send their

children to school, they will be out of a job. Of course, in order to hold their jobs they will not send them to school.

In one instance a member of a school board "came to school one morning with a gun to keep a Mexican child from attending![18] Thus, Manuel found that even though schools were "technically available" to the entire "white" community, the "policy of antagonism on the part of the other white population too often means that actually the Mexican child has no school open to him."[19] Manuel concluded that the fundamental reason for refusing education to the Mexican child involved the economic function of the family, as this district superintendent testified.[20]

> Most of our Mexicans are of the lower class. They transplant onions, harvest them, etc. The less they know about everything else the better contented they are. You have doubtless heard that ignorance is bliss; it seems that it is so when one has to transplant onions.

Thus far, we have discussed the major educational pattern afforded Mexican migrant children. Where districts allowed education, they did so only on a segregated basis. And even then, the amount of schooling fell far below the standards for the age of the child. In those districts where Mexican migrant children attended school they commonly encountered segregation for the first several grades, and generally they were obligated to attend the first grade for two years due to language and irregular attendance.[21] Consequently, the bulk of Mexican migrant children, when enrolled in school, found themselves in the first grades. Thereafter, a rapid tailing off of enrollment occurred. A study of Hidalgo County describes the dropout problem in clear and simple terms.[22]

> The ages of the enrolled children reflected the brevity of the school experience of most children of field workers in the valley.

Seldom were children enrolled before they were 7 or 8 and usually by the time they were 14 they had withdrawn.

Warburton, Wood, and Crane reported that in Texas, "Withdrawals from school began shortly after the opening of school in the Fall and continued at an increasing rate throughout the school year." By the end of the school year, less than three fourths of the fall enrollees still remained in school. Moreover, attendance "throughout most of the school year was exceptional."[23] Only 14 percent of the children under 16 years of age missed not more than 3 weeks of school. Only 39 percent "attended as much as 120 days and thus met the minimum attendance requirement of the compulsory-school-attendance law."[24]

The educational consequences for the population proved devastating. Menefee reported that in Crystal City, an important agricultural center of south Texas, figures taken from 1938 showed that "the average 18-year-old [Mexican] youth had not completed the third grade of school."[25] Thus, this led McWilliams to write that "so far as migratory children are concerned, the compulsory school attendance law might just as well never have been enacted." A Texas school superintendent stated that "the compulsory school attendance law is a dead letter—there is no effort to enforce it. Nobody cares."[26] And this shows precisely how an economy based on large-scale agriculture could operate profitably and efficiently, or as one farmer testified, "if they get educated a little, they don't make such good farm hands."[27]

On the other hand, children were often too poor to be satisfactorily dressed for school and often parents kept their children at work as a matter of basic survival. Under such circumstances the Mexican community deemed education a privilege, not a right. Thus, one migrant mother explained that she alternated attendance for her two sons because "I can't keep both my children in school every day . . . if their father works alone he can only make $4 a week, while if one of the boys works with him, they [i.e., the family] can earn $6 or $7." Whereas the Mexican parents preferred education for their children, their dire circumstances made schooling a marginal activity. The two conditions, basic survival needs structured by their poverty, and the actions of educators and employers, placed the right to education nearly out of the range of experience for several generations of Mexican migrant families.

The state funds allocated to local districts did not decrease as a result of Mexican nonattendance. The state allocated resources on the basis of school census, not school attendance. Thus, the exclusion of Mexican children increased the educational resources available to the Anglo community. In the school year 1944–45 "each Texas district received $29.00 per capita for all children between the ages of six and seventeen listed on its census enumeration."[28] Given that only half of the Mexican school-age population attended school at all, exclusion proved to be a windfall for the Anglo community. Pauline Kibbe cited this example to illustrate the point.[29]

> One central West Texas school district last year [1945] reported 2,000 children of school age in the district and collected the State apportionment on that basis, whereas the total seating capacity of school buildings in the district was only 1,350. The State of Texas is not morally justified in contributing to that district on the scholastic enumeration basis, when it is obvious that 650 children could not attend school if they so desired. It so happened that the Latin American children in the district numbered 650.

Migrant children thus not only shouldered a large share of the agricultural economy, but they also made important financial contributions to an educational system that excluded them and benefited only the dominant community.

Educational patterns for California migrant youths developed similar to those of Texas. In general, however, California did have a better record than Texas, but only in terms of quantity, not quality. Concerning the education of the Mexican migrant child, Texas and California had more in common than they had differences.

Segregation of Mexican migrant children in California generally consisted of two types—either in a Mexican school, or in a migratory school. Unlike other states of the Southwest, the California legislature created a special revolving fund for the establishment of schools for migratory children in 1927. The law did not mandate the creation of these schools, but county governments could establish them voluntarily upon the urging of the state Board of Education. In the great valleys of California and in the agricultural areas of southern California, numerous towns and villages contained thousands of Mexican field laborers. In general, wherever the Mexican population grew large enough, the state constructed a Mexican school.

In agricultural areas, the state-funded migrant schools were, in essence, Mexican schools. For example, concern for immigrant education and Americanization moved the Fresno County superintendent of schools to establish migratory schools with the aid of state funds in 1928. However, these schools (as most migratory and Mexican schools) did not interfere with the work patterns of the children. In fact, schools tended to complement the labor process. Children enrolled and left according to the crops and no one gave the irregular attendance a great deal of concern. Moreover, in the migratory school a special schedule ensured that children could join their parents and elders in the fields. One contemporary observer, favorable to migratory schools, wrote (1931):[30]

> In the migratory school, economics determine the length of the school day. When the first schools were established the hours were from seven-thirty to twelve-thirty which enabled Jose, Manuel, Carmelita and Maria to join their father and mother in the cotton field after the noon rest period. It takes the income of the whole family to insure food and clothing for the family of the itinerant laborer. True, the amount of cotton picked by each boy or girl after school hours is not large but the aggregate earned by three or four children means a considerable addition to the family income.

Since the five-hour day violated state educational regulation, such schedules as those in migratory schools needed the sanction of state officials, which they hardly ever denied. The 1924 Biennial Report of the superintendent for public instruction clearly indicated the compatibility of child labor and education.[31]

> When the agricultural work is very light and without hazards there should be an adjusted school day beginning not later than the field work. This provides for the whole family leaving the camp at the same time, the adults going to the field and the children to school. . . . It also means that the school day is over when the mid-day meal is ready. It provides also that children may work in the afternoon.

Thus, the five-hour school became the norm in the Mexican migratory schools, as well as in the segregated nonmigratory Mexican schools in citrus and nut-ranching areas, such as in southern California. Consequently, the condition of migratory education did not appear favorable to the child. For example, the Ventura County rural supervisor of education described the common routine for migrant children: "to work and attend school for a total of eleven or twelve hours per day."[32] Such an extended day violated California child labor laws, which limited work and study to eight hours per day. Yet no one felt compelled to terminate this practice, which was a particular feature of Mexican migrant education. Nevertheless, the rural supervisors of education in Ventura County appeared pleased with the outcome.

> The general results of this program of migratory schools have been: Increased ability on the part of the pupils in English reading and language; general Americanization work; higher standards of cleanliness established.[33]

On the eve of the depression nearly 37,000 children were migratory and "had no permanent place of residence."[34] The vast majority of these included Mexican children; however, many more permanently resident children also held migratory status for periods during the year according to seasonal labor. Many city dwellers followed the crops for varying lengths of time and thus received education in a number of different schooling environments. Residents of Los Angeles could move from an urban segregated, or "neighborhood" school, to a migratory segregated school and back during the year. One study found that in Los Angeles County schools 9 percent of the children were migratory.[35] In other cases, a child may move from a rural, or semirural Mexican school to a Mexican migrant school. In either case, whether the child was a city or rural resident, or an entirely migrant child, the educational program had severe limitations when compared to the education of the general population. One member of the National Child Labor Committee observed the Mexican migratory family movement in California of which children were "part and parcel."

> In the case of the families which go out from the cities to work on fruit and vegetable farms, the children often lose a month or more at both ends of the school year, because the migration takes place before school closes in the Spring and ends after it opens in the Fall. In the case of the entirely migratory families, the children are apt to have no schooling at all, or schooling of so poor a character and given under such adverse circumstances that it can not be effective, and the children are badly retarded.[36]

Thus, in the accounts of most observers, schooling for migrant children appeared not only inferior, but to a large extent it remained education in name only. At best, many children did enroll in a school for certain periods of time and did learn some rudiments. But generally they learned very little. However, by 1930, California was the only state in the Southwest that made an effort to extend schooling to migrant children. Nevertheless, severely ostracized and branded as outsiders, these children encountered a situation that relegated them to a segregated environment and subjected them to a chauvinistic Americanization curriculum that emphasized the elimination of Mexican culture.

In spite of the efforts at educating the migrant child; estimates indicate that only about half of migrant children actually enrolled in school.[37] Not uncommonly, public schools simply either discouraged or refused admission to migrant children. One writer reported that schools in Ventura County had signs that read No Migratory Children Wanted Here.[38] Those who could attend found themselves falling behind as the years went by, so that as a whole, Mexican migrants lagged well behind the nonmigrant Anglo child. In one study of 1,909 migratory children in Ventura County, nearly 88 percent of the children enrolled in grades that did not correspond to their ages. The average discrepancy was between 2 to 2½ years. The median age was ten, while the median grade was the low third.[39] Studies in Brawley, California, in the Imperial Valley, also demonstrated a serious lag between age and grade.[40] Undoubtedly, overage contributed to the high dropout rate recorded after the primary grades on the part of migrant children. In the El Monte Lexington School in southern California, 138 Mexican children enrolled in the first grade, and as the years progressed, a marked decline in enrollment occurred, so that by the seventh grade, 17 had enrolled, and by the eighth grade only 7 had done so.[41]

The high dropout rate occurred before the high school years, but, by then, the emphasis on vocational subjects was clearly established.[42] A combination of factors created the low level of participation by migrant children in California education. Irregular attendance, shortened schedules, high dropout rates, high nonenrollment figures, and poor physical resources, made the schooling of migrant agricultural child laborers in California seem without substance. In essence, these children belonged to an industrialized agricultural economy and satisfied cheap labor requirements—as in Texas where their education was not a right but a nearly impossible to attain privilege. The record in Colorado is of the same cloth.

The introduction of migrant family labor into Colorado followed the passing of protective sugar tariffs, especially the Dingley Tariff, which made domestic sugar beet production profitable. Once sugar beet farming entered into western agriculture, the sugar oligopolies, the Spreckels Sugar Company of California and the Great Western Sugar Company among them, contracted with existing farming enterprises for the production of beets, rather than electing to enter into direct owner-ship and production. The method employed by the companies allowed them to shift the costs and management of production upon the farmer. The companies set the acreage to be worked by the type of labor required and the price to be paid per pound of sugar beets. Once they introduced this method of production, it obligated the farmers to hire the necessary labor at the price commensurate with a profitable return on the use of the land. Under such conditions family labor became the principal laboring unit in the Colorado beet fields.

In northeastern Colorado, an area of concentration for sugar beet production, all thirteen sugar factories were "owned by one company, the Great Western Sugar Company."[43] Consequently, this type of situ-ation forced all beet growers to contract with Great Western, which established the general contours of the production and marketing of sugar beets in Colorado. The company also determined the type of labor that the growers could utilize, thus Great Western "required that ninety percent of each (labor) shipment should consist of family labor...."[44] and in 1921 no less than 10,000 Mexican workers, including men, women, and children, were shipped from the Mexican border and areas of the Southwest to the beet fields. In 1924, 1926, and 1927, 12,043, 14,538, and 10,576 workers, respectively, were shipped.

Recruiting such large numbers of workers required 55 labor agents, "extensive advertising, including thousands of booklets, billboards, hand-bills, calendars and newspaper advertisements."[45] Indeed, Mexican family labor attained a virtual monopoly of unskilled work in sugar beets. A nation-wide survey showed that in 1935, two thirds of all sugar-beet workers were Mexicans.[46]

Despite the desirability of migratory families, both Great Western and their growers found that costs of transport exceeded acceptable levels. Thus, during the 1920s the companies established Mexican *colonias,* or company towns, on the fringes of towns allowing workers to "stay over" during the winters. By 1928 the "movement to build up the resident supply of Mexicans" had achieved quite a bit of success. Resident family members "increased an average of 258 families per year" between 1921 and 1928; raising the number of families from 537 in 1921, to 2,084 in 1927[47] living in northeastern Colorado. Under the *colonia* arrangement, workers purchased company lots at minimal prices and companies then provided material for adobe construction. These supported themselves as casual laborers during the winter, but their principal means of support remained in sugar beets. However, whether labor was resident or migratory the patterns of labor employment, that is, the extensive use of Mexican family labor, continued as the policy of the Great Western Sugar Company.

Children proved much more vital and integral to beet production than cotton and vegetable farming. Sugar beet production was labor intensive, much more so than even cotton production, thus necessitating the greater need for the cheapest form of labor—the unpaid labor of children. In one case study of beet production, children made up 38 percent of the entire laboring force, and in another study they constituted 49 percent and provided half of the total laboring hours in both cases.[48] Beets were such a labor intensive endeavor that child labor became synonymous with it. One study compared labor requirements of beets to wheat and found that the former required from 117.3 to 123.9 labor hours per acre; wheat, on the other hand, required 10 labor hours per acre. However, in certain areas of Colorado's beet areas children performed approximately half of the beet labor hours, whereas children worked only about 3 hours per acre in wheat.[49] The labor requirements differed because beet work consisted of tasks performed almost entirely by hand. (Machinery in this instance did not lead to family labor, but rather, the combination of large monopolistic companies protected by tariffs engineered the development of beet production and the use of family labor.)[50]

In the beet areas of Colorado, agriculture included hay, melons, onions, beans, corn, and fruit. However, there existed a system of labor according to tenure and type of production. The four economic groups in the area included land owners, renters, wage workers, and contract workers. The landowners, renters, and wage workers generally consisted of native Anglo-Americans, or European immigrants, especially Russians and Germans. Generally, Mexicans comprised the contract workers, although in some areas Russians and Germans were also represented. The labor intensiveness of beet production manifested itself in monotonous, repetitive, and arduous manual labor. Since slow periods separated the several processes of beet-work—bunching and thinning, hoeing, and pulling and topping—the labor process consisted of both speedups and complete inactivity.

The education of the children in beet production was marked by its absence, due to the necessary amount of time devoted to work. Failure to enroll children in school usually followed the contours of the economic groups. In one area, school record information revealed that of 121 children not in school, 14 were owner, 15 renter, 2 wage, and 90 contract children. A larger study of 354 children found that 75 percent of contract children failed to attend school due to work. By and large, Mexican children worked much more than their non-Mexican counterparts in agriculture, and even when owners engaged in beet production, their children worked only half as much as contract children and generally avoided the arduous tasks and long hours. This was due to the fact that beet work was largely reserved for Mexicans. Contract "families worked on an average thirteen acres more than tenant families, and sixteen acres more than owner families."[51] In the Arkansas Valley of Colorado (1929) education received by the contract and owner children differed decidedly. At the time of the study, which was done during the work season, the "children of the contract labor families should have been in school on the average 61.5 days, and had been actually in attendance only 21.9 days. Their average loss was 64.4 percent."[52] On the other hand, the figures for the farm owner families showed that an opposite trend: these children should have been in school the same number of days (61.5), "actually attended an average of 50.3 days, making a loss of 11.1 days." Farm owner children thus missed only 18.1 percent of the time that school had been in session. In one study of 1,160 children, 280 were contract children and 69 percent were behind 1 year; most were behind 2 or more years. Of 759 owner children, 35 percent were behind, generally less than 2 years. The rate of retardation "was roughly twice as great among the contract labor children as among farm [owner] children."[53]

Farmers, sugar companies, and merchants felt little need to extend education to Mexican children and, in fact, saw education as a detriment to their financial interests. A South Platte Valley, Colorado, principal stated that schools "never try to enforce compulsory attendance laws on the Mexicans. . . . The banks and the company will swear that the labor is needed and that the families need the money."[54] One analyst explained the situation further.

> The general belief is that the beet industry is a valuable commercial asset which brings prosperity to the region as a whole. It is believed that a cheap labor supply is necessary for this industry and that the Spanish-American or Mexican is the one to furnish it. Too regular school attendance would not be compatible with this.[55]

Merchants and growers often established a debtor-laborer condition upon the Mexican family, which further obstructed observance of compulsory attendance laws. Taylor cited the following case to demonstrate a point:

> [A] Mexican laborer whose children were kept out of school to work beets received notice from local authorities that his children must return to school. The following Sunday the farmer who employed the Mexican and the merchant who sold him the provi-

sions came to the home of the superintendent of schools. The farmer said: "I have advanced one hundred dollars for Martinez' provisions and unless he has his children to help him complete the contract he won't have enough to pay me back." And the merchant added: "Yes, and I have given him $54 credit in addition which he won't be able to pay me."[56]

Taylor further found that this "case was not an isolated instance," and that it was customary to extend advances and credit to Mexican laborers, thus tying the laborer to growers and merchants via indebtedness.

Contract workers frequently encountered social ostracism in the communities within which they worked. Thus while they proved economically integral to the community, socially they remained segregated. The lived in shacks on the outskirts of towns provided by the growers or farmers during the season, and returned to their equally marginal *colonias* in the off season. In either case, they lived in extreme poverty, enduring meager diets, overcrowding, poor sanitation, negligible health care, and the hostility of the permanent residents. One report stated that

> . . . the Mexican . . . is not wanted by the local people. The root of the trouble lies much deeper than the Mexicans shortcomings; it is the fact that he is a Mexican. The expression "whites" and "Mexicans" are common terms as though there might be a racial difference. The situation was well put by one man who said "The Mexican is a necessary nuisance," meaning that he was necessary because of beets demanded him, a nuisance because he was a Mexican. . . . He is wanted because of his work and that only. The local people feel practically no responsibility towards him. . . . During the summer, signs were in the windows of restaurants, barber shops, etc. which interpreted meant the Mexicans were to stay out. . . .[57]

Consequently, the compulsory schooling laws were dead-letters as they were in Texas and California. School authorities expressed little sense of responsibility or concern toward the migrant family. In fact, they considered migrants a special problem that upset and disrupted the educational program. Often "no effort was made to get the migratory Spanish-American or Mexican into the school, or at least until the beet harvest season was over."[58] When schools admitted contract children, authorities generally placed them in a special room designated for such children, called simply, the opportunity room. Generally opportunity rooms functioned only during the off-season—thus, it was commonly accepted by authorities that contract children would not enroll, nor would schools expect them, during the working months. One writer described this unwritten, exclusionary practice as "extremely bad at the present time, and the laxity in regard to the enforcement of the school law, especially in regard to the Spanish-American and Mexican children, is striking. . . ."[59]

By the end of the depression, child labor had diminished in the beet fields due to the passage of the national sugar production law in 1933 and supplanted in 1937. The law contained provisions for the regulation of child labor effecting a decrease in the prevalence of child labor. In 1933, 13 percent of the nation's beet workers were under 16; a 1938 study of beet workers in Crystal City, Texas, showed that only 2 percent were under 14, although 15 percent were from 14 to 18 years of age.[60] Nevertheless, all accounts found that child labor in sugar beets decreased due to regulatory legislation but little changed the working and living conditions of those who had passed the age of 16 and continued working in the beet fields.

In addition, while child labor in the beet fields diminished, the New Deal legislation did not terminate it. One study of family beet labor published in 1939 showed conclusively, that beet production continued to rely on the labor of school age children. It cited data on "children 12 and under 14 years of age" that demonstrated that 50 percent of this group was employed, and that despite an 8-hour maximum workday, more than half of the working children under 16 years of age worked usually for longer than 8 hours a day in the beet fields, ". . . usually 12 or more hours a day."[61]

Another study of Mexican family beet workers in Michigan published in 1946 demonstrated similar findings. It found that of total of 1,397 Mexican children in four selected counties, only 184 enrolled in school on the first day of class. The study states, "It is evident that attendance laws are not enforced for Mexicans."[62] Bear in mind that the year was 1946, twelve years after the passage of federal legislation designed in part to eliminate child labor in beet production. One reason that Michigan school officials gave for not enforcing compulsory school laws for Mexican children maintained that the Mexicans were "really Texans and [were] in the state [only] during the winter months. . . ."[63]

At midcentury not a great deal had changed in relation to the education of the children of beet workers. It appears that the effect of New Deal legislation, especially the WPA (Work Progress Administration), created greater control of the regulation and recruitment of beet labor, their wages, ability to organize, and freedom of movement.[64] Thus, the sugar beet companies recovered the labor slack they encountered with the loss of child labor.

However, the pattern of discrimination and exclusion continued through the depression and into the forties. Thus, if education had any effect on socioeconomic backgrounds, we could expect the schools of Colorado during this period, to contribute to the reproduction of a supply of cheap, migrant family labor.[65]

Seasonal family migration resulted from the development and spread of large-scale agriculture in the Southwest. The principal source of this family labor was Mexico. Thus, Mexican migrant families became a characteristic of rural communities in the Southwest as well as in some states of the Midwest. Migrant families became an indispensable labor unit— as opposed to a single laborer—in cotton, fruit, beet, vegetable, and nut farming. Corporate farming enterprises stimulated the buying, selling, and transporting of families as labor from urban and rural residences to agricultural work sites. Thus, because the labor process involved the entire nuclear family, plus other relatives, the educational opportunities would necessarily be reduced to accommodate the social relations in production. In fact, universal compulsory education—either full- or part-time—presented a barrier to the efficient utilization of family labor. Consequently, education was either entirely eliminated, or it was reduced to a mere tangent in the lives of migrant families. This feature of the educational life of migrants gave their lives a "castelike" character—for in communities where basic class divisions separated Mexican from Anglo, the schooling process divided accordingly. The separation between those children to be educated and those children destined to participate in society mainly as labor, was largely a class question that also divided nationalities.

The migratory educational experience most clearly illustrates the correspondence between education and the economy. The relationship is more easily recognized because the educational institution consciously elaborated programs that were openly based upon the socioeconomic relations in agriculture. In the urban context educators referred to abstract theories that meshed schools and the economy. In the countryside educators designed their programs based upon the immediate economic demands of local farmers and agricultural corporations. These "practical" economic necessities and local demands formed the basis for the denial of educational opportunity for the Mexican migrant community. A wide array of forces were mobilized to insure that the migrant family continued as a migrant family. Every governmental institution that came into contact with the migrant family seemed to reinforce the migratoriness of the family.

Indeed, during the period under study, the schooling process became in essence an extension of the immigration process. As employers recruited and imported Mexican peasants to satisfy the demand for their labor, the educational process conveniently aligned itself so as not to interfere with this trade in human labor. As such, each school, whether by refusing to admit Mexican children or even when it did admit them, ensured that it would contribute to the reproduction of the Mexican child as cheap labor. By doing so, the educational institution assumed the function of an international border. Each year employers felt less pressure to seek new immigrants. They could trust that the school system would provide cheap labor locally.

CHAPTER 6

INTER-AMERICAN AND INTERCULTURAL EDUCATION

The problem of inequality in educational resources and achievement has long been a source of conflict between the Mexican community and the Anglo-dominated educational system. Analysts on all sides have generally interpreted the problem as stemming from either local, regional, or national contexts. No one has, however, offered an analysis incorporating two critical conditions affecting educational policy beginning in 1940. The first condition originated as an impact of the international context, a context defined by the struggle for world power by the United States; the second emerged as the increasingly apparent potential for independent political action held by minorities,[1] especially blacks and Mexicans. I argue that in the minds of domestic and foreign policy officials these two conditions interconnected and beginning in 1940, government officials formulated federal domestic policy affecting minorities in relation to wartime and, later, cold war objectives. This federal activity represented indeed a new political relationship destined to affect the political behavior of the Mexican people, and this relationship became clearly established in formal and informal educational policy affecting the Mexican community.

In the historical accounts of Rodolfo Acuna,[2] Thomas P. Carter,[3] Meyer Weinberg,[4] Charles Wollenberg,[5] and Carey McWilliams,[6] little or no discussion takes place concerning the international dimension as a critical factor in Chicano educational history. In addition, although historians have focused much attention on World War II as a historical watershed in the development of Mexican political consciousness and activity, little research has focused upon those programs applied by the federal government that affected the Mexican community during that same period. McWilliams's modest analysis of the State Department's Office of Inter-American Affairs in *North from Mexico,* probably makes the major statement on the role of the federal government in the educational and political experience of the Mexican community. Yet McWilliams downplays the significance of the international factor as well as the significance of the federal intervention into the Mexican community. Wollenberg includes some discussion of the effect of World War II upon social science thought and the practice of segregation, but does not emphasize sufficiently the international question, nor the role of the federal government in regional education.

San Miguel's recent work on educational reform in Texas devotes a chapter to the inter-American phase, but interprets it as an aspect of the Mexican-American struggle for educational equality. This study interprets inter-American education as shaped by the foreign policy interests of the United States, within which certain educational reforms became desirable, even necessary. This interpretation of the international factor places emphasis upon the role of the state in shaping the agenda of educational reformers in the Mexican community. The paucity of research upon this significant historical relationship, that is, between the federal government and the Mexican community at the World War II juncture, places it on the agenda as an important research topic.

I will now demonstrate that since the Second World War the international concerns of the United States, especially its policy interests in Latin America, have proven fundamental to the altering and shaping of formal and informal educational policies affecting the Mexican community. I will explicate the relationship between the inter-American and intercultural educational programs, which significantly affected the Mexican historical experience during and after World War II. I will also explain the need to politically socialize the Mexican people, and the causes of the international struggle for power waged first between the Allies and Axis powers, and later between the United States and Soviet blocs.

The Economics and Politics of U.S. Foreign Policy

This interrelation manifests itself clearly in an examination of economic and political relations between the United States and Latin America. Based on this immediate relationship, educators and other authorities formulated several long-range educational objectives for the Mexican people. The general purpose of that foreign policy included maintaining and developing economic ties between the United States and Latin America and preventing the establishment of political forces that would endanger those ties. Because that foreign policy targeted the Mexican community, an educational emphasis developed that would affect the political culture of the Mexican people. One of the methods proposed by the State Department to ensure such ties involved an innovative application of the culture concept, breaking the last strongholds of the biological determinists within the social sciences and leading consequently to an incorporation of cultural programs to promote "hemispheric solidarity." One of the principal forms of cultural activities included formal and informal educational reform in Latin America and in communities with significant Mexican populations in the Southwest.

The foreign policy under discussion spanned two related, yet distinct periods: the war against the Axis powers and the cold war with the USSR. The two have remained related because the fundamental economic and

political concerns of the United States continue, but with some variation. During World War II the economic concern became the maintenance and increase of the flow of raw materials to supply the war effort;
the political concern held that foreign governmental policies conform to
U.S. objectives and that Nazi sympathy among the people remain at the
lowest possible level. In the postwar period, the developmental theories
and programs that applied to the Third World encapsulated these general
policy objectives. However, a shift in emphasis reflected a heightened
concern with modernization of the Third World and the utilization of
foreign capital and technology to finance and construct that modernization. The practice of exchanging foreign capital for raw materials did
not represent anything new, and as J. Fred Rippy demonstrated in an
article on the "Historical Perspective" of foreign aid, much of the motives
of postwar development programs abroad was well established by the
1920s.[7] Rippy notes, for example, that the export of capital in the form of
loans for the purchase of U.S. manufactured goods and indirect investments by corporations in the twenties and thirties, held central importance in the formulation of foreign policy, and continued to do so within
developmental policy concerns in the forties and fifties. However, beginning in 1940, foreign policy incorporated a new dimension—an emphasis
upon the ideo-cultural outlook of the peoples of underdeveloped countries.

The key to the development of this ideo-cultural emphasis predated
the 1940 period. In many underdeveloped nations, and especially in Latin
America, anti-American feelings ran high and political parties formed
on the basis of stands against U.S. economic exploitation of national
resources and political intervention, including military occupation. Latin
America's first labor unions formed where U.S. enterprises began to
exploit natural resources, such as bananas, copper, oil, and rubber.
Strikes against these enterprises occurred with great frequency during
the twenties and thirties. Often out of such labor struggles came broader
national political parties, such as the Communist party of Colombia. In
general, Latin American workers not only held the Yankee in low esteem,

but Yankee capitalists became the target of militant labor action, and anti-American and radical or communist unions and parties began to grow and engage in national politics. This process continued unabated, except where national governments willingly intervened. The United States considered this a potentially risky situation if allowed to continue. Consequently, foreign relations mirrored the New Deal through the Good Neighbor Policy, which promised an end to militaristic intervention and a policy of international fair play. However, as the United States and Latin America forged stronger economic and political ties, especially during the war years, the cultural and ideological outlook of the populations of the Latin countries became increasingly critical factors for the maintenance of those ties.[8] In the 1940s a means of directing that political outlook away from anti-U.S. stands and action and towards "hemispheric solidarity" developed through a program of cultural understanding, and later in the postwar developmental phase of U.S. foreign policy, through educational reform aimed at modernizing the culture in Third World nations to conform to the economic and political objectives of the United States.[9]

U.S. FOREIGN POLICY AND THE OFFICE OF INTER-AMERICAN AFFAIRS

Events leading to the outbreak of the Second World War created the immediate need to stabilize the Latin American political atmosphere. Thus, in the late thirties the State Department reacted to Nazi propaganda programs with efforts of its own to attract Latin American peoples. It was "largely in response to Nazi and fascist efforts to win support in Latin America," writes Charles Frankel, "that a formal agency was created by the federal government specifically for the purpose of conducting educational and cultural relations."[10] The Division of Cultural Relations was formed within the State Department, and within the division, the Office of the Coordinator for Inter-American Affairs was created in 1940. President Roosevelt assigned the young and energetic Nelson A. Rockefeller to head the Office of Inter-American Affairs (as the Office of the Coordinator was later renamed). The "Rockefeller group" (as the OIAA was popularly known) had the responsibility of providing information "through press, radio, and motion pictures, but gave a strong push as well to . . . cultural activities. . . ."[11] Rockefeller summarized his official responsibility, and that of the OIAA.

> The republics of the Western Hemisphere have tapped their forests, mines, jungles, and soil to pour an ever-increasing stream of raw materials into the arsenals of democracy in the United States and other allied nations. In this process, with its numerous ramifications, the people of all Americas are learning more and more about each other and the significance of their interdependence.[12]

Carey McWilliams wrote that the OIAA did not initially include the Southwest in its programs and that it did so only at the behest of numerous individuals (including McWilliams) hoping to utilize the OIAA as a leverage to improve the situation of Mexicans in the Southwest.[13] Nevertheless, after the U.S. policy toward Latin America incorporated the Southwest, the issue of "who initiated what," became moot. The main point is that the State Department independently shaped a foreign policy design that included a large population of people within U.S. borders. It consequently launched an educational program to improve U.S.-Latin American relations that dealt with the Mexican population within its borders. The activities of the office encompassed several major forms. For example, it promoted a set of common political and economic policies and objectives within the educational systems of the Western hemispheric nations.[14] The OIAA also pushed for educational reform in Latin America aimed at dissolving socio-political conflict, intended to eliminate political radicalism and to promote hemispheric unity. An economic exchange conditioned each of these activities: the export of raw materials to the United States and the import of technology and capital from the United States. Thus, a program labeled "inter-American" education came into being in 1940 and dovetailed with intercultural education, an emerging and quite related program aimed at dissolving minority militancy in the United States.

Just as inter-American education concerned developing friendly relations among the peoples of the Americas, the intercultural education promoted by the U.S. Office of Education during the 1940s concerned constructing peaceful relations between minorities and nonminorities in the United States. That concern emanated from the possibility that Axis enemies (and later Soviet agents) would exploit racial conflict and weaken national unity. In a period when the United States promoted "goodwill" in underdeveloped, raw materials-producing nations, minorities in the United States, many of them either descendants from, or natives of, nations where goodwill ties were to be established, encountered the severest forms of discrimination and oppression. Moreover, in many of these nations strong anticolonial and nationalist movements had begun to develop. Thus, as the colonized nations and underdeveloped nations began to stir, representatives of those nations in the United States became a serious concern for foreign policy planners. During the war apprehension arose over the potential success of Axis powers in generating favorable responses around the world among discontented colonial and minority peoples; after the war, that concern shifted to the possibility that nationalist stirrings might move newly emerging as well as independent underdeveloped nations toward socialist models for development. American officials evaluated social relations within the United States in light of these concerns. Adolf A. Berle, Jr. voiced serious misgivings about racial discrimination and its effects on foreign policy.

> To say that race discrimination damages the Good Neighbor Policy is a masterpiece of understatement. . . . It is no exaggeration, I think, to say that the habit of race discrimination practiced in considerable parts of the United States is the greatest single danger to the foreign relations of the United States, and conceivably may become a real threat to American security.[15]

Berle was one of many social scientists, educators, and government officials addressing the need to control minority discontent through social reform. Robin M. Williams, Jr., writing for the Committee on Techniques for Reducing Group Hostility of the Social Science Research Council, underscored a related need for the elimination of racial conflict in order to further foreign policy objectives.

> . . . the role of the United States in the international scene may be profoundly affected by developments in the relations of domestic groups. American statesmen who deal with world problems have to contend with world wide press coverage of intergroup relations in the U.S.[16]

Paul S. Taylor, an economist with much research experience on Mexican labor in the United States, also addressed the political relationship between white and nonwhite peoples in the United States and of their bond with the international relations between white and nonwhite nations and peoples.

> Whether we like it or not, we face a new world. In the past it was not very important to us that we European-stock white were outnumbered in the world by about 2 to 1. That fact will be very important to our children, to their places in the world, and to their peace. . . .

> History has placed representatives of some of these people in our midst as small minorities. . . . By the way in which we get along with these few people we have it in our hands to help to make or mar our own children's future. For those intercultural problems . . . which remain unsolved . . . can inflame men to the path of war.[17]

A basic concern of inter-American education, as one writer put it, dealt with the "imminence of social explosion" and thus the control of volatile social forces became a paramount objective.[18] In a 1945 address to a conference on "Approaches to National Unity," Talcott Parsons argued that racial "interest seems in many ways to operate like gasoline" but that if such interest can be "controlled and canalized in a well integrated institutional structure" it can become a positive social force.[19] However, in a "disorganized situation . . . it can be an explosive and destructive force." Parsons, like most social scientists of the period, engaged in research to solve the "Race Problem," suggested the creation of "mechanisms which tend to keep down aggressive impulses and steer them into harmless channels . . . perhaps the most important [mechanisms] are the value patterns and accompanying sentiments which forbid hostility to other groups."[20]

THE OFFICE OF INTER-AMERICAN AFFAIRS IN THE SOUTHWEST

The concerns of officials and educators responsible for shaping inter-American and intercultural education centered on the political control of minorities.[21] Prior to 1940, little federal intervention into the social processes of the Mexican community occurred, with the exception of immigration and land legislation. However, the Mexican community served notice in the late twenties and thirties that they were prepared and willing to organize themselves for bitter labor union battles as well as civil rights issues. The intensity and prevalence of militant labor union activity, and the willingness to work with radicals and Communists to carry out long strikes in the face of severe repression at once dispelled the notion of the docility of the Mexican people. As McWilliams pointed out years ago, the most militant union activities during the depression came from the organizations of Mexican agricultural labor. Indeed, Mexican labor militancy caught the government by surprise, for until then, the official response consisted of either repression or deportation. Given the permanent character of the Mexican community in the Southwest, a need for a new approach anticipating all possible forms of political action became readily apparent. Consequently, the decentralized laissez-faire approach no longer held sway in the early forties and a policy of active intervention into the political life of the Mexican people *on a permanent basis* became a characteristic of contemporary relations between minorities and the state. Expectations held that intervention into Mexican political activity succeeded through a formal and informal educational reform program that reduced social and class conflict, increased political solidarity, and corresponded with regional economic demands for particular skill training. The OIAA, therefore, actively engaged in the promotion of particular educational programs in the Southwest to reduce the potential for independent political activity by the Mexican people, and consequently campaigned against some forms of racial oppression and discrimination, particularly school segregation.

A representative of the office succinctly summarized the two main lines of approach taken by the OIAA:

> 1.Stimulating and coordinating public and private rehabilitation programs aimed at preparing our Spanish speaking people to participate more effectively in American life and economy.
>
> 2.Educating English speaking citizens to discontinue discriminatory practices that are injurious to the war effort and to our relations with the other American Republics.[22]

Harold E. Davis, the director of education and teacher aids of the OIAA, outlined the objectives of its southwestern activities in an article in *World Affairs*. First on the agenda, these activities sought to insure that organizations such as the Alianza Hispano-Americana, LULACS, and the League of Loyal Latin Americans do not become problems "where they have been particularly active."[23] The political objective included "that of making such organizations a valuable and useful part of the cultural pattern and preventing them from becoming disruptive or divisive factors."[24] Second, in order that the Spanish-speaking communities assimilate "into the pattern of living and the social structure of the United States, important social psychological, as well as economic adjustments" needed to occur.[25] First, among these adjustments, the Anglo majority had to accept certain features of Hispanic culture, possibly including some forms of bilingual programs. Additional adjustments consisted of developing a program to "overcome the misconceptions on the part of some United States residents about the peoples of the other Americas"[26] and a program to change "several attitudes on the part of Spanish-speaking groups."[27] Davis pointed out that Hispanic residents needed a cultural adaptation to living in the United States.

> Their feelings of hostility, growing out of the Mexican War, the Mexican Revolution and attendant border disorders need to be replaced with more receptive and cooperative attitudes. In the past these factors have led the Spanish-speaking groups to retire within themselves—psychologically and culturally. Such cultural resistance can be overcome partly through the schools, but it is also the major problem of adult and community education.[28]

Davis recommended that schools prepare pupils more efficiently for the kinds of economic activities Mexicans engaged in. Education should "play an important role in long-range occupational planning."[29] Consequently, attention "should be given to occupational adjustment in the elementary schools in most Spanish-speaking communities as long as the school life of the majority of the pupils is limited to the elementary grades." Davis advised that the "development of agricultural skills through school programs is one of the chief ways to raise the living standards of the population," but he also advocated the training of a surplus Mexican labor supply for opportunities in "technological fields."[30]

Because both inter-American and intercultural education resembled each other in objectives, they often appeared combined and undistinguishable in practice. Applied activities spanned formal and informal educational projects and included the Texas Good Neighbor Commission, numerous educational conferences, scholarly research studies, community goodwill events, intercultural education projects in schools and communities, publications, news releases, movies, and a concerted effort by social scientists to develop methods to reduce tension and conflict and increase political solidarity.

The scope of the OIAA activities also went beyond those agencies commonly responsible for social service, and included private organizations such as the Texas Junior Chamber of Commerce. However, the OIAA focused upon social services and therefore funded such projects and organizations as the Chicago Immigrants Protective League, the Hogg Foundation, the New Mexico Barelas Community Center, and special training programs at the University of Texas and the University of New Mexico. An example of OIAA funding was the grant-in-aid, which the office awarded to the Chicago Area projects "to enable them to establish two community houses in regions of heavy Mexican population." The houses conducted "such activities as adult education, Americanization course, and teaching leisure time activities to adolescents."[31] The evidence clearly indicates that the objectives of inter-American and intercultural education did not encompass social change, that is, alterations in the distinctive socioeconomic relations between Anglos and Mexicans. Instead, the objectives emphasized social control and the channeling of the political consciousness and actions of the Mexican people and thereby reinforced existing social relations in the Southwest. As such, inter-American and intercultural education did not fundamentally break with the educational objectives of the previous period (1900–1940). However, it did incorporate new methods to achieve political integration and reproduction of labor power; certain added objectives, such as "hemispheric solidarity" gave a new dimension to education in the Mexican community.

The OIAA stressed formal and informal education as the principal methods to achieve its overall goals of hemispheric solidarity. As mentioned earlier, the Mexican population in the United States was defined as part of the Latin American aspect to the question of regional unity, especially U.S.-Mexico relations. Consequently, in its vision of a new international and intercultural relationship based on harmony and cooperation, education would play a key role. In the Southwest, the objectives seemed simple. ". . . Our purpose must be to assimilate them into the pattern of living and social structure of the United

States to reduce conflict and tension, and to eliminate a militant political consciousness."[32] As a means for these objectives, the OIAA organized, sponsored, and funded commissions, conferences, research projects, and teacher-training workshops on the question of formal education in the Mexican communities.[33] As described by one observer, these activities consisted of a "mounting wave of Inter-cultural Workshops."[34] Helen Heffernan, chief of the Division of Elementary Education for the State of California and an active participant in the inter-American unity campaign wrote:

> Under the far-sighted leadership of Mr. Nelson Rockefeller, the place of the school in building inter-American understanding and enduring friendship was immediately recognized. Many projects of an educational nature were established under his direction to help the teachers of the United States to come quickly into possession of necessary content through which . . . inter-American relations may be developed in the children, youth, and adults of their largest North American neighbor.[35]

In addition, she stated, "The treatment accorded to children of Latin American background . . . will have great influence on the confidence on the citizens of other American republics. . . ."[36] An examination of a few of the major areas of action reveals the nature of this stepped-up tempo of state intervention into the educational and political life of the Mexican community.

THE TEXAS GOOD NEIGHBOR COMMISSION

In order to discuss the OIAA, we must examine the Texas Good Neighbor Commission, one of the key projects underwritten and funded by the OIAA. Although a number of studies have focused on the commission, none (with the exception of Pauline Kibbe's work, *Latin Americans in Texas*) have placed it into its proper context, that is, none have adequately defined it within a larger program of Inter-American education emanating from Washington. Thus, the commission, a prime

example of an informal educational program, deserves a broader inter-
pretive perspective than it has received. Although the state of Texas
established the agency in 1943 "to deal solely with the problem of
discrimination and its effects on relations between the United States
and Mexico,"[37] the OIAA directly and indirectly involved itself in the
creation of the commission. Consequently, the commission consciously
followed the policy guidelines elaborated by the OIAA. Moreover, the
office provided grant moneys to fund the establishment and operation
of the commission's first three years. The office also exerted administrative leadership. The former director of the Texas branch of the OIAA
headed the commission from 1948 until its termination in 1951. The
commission members knew very well that the local task had international implications, as evidenced by Kibbe's 1947 work, which she based
on her efforts as the commission's first executive secretary. Her discussion on the problems of Mexicans in Texas is preceded by six chapters on
the international situation, focusing upon the importance of maintaining
and developing existing economic and political relations between the
United States and Latin America. In explaining the need for the commission, she followed precisely the policy design outlined by Nelson Rockefeller in his 1938 memorandum to President Roosevelt urging the establishment of a special office to improve U.S.-Latin American relations.[38]

According to Thomas Sutherland, who served as executive secretary in
1947, the idea behind the commission did not originate entirely with the
threat of Mexico blacklisting Texas from access to bracero labor, as some
authors have claimed, but it began, to a larger extent, with the general
need for the United States to strengthen relations with Latin America and
to control the issue of Mexican civil rights in Texas. Heavily attacked in
the Mexican press, the problem of the discrimination against Mexicans
in Texas received a great deal of publicity, and, as a consequence, the
Mexican government threatened to hold back much needed bracero labor
if conditions did not improve. However, the Mexican blacklist did not
result entirely from the Mexican government decision to force improvements in civil rights. The evidence indicates that a vocal and critical

independent press made it imperative that some official action be taken. The Mexican government, however, actually voiced little criticism of Texas' civil rights and probably would not have engaged in blacklisting at all had the press not widely disseminated reports of discrimination.[39] Finally, the blacklist had no effect on the numbers of Mexican workers in Texas; the border patrol simply did not enforce any entrance requirements, allowing an open entry of "illegal" labor.

Nevertheless, the commission took shape as a fact-finding body without powers to recommend legislation, intervene in disputes, mediate conflicts, or file legal proceedings. In essence, the commission's charge was so vague that members initially wrangled for several months over what it was expected to accomplish and what it could do. During its several years of existence from 1943 to 1951, it had done little to end discrimination against the Mexican people. Kibbe encountered such criticism by her strong sympathetic stand to the Mexican side on substantial issues, that she resigned in 1946. Even though the commission proved in many respects to be a token effort at improving the image of Mexican-Anglo relations, it functioned as an important political device that took the wind out of the sails of a vocal element in the Mexican press and thereby in Mexico as well. Setting the stage for political action relating to Anglo-Mexican relations in Texas, stands out as a most significant accomplishment of the commissions' program and activities. The commission saw itself, and was perceived by the state government, as the political leadership of civil rights in Texas. Its primary responsibility, as such, consisted of effecting a sense that something was being done to alleviate conditions that raised the ire of the Mexican people in Texas and the activists in the Mexican press.[40]

Since the commission never wielded any power, and only carried with it the responsibility to "promote goodwill and understanding," it never contributed any significant changes to the pattern of discrimination affecting Mexicans. Indeed, the commission attempted to establish Good Neighbor councils in local communities and the first of these councils aimed "to promote the principles of Christ in human relations throughout the state of Texas."[41] The remaining seven were not as vague, as evidenced by the eighth, which sought to "eliminate prefixes and hyphens, in order that we may become Americans in the truest and broadest sense."[42] Essentially, the commission steered clear of fixing blame, pointing to the need for voluntary action, and for slow, gradual, peaceful solutions to the Anglo-Mexican problem in Texas and shunning the use of "punitive measures or the application of civil or criminal sanctions."[43] Thus, the role of the commission was educational—as if to say, that the more each side, Anglos and Mexicans, learned about each other, the less friction, discrimination, tension, and discontent, would exist.

The commission published pamphlets urging the voluntary integration of schools, and the incorporation of courses in Latin American culture in school curricula, while underscoring the need for special efforts (without designating them) to relieve poverty and its social effects among Mexicans. By 1948 the commission's work "seemed to lie in the process of exhortation for better behavior and attitudes between Anglos and Latinos."[44] However, it exhorted a particular type of behavior— that being, peaceful, nonantagonistic relations—without proposing and, much less, carrying out, alterations in the existing economic, political, or social relations between Anglos and Mexicans. In spite of the tokenist measures, the Mexican government acquiesced to the commission's work and cooperated with it. In 1947 the Mexican secretary of the interior in a letter to Texas Governor Beauford H. Jester, expressed satisfaction at the commission's "efforts" at handling discrimination cases and urged that it continue its educational campaign to end segregation in schools.[45]

Then-executive secretary, Thomas Sutherland, confidently (and rather unbelievably) stated in 1948 that there existed little "justification for anti-Texas feeling in Mexico. . . ."[46] However, as Kibbe convincingly demonstrated in her 1947 work, discrimination in Texas remained as strong as it had ever been—contrary to the impression the commission attempted to convey. The commission undertook an informal educational campaign to solve long-standing discriminatory practices against the Mexican population. However, it proved most successful in the effect it had upon controlling the issue of civil rights and of taking the wind out of sails of critics, especially the Mexican press, and polishing the tarnished image of the Yankee in the Mexican mind.

Everett Ross Clinchy, Jr., summarized the work of the commission well.

> In a certain sense, then, the Good Neighbor Commission has had to be a "front." Officials have frankly admitted that it was hastily created to point out to Mexico that Texas was indeed a "good-neighbor." The state government had to thread its way between the demands of Mexico on the one hand and the tenacious interests of local groups on the other. The result has been that the commission has had to do its work in the less controversial area of "education for better understanding." Thus, it could show Mexico that it was anxious to solve the problems of Latin Americans and it could at the same time not get involved in the "forbidden" areas of Texas politics, namely, . . . state interference in social and economic affairs.[47]

CONFERENCES, WORKSHOPS, AND RESEARCH

While the commission served as a kind of "centerpiece" of OIAA activity, several broad forms of action took place that demonstrated extensive application and proved more effective and significant than the commission. One of these included the sponsorship of regional and local educational conferences for the purposes of altering the educational programs as they affected the Mexican community.

A state of California school administrator active in the OIAA campaign, lamented the fact that current educational research on the Mexican child "has little to contribute," as he called out for new "research on the problem" so as "to revamp curriculum and teacher training programs."[48] Many had expressed this same message, including a leader in the field of education in the Mexican community, Dr. George I. Sanchez. A longtime critic of discrimination in education, Dr. Sanchez had written about the fallacy of racial intelligence (as well as weaknesses of IQ testing), the evils of segregation, and the need for a special curriculum adapted to the needs and culture of the Mexican child. Dr. Sanchez gained a reputation as a reformer, author, administrator, and professor, and eventually held the position of educational consultant to the Office of Inter-American Affairs. When supporters first proposed the campaign for inter-American education, he did not hesitate to take part in it and actively promote it. Out of this movement, the First Regional Conference on the Education of Spanish-Speaking People in the Southwest emerged and convened at the University of Texas, Austin, in 1946. Called by the Texas General Education Board and the University of Texas, and funded by the OIAA, the conference brought together twenty-nine educators and administrators from the Southwest (and representatives of the Office of Inter-American Affairs). In the foreword to the *Report* on the Conference, Dr. Sanchez described the objectives precisely in those terms advocated by the Office of Inter-American Affairs: that is, the education of the Spanish-speaking people represented a "keystone in the structure of cultural relations between the United States and the other American Republics."[49]

The conference soundly criticized segregation as a method of acculturation and focused on long-standing problems such as bilingualism, vocational guidance and training, relevant textbooks, and curriculum. In spite of its conciliatory tone and reformist approach toward the Spanish-speaking, there remained old chauvinistic traditions in the inter-American phase as evidenced by a recommendation by the panel on "Remedial Measures" that Mexican children learn middle-class Anglo culture. It held that it was impossible for Mexican "children to learn the ways of American living when they are not in contact with people who live in that manner. This applies particularly to language and the more subtle forms of intercourse."[50] The report consequently recommended the ending of segregation. That the conference would adopt such recommendations seemed inevitable given the policy thrust of the period and the embracing of that policy by the participants. As expected, the emphasis upon reshaping Mexican culture to fit American standards continued, not just because only four of the participants possessed Spanish surnames, but because, as Davis had pointed out, the country needed assimilation to achieve national and international political unity. Moreover, assimilation could not effectively proceed in a segregated environment, and as one participant observed, segregation "does more to make Communists than all the direct methods of indoctrination the Soviet government can employ."[51]

The OIAA also sponsored research projects that delved into the education of Mexican children. One of the more lasting and significant studies was carried out under the auspices of the Texas Committee on Inter-American Relations and titled, "Spanish-Speaking Children in Texas." The research, directed by Wilson Little, defined the First Conference on the Education of the Spanish-Speaking as an educational program to meet regional, national, and international concerns. Little's study nevertheless provided much valuable statistical and demographic information of the nature of the education of Mexican children and concluded, like almost every other writer concerned with inter-American education, that segregation was counterproductive, that curricula should recognize the cultural traits of Mexican children, and that instructors should undergo the necessary training to insure better skills among teachers of Mexican children.

The Office of Inter-American Affairs also supported numerous local and subregional projects. In 1943, for example, 67 "colleges and universities . . . held special Inter-American institutes to assist students, faculties, and college communities in increasing their background knowledge of the other Americas."[52] In that year the office sponsored 500 lectures and discussions on Inter-American subjects. In 1944 some 80 colleges and universities participated in lecture and institute programs, and teacher workshops were scheduled at 27 normal schools and teacher-training colleges.[53] The office also sponsored student-teacher exchange programs in the Americas, as well as fellowships for advanced Spanish-speaking students of the Southwest who were identified as future political leaders in their respective communities.[54]

In July 1943 and in October 1944, the National Catholic Welfare Conference held its second meeting in San Antonio (the first in Denver) attended by a selected group of 43 leaders from Colorado, New Mexico, Arizona, California, Texas, Wyoming, and Utah, which concluded with a report outlining the recommended role of the Catholic Church among the Spanish-speaking. The first resolution decided upon at the second meeting reflected the interests of the participants. "We recommend that regional seminars of the Southwest be held annually to plan a program for the betterment of Inter-American relations."[55] In general, the meetings (funded by the OIAA) recommended a kind of "New Deal" for the Mexican community. Some of the suggestions included: better working conditions for the Spanish-speaking; enforced child labor laws; priests and laity encouragement for labor organization among farm workers; and church support for protective legislation, such as social security benefits for farm workers.

Throughout southern California, inter-American projects and conferences predominated on the educational landscape. The Los Angeles, Santa Barbara, San Diego, and San Bernardino Boards of Education engaged their own versions of a Good Neighbor Policy.[56] The OIAA managed to disseminate its message widely and to incorporate many distinctive and separate activities into its campaign. The example of the Los Angeles County Office of the Superintendent of Schools provides a case in point. In March 1942 the county sponsored an address by the field representative of the Western Division of the OIAA, to its teachers and administrators entitled, "Developing Understanding Through Inter-American Education." In its official publication, Los Angeles County noted that it was "making every effort to help boys and girls better understand and appreciate the cultures and problems of the Latin American people."[57] As part of that effort, the county held workshops, inter-American courses, addresses, and a Mexican demonstration school for developing methods of instructing Mexican students. The OIAA awarded a grant funding the "secretarial help and one-half the salaries of teachers." According to the district's official publication, the *Monthly Bulletin:*

> The major purpose of the school is to serve as a laboratory in the learning of English by Spanish-speaking children. Such a school will provide an intimate opportunity to observe and record day by day the children's reactions to various situations. . . . These observations and tryouts of material will serve as a direct stimulus to those who are preparing the manual for teachers.[58]

As early as 1942 (ironically the year before the anti-Mexican riots by armed forces personnel swept the area), Los Angeles County, following the cues by the OIAA, had developed a comprehensive and critical reappraisal of the educational program for the Spanish-speaking and arrived at specific recommendations for reform encompassing four areas: teacher training, curriculum, school adjustments to the culture of the home, and effective counseling. The Los Angeles County program attacked segregation, prejudice, and discrimination in general, as was to be expected of an inter-American effort. But while it did so, it proposed reforms that would not appreciably improve the schools' record in the Mexican community. For example, schools continued to define true bilingualism as a barrier to effective acculturation and, therefore, recommended the teaching of English, although via a more open environment that did not penalize the use of Spanish while the child transferred to English. Officials declared the home-culture deficient and therefore advised the school to take necessary precautions to change it without offending the sensibilities of parents.[59] The advice by the superintendent's office regarding counseling seemed the most significant as it related to the future lives of the students and as the essence of the educational program in Mexican communities. The superintendent and his top aide wrote:

> ... counseling must be realistic. He will face difficult adjustments. After all, it doesn't seem wise to ignore the fact that only his lighter-skinned classmates were hired by the stores during the Christmas vacation. Nor can we ignore the fact that his father was one of the first to be let out of the plant as times grew slack. In some way we must help him face these realities, help him prepare himself. . . .[60]

Again, the advice, as in the twenties and thirties, insisted that education for the Mexican child should concentrate on the vocational side of the schooling program. This kind of one-sided education preceded the inter-American campaign and was incorporated with modifications into the Inter-American program.

Los Angeles County put its program into practice through teacher-training workshops. In large assemblies, participants underscored the basic issues of hemispheric solidarity, the need for understanding Mexican culture, and the "social and economic barriers raised against Mexican youth in this country"[61] and discussed them later in study sessions. At one workshop, held at Lincoln High School in 1943, the organizers invited Mexican youths, community leaders, and workers to present and discuss their views on prejudice and discrimination. According to the principal of Lincoln High, one community speaker "challenged our prejudices, our preconceived ideas, and urged us to build an American symphony in which the Mexican theme will be significant and respected."[62] The thrust of that workshop reflected the general objectives of war and postwar domestic policy toward minorities in attempting to create peaceful relations between races and nationalities. Leadership in the resolution to fundamental economic and social problems rested, for the time being, in the hands of the federal government in Washington.

The Office of Inter-American Affairs directly sponsored a similar teacher training workshop held in El Paso in 1945. The El Paso project undertaken by the El Paso school system focused exclusively on the problem of teaching bilingual children. Since educators and others considered bilingualism the barrier to educational achievement, the effective learning of English would significantly reduce failure, thereby furthering "the educational progress of the non-English speaking child."[63] The workshop produced a number of material that later appeared in publication under four separate titles: *Workshop of Developing Teaching Aids for Non-English-Speaking Children, A Manual of Aids and Devices for Teaching Beginning Non-English Speaking Children, Manual of Supplementary Aids for Teachers of Bilingual Children;* and *A Guide for Remedial Work in English Pronunciation.* The publications were utilized throughout the El Paso public schools and eventually were distributed to many cities in Texas. Indeed, in the opinion of the assistant superintendent of the El Paso schools, the publications made a "distinct contribution to education in the Southwest" and represented "the concerted thinking and planning of a group of teachers who set about to solve some problems confronting the entire school system."[64] While the teachers may have been concerned with a more productive method of English instruction, the OIAA found interest in a more effective method of eliminating minority consciousness, and their bilingual policy leaned toward this end.[65]

Smaller conferences convened at a number of colleges and universities and followed similar themes. In 1942 the Claremont Colleges in California, sponsored a conference on Hemispheric Solidarity, held in conjunction with local community efforts to improve relations between the Mexican and Anglo communities. As a consequence of this joint effort, both communities reached a decision to end segregation of Mexican children in the San Dimas, California, grade-schools, and they launched adult and youth recreational and intercultural programs as well as programs aimed at "increasing knowledge . . . of the Latin American countries."[66] In addition, members of these communities organized a preschool program for non-English-speaking children with funds made available from the Office of Inter-American Affairs.[67] The long-term effects of these types of programs remain unknown; however, it is most significant that the OIAA extended its influence widely, reaching such small communities as San Dimas, California, with a population of twenty-seven hundred. The most obvious aspect of the San Dimas program, was that it, like the Texas Good Neighbor Program, operated based upon the belief that an educational program could generate goodwill alone, whether it be adult, youth, or community oriented.

Such expectations appear remote, given the deeply rooted economic and social problems that had largely shaped the historical experience of the Mexican community in the Southwest. Thus, while programs in inter-American relations and solidarity took shape, hundreds of thousands of bracero contract laborers, along with a similar number of undocumented workers, met the labor needs in the southwestern economy. The historical force that had the most to do with shaping Anglo-Mexican relations in the United States flowed onward without obstacle to its course, while the OIAA charted a control of those relations based on education. The office however had not charted a reform of that economic force shaping the Mexican experience, and it seems more likely that the office intended, among other things, to eliminate potential obstacles to the maintenance of Mexican labor in the southwestern marketplace. This is evident from the emphasis on vocational education proposed by the office, which coincided with the nature of the economic function of the Mexican community in the regional economy. In addition to those just mentioned, numerous publications also appeared directed at educators and the promotion of Inter-American objectives. The most noteworthy featured the Seventeenth Yearbook of the California Elementary School Principals' Association, a compilation of twenty-six articles, including those written by the anthropologist Ruth Tuck, University of California Vice President Monroe E. Deutsch, and the Claremont College historian W. Henry Cooke.[68] With "Education for Cultural Unity" as its theme, the 1945 publication discussed the general objectives in inter-American education and also provided views on specific topics, such as "Techniques for Developing Intergroup Understanding, Cooperation, and Goodwill." It urged teachers and administrators to initiate a new type of educational program based on intercultural objectives and structured upon new instructional methods, such as adjusting to the reality of Mexican "folk culture," as defined by Ruth Tuck. In addition, scholarly publications such as the *Journal of Education, Hispania, School and Society, The Educational Forum,* and *The International Quarterly,* regularly published articles on inter-American subjects and stressed the value of education for hemispheric unity. The U.S. Office of Education also engaged in the effort and sponsored publication of materials suitable for incorporation into elementary, secondary, and higher education in its Education and National Defense Series publications.[69]

THE OIAA AND THE CRITICISM OF SEGREGATION VIA THE CULTURE CONCEPT

Most significantly, the inter-American solidarity campaign and its emphasis on cultural harmony, generated a climate of opinion against the segregation of Mexican children. That consequence undoubtedly affected the courts in their anti-segregation decisions of the 1940s.[70] However, as Wollenberg has pointed out, the objectives behind the anti-segregation drive bore a striking resemblance to the objectives of segregationists. In fact, proponents of cultural harmony viewed integration as a method of eliminating the significant and dynamic elements of Mexican culture. The director of the Division of Elementary Education for the California schools on temporary leave as field representative to the OIAA wrote:

> Assimilation is a long-time process but it will be even slower if hindrances such as segregation for educational purposes persist. . . .
>
> . . . . in many instances . . . the school must strive to improve the health, manners, and behavior of the minority group itself in order to remove the only legitimate justification . . . for policies of segregation.[71]

The inter-American effort certainly demonstrated a host of positive aspects: for example, in Colorado numerous community organizations dedicated primarily to "bread and butter issues" formed as a result of OIAA support;[72] throughout the Southwest, a campaign critical of segregation and discrimination had some effect, at least it affected the thinking of the courts; the OIAA also allowed for numerous reformers to utilize the organization to create better social conditions for the Mexican people, one of these was Sanchez; lastly, the OIAA promoted a new social science outlook critical of the biological determinist position and worked to supplant it with the culture concept. The culture concept molded and promulgated by liberal forces in politics and the social sciences, supplanted the biological justification for socioeconomic inequality, and provided the methodological foundation for shaping educational objectives in relationship to the Mexican community. Much of the basis for its rapid integration into the educational process, and for its continuation as guiding principles behind the education of Mexican children can be traced to the early efforts of the Office of Inter-American Affairs.

The postwar program for Third World economic development proposed by the United States, represented one other aspect to federal intervention into the educational process in the Mexican community, and it related to the culture concept, which merits discussion. This program for economic development coincided with two critical factors: a planned postwar expansion of the U.S. economy combined with the need to modernize Third World economic infrastructure to correspond to expected increases in exports of necessary raw materials; second, contention from the Soviet model for economic development, which seemed a doubly dangerous factor since in the minds of many leaders and peoples in the Third World, socialism and independence from the United States constituted twin objectives on the immediate Soviet political agenda. The United States moved swiftly to forestall the latter possibility through a program based largely on the culture concept formulated by leading social scientists. Essentially, the culture concept within U.S. foreign policy proposed that cultural variables formed the basis of both developed and underdeveloped societies and that a process of cultural reform (linked to economic reforms) could eliminate underdevelopment. According to theorists of underdevelopment, such as Parsons, Seymour Martin Lipset, Hoselitz, and McClelland, the Latin American value system was at variance with the modernization process that the industrialized nations experienced. Lipset argued that Max Weber's value theory accounted for the resistance of traditional elites to modernizations.

> The general Weberian approach has been applied to many of the contemporary underdeveloped countries. It has been argued that these countries not only lack the economic prerequisites for growth, but many of them perceive values which foster behavior antithetical to the systematic accumulation of capital. The relative failure of Latin American countries to develop on a scale comparable to those of North America or Australasia has been seen as, in some part, a consequence of variations in value systems dominating these two areas.[73]

Theoretically, the core of the underdevelopment problem consisted of "the continuation of pre-industrial values" supported by an agrarian rural social structure. Thus, the social agents who impelled modernization, the entrepreneurs, lacked both in terms of number and depth in their entrepreneurial value orientation. In the minds of developmental theorists, Latin Americans unfortunately "discouraged entrepreneurial activity, while [the value system] of the English-speaking Protestant world of the United States and Canada fostered it."[74]

Those who studied the problem of Mexicans in the southwest inevitably linked it to the principles of Latin American underdevelopment and they ultimately arrived at the expected conclusions. When Kibbe wrote her stinging criticisms of racism and discrimination in Texas, she also found it necessary to critique Mexican culture as a source of the general "Mexican problem" in Texas. She characterized Mexicans as self-pitying; fatalistic, unable to work together; tending toward envy; unable to maintain social enterprises; and incapable of developing

"strong, permanent, widespread, and economically powerful organizations, tending instead to numerous small, ineffectual clubs and societies."[75] Kibbe called these and other characteristics, such as retaining
the Spanish language over English, "Errors."

Florence Kluckhohn arrived at similar conclusions regarding Mexican
culture utilizing the "pattern variable" approach described by Lipset.
Again, Anglos stressed positive cultural values, while Mexicans adhered
to a culture that impeded success. According to Kluckhohn, the value
orientations of the Mexicans—fatalism, individualism, personalism, and
familism—those same characteristics that prevented economic development in Latin America, "tells us why a hundred years of American rule in
our Southwest have not made typical Americans out of very many Mexicans."[76] The problem of poverty among the Spanish-speaking had its
roots in the culture: "without achievement concepts" the "dispossessed
Mexican migrant" could not be expected to compete.[77] Schooling therefore must acknowledge three factors if educators expected it to succeed
in its acculturationist objectives: first, "the enduring quality of cultural
orientation" in conditioning individual and social behavior; second, that
irrationality in the behavior of the Mexican population derived from its
culture; third, those managing education (Anglos) failed to recognize the
fundamental distinctiveness and significance of their own middle-class
culture from that of Mexican culture.[78]

A major figure in inter-American education and specialist with the
American Council on Education's Intergroup Education Project, Marie
M. Hughes, stated that

> when any group is segregated, the major learning process of
> imitation is circumvented. The minority group cannot learn
> accepted ways of middle-class culture in America. . . .[79]

This, of course, had another side to it: the culture of the Mexican
community exhibit something deviant. Kluckhohn, like many social
scientists and educators of the period, felt that cultural pluralism worked

against the interests of minorities and in fact contributed to their lower-class status. She summed up the heart of the problem as addressed by the Inter-American Program.

> We cannot simultaneously accept the diversity of Mexican cultural orientations and expect Mexicans to become well enough assimilated for at least some sizable proportion of them to become successful Americans. Mexican orientations—in our system—assure very little for individuals except a lack of mobility and a general lower class status.[80]

The culture concept therefore placed into perspective the ultimate objective in education: a peaceful process of assimilation, the weaning of the Mexican community away from core values of the Mexican culture and toward the core values of middle-class Anglo culture. The Mexican population could retain acceptable cultural elements and integrate them into the American culture under a policy known as "cultural democracy," but these were superficial aspects: food, music, dance, architecture, and idioms. Precisely, this theoretical approach undergirded the efforts of the Office of Inter-American Affairs in wartime and continued into the fifties and sixties.

Although culture concept had an enduring quality to it in practice, it did not accomplish the desired ends. The political goal of inter-cultural and inter-American education (i.e., political solidarity) faced severe threats from the mass minorities' movements of the sixties, which established their own visions of a democratic society and challenged the precepts of the liberal social sciences. The response of the federal government in its 1960s civil rights legislation continued to maintain the political objective of eliminating conflict and independent political action and militancy. Nevertheless, social reforms of far greater magnitude than those envisioned in the forties and fifties by social scientists proved necessary to dissolve the conflicts and civil disorders typical of the 1960s.

Chapter 7

De Jure Segregation

Its Rise and Fall in the Southwest

The practice of segregation created its political opposition, and although this study has focused on the action of segregation, the social movement to end segregation is of critical importance to understanding the era of segregation. Furthermore, we cannot fully appreciate the process of desegregating American society without recognizing the role of the Mexican community acting through the *Mendez* case within the legal system. The historical accounts that have addressed the *Mendez* case, such as Francisco Balderrama,[1] Charles Wollenberg,[2] and Thomas P. Carter and Robert D. Segura,[3] have not engaged in any discussion of the actions taken by the Mexican-American parents, community, and community organizations that led to that successful desegregation court case. The case proved significant by itself, but its legal ramifications alone did not make the case a historical landmark. Also, the plaintiffs and the local community breathed life into the legal system as a result of the case as they brought it to bear upon the desegregation of California schools. I shall now examine and document this aspect of this important legal juncture. In doing so, I will highlight the political behavior of the Mexican community as a key factor in this case. The legal arguments and their consequences did not provide the only lessons from this case.

The actions of the community also figured decisively in the termination of de jure segregation.

While this historical approach is not new, however, in the literature on the *Mendez* v. *Westminster* case, such an analysis certainly is long overdue. I want to know what it took in terms of the parents, the community, and organizations, to bring this case to court. I want to know how they decided to file suit, who actually made the decisions, and the support given (beyond the plaintiffs) which furthered the cause. I want to examine the social side of this essentially political conflict resolved in the courts. For if indeed a political conflict did take place, then we should acknowledge the principals who won this battle for democracy in education.

Given the significance and wide effect that this case had on subsequent desegregation decisions affecting Mexican children, it becomes important to sharpen the analysis and also to bring forward the social aspect of this process that has not been discussed in the literature.

THE DEVELOPMENT OF SEGREGATION IN A SOUTHERN CALIFORNIA CITY

Our attention turns first to the process of the development of the segregation of Mexican children in a single community. I have decided to use the history of the segregation of Mexican children in Santa Ana, California, given that it was a key defendant in the *Mendez v. Westminster* case. I gleaned the information contained in this chapter primarily from the minutes of the Santa Ana Board of Education. The clear images of the development of the segregation of Mexican children, of its justification, methods to maintain it, and the controversy over the eventual court order dismantling it, also appear in the minutes.

Located forty miles south of Los Angeles, Santa Ana is the county seat of Orange County. Until the 1950s wave of urbanization, Orange

County was predominantly agricultural with Santa Ana as the hub and largest city. The county grew prosperous on the production of oranges, lemons, nuts, beans, and vegetables. Within this rich agricultural area, a large and mostly permanent population of Mexican agricultural labor (some 17,000 in 1930) settled in the various cities and towns migrating within the county and to neighboring counties to harvest and tend the crops. As the economy grew, so did its reliance on Mexican labor, and as one student wrote, "In the development of a large part of the citrus industry in Orange County, California, the Mexican has played the role of . . . Atlas, bearing upon his shoulders in an inconspicuous manner the foundations of this prosperity."[4]

The largest Mexican settlement lived in Santa Ana, and in the late twenties, 4,000 dispersed into three main barrios: Artesia, Logan, and Delhi. In 1930, Mexicans comprised about 14 percent of the county population (17,000 of 288,000) and constituted about 15 percent of the Santa Ana population. The schools of Orange County generally segregated Mexican children in the larger districts, although in cases where the Mexican population remained relatively small, mixed facilities were used.[5] In the midforties about 80 percent of Mexican children in the elementary grades attended 14 segregated schools. In all, 4,037 Mexican children enrolled in elementary schools, or one quarter of the county school population.

Discussion of the segregation of Mexican children in Santa Ana first appears in the superintendent's Annual Report of 1913 and coincided with the initial phase of Mexican migration to the Southwest. That report revealed that administrators set special rooms aside for "Spanish" [sic] children at the Washington School. This first form of segregation appeared to be an ad hoc arrangement setting up a Mexican classroom on the grounds of an otherwise Anglo school. The report also showed that the Mexican room had a substantially different curriculum. Schools expected both boys and girls to study manual training and according to the expenditures of the "work done at Washington School by the Spanish pupils,"[6] Mexican boys engaged in gardening, boot-making, blacksmithing, and carpentry; girls were involved with sewing and homemaking. The school district carpenter instructed the boys. The separate room arrangement soon became too cumbersome to manage because of the increasing Mexican enrollment, so it evolved into the construction of separate schooling facilities. In 1913 Superintendent J. A. Cranston recommended that the district use Washington or Central School exclusively during the coming year, for the accommodation of those "Spanish" children who can't understand or speak the English language in order that they receive special attention and the progress of other children continues uninterrupted.[7] The superintendent contended that the focus on manual training in the separate room arrangement should also extend to the separate school.

> This past year, in giving instruction to this class of children, special emphasis has been laid upon the use of spoken and written English, reading, writing, spelling, the most simple and practical use of numbers, sewing and mending for the girls, and manual training for the boys, and better habits of living for both. The manual training for the boys has taken varied lines of activity, as carpentry, repairing shoes, basketry, haircutting and black-smithing.[8]

The school divided students into classes according to economic function—that is, manual training for Mexican children, academic preparation for white children—and it also divided students along sexual lines within the segregated classes. Thus, the pattern of segregation tended to reinforce the traditional sexual division of labor within the Mexican family and to add and develop those divisions particular to an advanced capitalist society.[9] Training for girls emphasized domestic work and certain kinds of unskilled industrial employment open to women. Boys prepared for manual labor traditionally relegated for males. In fact, the emerging curricular track, known as industrial preparation, became the lone curricular program available to the Mexican children.[10]

For nearly two generations, from 1911 to 1947, the school district practiced segregation until ended by the Ninth District Court decision on
a suit brought by a group of parents whose children attended segregated schools in Westminster, Orange, El Modena, and Santa Ana in
Orange County, California. The schools educated Mexican children by
molding them into a source of labor for the lowest-paid and most phys-
ically demanding productive tasks in the local economy. These institutions practiced a channeling function that ignored the need and yearning
for knowledge of the Mexican children, and instead altered the child's
interests to fit the expectations of the school.

The educational system's cultural and political manipulation and
Americanization programs also targeted Mexican parents. Thus, just as
schools established Mexican rooms for the young, they also established
Mexican rooms for the older generation. As early as 1913 the board
"agreed to grant the request for two rooms at Roosevelt School as a night
school for the Mexicans."[11]

In 1916 the board deliberated further on the practice of separating
Mexican children. The Committee on Buildings "reported favorably for
a six room building to be located near the present Fifth Street building,
and a two room building for the East part of the city for the use of the
Mexican children."[12] However, the district often referred to classrooms
for Mexican children as the "Mexican School," and the teacher in the
"Mexican School" as the "Mexican teacher"; if such a teacher headed
the "Mexican School" she (always she) became known as the "Mexican
School principal." Thus at Roosevelt School, two parallel administrative and educational units existed, each functioning separately and for
distinct educational objectives.[13] By the early 1920s the school district
established a Foreign Adult Education Department and an Americanization Department for Elementary and Secondary Schools, each with
a director and staff to administer the education of the Mexican community. The district hired teachers either for a "Mexican School," or for
an Anglo school. Clear distinctions emerged between the faculty of the

Mexican and Anglo schools and their hiring practices. By 1918 the practice of segregation was in full swing, characterized not only by physical separation, but also by distinct and unequal curricular programs.

The Superintendent's Report of 1918 proudly pointed out its new program of IQ testing and classifying of pupils under the tutelage of Dr. J. Harold Williams of the Whittier State School.[14] In addition, this program would devote increased attention to vocational guidance in the intermediate grades with course work in the occupations, preparing students for the type of study selected in the high school. High school freshmen would place in a course level according to the vocabulary test of the Stanford Revision, and information gained from the "so-called Otis Group tests in addition to class marks and teacher's estimates of intelligence. . . ."[15] This selection procedure characterized the education of the Anglo child. Under the heading, "The Industrial School," the superintendent reported on the selection process of the Mexican children.

> You have already approved my recommendation for a new school for those Mexican children who are unable to speak or understand the English language. This school will make it possible to give such children personal attention and a kind of training suited to their needs, a training that is impossible when they are placed in the same class with pupils who are not thus handicapped by language and culture.[16]

For the Mexican parents, the report continued, a special night school was established for "instruction in oral and written English, Arithmetic, Writing and Spelling and in the history and laws of our country, and in hygienic methods of living." In addition, the schools hired a Mexican nurse, a Mrs. Rodriguez, as an experiment "in connection with the home life of our Mexican people." Her task required, among other things, that she "visit the homes, study their mode of living and teach them sanitary methods." Authorities deemed the experiment a success; consequently they decided to continue the program.

> Mrs. Rodriguez has done . . . a wonderful work for her people
> in teaching them more sanitary ways of living, in arousing their
> interest in American life, its opportunities, and advantages. . . .
> She has succeeded in interesting many of the mothers in work,
> in taking lessons in cooking and sewing, and during the past two
> years has conducted a very successful Mexican PTA in which
> the fathers and mothers took a lively interest in learning better
> methods of bringing up and educating their children.[17]

However, that cultural intervention did not pose an immediate danger
for the basic division of labor within the Mexican family. Instead, it
worked to reinforce certain features of it. On the other hand, by spon-
soring courses in vocational work for girls, the schools promoted the
entrance of Mexican women into the ranks of labor, thereby effecting
subtle but significant alterations in the family structure and in the sexual
division of labor within the Mexican community.

The early process of segregation evolved not without conflicts and
antagonisms. For some Anglos, the program to build Mexican schools
seemed too slow, while many Mexicans demanded its termination.
Consequently, the board felt pressed to examine the legal basis for its
segregation practices and to provide some justification for its practices.
The first salvo came during the summer of 1918 in a lengthy resolution
from the (all Anglo) Lincoln School PTA, urging "that the Board do something in regard to the Mexican School, . . ." and that read in part that
"segregation is eminently desirable from moral, physical and educational
standpoints," and that it "would be a rank injustice to our school, our
teachers and our children"[18] if Mexican children continued to attend.

Sufficiently moved by the resolution, the board instructed the board
president to "procure bids for material for [the] Mexican building."
However, in order not to unwittingly create more reactions, the board
met at a later date with representatives of the Anglo PTAs and "talked
over the Mexican segregation question."[19] There, the board and Anglo
PTAs came to an agreement: all Mexican children would hereafter

attend Mexican schools. In essence, the plan outlined by Superintendent Cranston in his June 1913 Annual Report for the segregation of Mexican children, provided the basis for agreement.

The Mexican community also attacked the board's policies. The board minutes record that in 1919 a local Mexican patriotic organization, the Pro Patria Club, "was objecting very strongly to segregating their children in the Schools and asked that they be allowed to return to their respective schools."[20] The superintendent subsequently invited the city attorney Scott, to present "an opinion on the legality of conducting separate schools. . . ."[21] On one side stood the segregationist board, backed by the Anglo community, and on the other, a small, but vocal group of Mexican parents who demanded freedom of choice and nonsegregation. The city attorney provided the legal defense for the board's segregation policies. He informed the board that although the law of the state permitted separate schools for "Indians, Chinese, and people of Mongolian descent," that it contained no provision to "maintain separate schools for Mexicans." However, he continued, it was legal to segregate Mexicans on the grounds of language, age, or regularity of attendance. Therefore, from a legal standpoint, the current practice of segregating Mexican children appeared "fully supported by the law."[22] A motion to continue segregation unanimously passed, and it read, ". . . agreed, that for the best interest of the Schools and especially for the great benefit to the Mexican children, to continue the Mexican school work as at present," that is, in segregated facilities.

The Santa Ana Board of Education never again faced a need to defend segregation until 1943 when Mexican parents raised the demand for nonsegregated schooling. During that span the board classified three schools, Artesia, Delhi, and Fremont, as Mexican schools. On 5 June 1919, the "plans and specifications for the [just permanent] Mexican school buildings were approved and the secretary was instructed to advertise for bids. . . ."[23] The temporary arrangement evolved into the first Mexican school building in Santa Ana, named the Santa Fe School. Thus, the process of segregation, begun in 1912 with separate classrooms, reached its completed form in 1920 with the establishment of a separate Mexican school. In 1921 the district added Logan, another Mexican school, and incorporated a third, Delhi, in 1924. The Santa Fe School was later renamed Artesia in 1924, closed down in the late twenties, and redesignated as Fremont. Thereafter, one thousand Mexican children faced busing if necessary to achieve the segregation of the nationalities.

The district hired instructors for the Mexican children according to not only their particular tasks, but also to a particular hiring policy and wage scale. The pay for teachers at the Mexican schools, on the average, ranged from $80 to $100 less per year than teachers at Anglo schools.[24] The principal at the Mexican school received $135 less per year than principals at the Anglo schools. This salary differential implied that Mexican schoolteachers, although all Anglo, held a less important status and because of such, seemed responsible for less demanding teaching assignments. Although its policy restricted the board from hiring married women whose husbands could support them, it made an exception in the case of the Mexican schools. By 1923 the board had established a policy allowing the hiring of married women with or without husbands "able to support them" to teach in Mexican schools. We can only speculate as to why the board encountered difficulties in employing teachers for the Mexican children and consequently changed its criteria in order to enlarge its pool of applicants. On the other hand, through hiring married women with existing means of support, the board could impose a substantially lower wage scale for Mexican school teachers upon unemployed teachers.[25] In general, the board not only applied differential criteria to the people of the community, but it also used a differential hiring and wage scale for teachers of segregated and nonsegregated schools.

The most controversial issue relating to segregation until the desegregation decision of 1947 concerned the recommendations made based upon an educational survey of Santa Ana conducted by two University of

Southern California professors, Drs. Osman R. Hull and Willard S. Ford. After much fanfare and to-do, the board contracted with Hull and Ford to carry out a survey of the educational facilities with the purpose of formulating a comprehensive building program, taking into consideration immediate and future needs and conditions. Their study completed in 1928 affords insights into the quality of the physical buildings in the Mexican and non-Mexican schools. The controversy raised by the study also tells us how low Mexican children placed on the list of educational priorities in Santa Ana and underscores the overwhelming inequality between Anglo and Mexican educational facilities. The report, entitled the *Santa Ana School Housing Survey*, proved a bombshell, in spite of its thorough and professional quality. The board vehemently rejected the survey's recommendations to tear down two Mexican schools and build two entirely new ones. However, Hull and Ford had good reason to make such recommendation: the Mexican schools, from a physical standpoint, represented the worst schools. Of the twelve elementary schools, the survey rated the three Mexican schools, Artesia, Grand Avenue, and Delhi, the least fit for educational purposes. With all schools graded on a 1,000-point scale, the Mexican schools received the lowest ratings: Artesia scored the lowest with a 191 rating, followed by Grand Avenue with 217, and Delhi with 330; the Anglo schools scored between 433 and 699. The descriptions of the Mexican schools contained in the report provide a commentary on segregation.

> The Delhi school is a wooden structure which is a fire hazard and poorly constructed [and] provides less than one-third of the required amount of light. . . .

> The Grand Avenue School . . . is a two story frame structure entirely unsuited to school use . . . it had been condemned for years.

> The most unsatisfactory school that is now being used . . . is the Artesia school. . . . It is a frame building with no interior finish. It has a low single roof with no air space, which makes the temper-

ature in many of the rooms almost unbearable. Since no artificial light is provided in the building, it is impossible to do satisfactory reading without serious eye strain on many days of the year.[26]

The board met, along with an Advisory Committee of the Chamber of Commerce, to discuss the recommended program. The suggestions to replace two Mexican schools with new plants proved to be a lightening rod of criticism. Harvey Gardner, of the Chamber of Commerce, reportedly objected to so much money spent on a Mexican school; he especially claimed, "When we do not have proper facilities for the American school children." Cushman, also of the chamber, also found that the recommendation for the Artesia School to be excessive. Thus, the board unanimously and decisively rejected plans for improving facilities for Mexican children.[27]

The board commissioned the survey in order to utilize the information as part of an argument in upcoming bond elections. However, the researchers made a fatal error in requesting too much for the Mexican community. Consequently, the board requested that they prepare a second set of recommendations, one that both the board and the voters could support. On 27 March 1928 Dr. Ford presented a revised program to the board and to the Advisory Committee of the Chamber of Commerce. It reduced the elementary building programs to one, instead of two Mexican schools, and it lowered the amount of money earmarked for the Artesia School from $170,000 to $112,000. Not sufficiently impressed, the board and the Advisory Committee again requested a revision of the Artesia School figure. "There seemed to be the unanimous opinion that Drs. Hull and Ford allowed too much for the Mexican School," read the minutes.[28] On 20 April 1928, the board addressed the third Hull and Ford program, which was also rejected and led to their abrupt termination as consultants to the district. "Superintendent Cranston consequently recommended that the President appoint a committee to decide on a Mexican school."[29] The committee recommended a new $65,000 Artesia school building (down from the original $170,000 Hull and Ford estimate), a new kindergarten for Delhi at a cost of $500, and rather than build a new Grand Avenue school, it suggested the restoration of the old and vacant Logan school and an addition made to it at a cost of $32,000. The committee reported further that

> in the Mexican situation, we believe Artesia should be developed as a permanent school, with the new buildings of a fair construction. We have gone over the Lincoln-Logan-Custer district situation carefully, and feel that any effort to locate a Mexican school outside the district itself will meet with decided and instant opposition. We, therefore, suggest and recommend that the old Logan school grounds be enlarged to include lots to the East on Lincoln Street, and one or two lots on the north. We would regard this school as temporary as the Mexican will likely be crowded out soon.[30]

However, the committee's revision to the Hull and Ford plan angered Anglo residents near the Artesia School, and on 22 May, two representatives of the area met with the board to discuss relocating the Artesia School within a Mexican neighborhood.[31] The board decided to take up the matter in consultation with the Advisory Committee of the Chamber of Commerce "for further consideration."[32] During the following year, the critical school buildings issues that administrators debated, included relocation of the Grand Avenue School to the vacant Logan School site and a new addition to existing school buildings constructed. In addition, the new Artesia School continued to face opposition from Anglo parents, and on 29 January, they presented a petition of two hundred signatures at a regular board meeting urging the relocation of Artesia to a Mexican neighborhood. In spite of the petition the board split over the site of the Artesia School. Their discussion sheds light upon the political relationship of school to the Mexican community during the era of segregation.

> Dr. Horton expressed his opinion that the people of that District had a just argument but said the big question before the Board is that of finding a better site than the present site. Mr. White . . . spoke of all properties around the Artesia school carrying race

restrictions and felt the school should be moved, nearer the center of the Mexican population. Dr. Ball spoke of the disadvantages found at other Mexican schools in being located in the center of the [Mexican] population, stating adults lounged around the buildings during the day as well as it night and were a public nuisance. After discussion Mr. White stated that if the Board of Education persisted in locating that school where it is now, all the voters in that district would do all in their power to defeat any school bonds which come before the people.[33]

The debate continued long into the night without a final resolution. Board members agreed, however, to defer final decision until residents of the Artesia district conferred at length with the Advisory Committee of the Chamber of Commerce and the board.

On the matter of the Grand Avenue School, board members raised a similar set of points. The central issue centered on whether to relocate the Grand Avenue School on the Logan School grounds, and to purchase additional properties for expansion, or to move the school out of the Mexican barrio and "across the tracks." On 26 April 1929, a special meeting convened to discuss "the status regarding the building site and buildings for the new Mexican school, final settlement of the question being the reason for which this meeting was called."[34] The discussion followed similar lines as in the past; Herbert L. Miller of the board, expressed the opinion of the majority at that meeting.

Mr. Miller had not changed his opinion from that of the previous meeting and stated that he felt a definite line should be drawn and the school kept on this side of the tracks; buying additional lots and squaring up the property would clean up a "bad hole"; it would also avoid the criticism which would be bound to come if the school were placed across the track as the section East of the track is going to be a [Anglo] residential property in the near future. . . .[35]

When the board asked the Chamber of Commerce Advisory Committee for their opinion on the proposed Logan School, all agreed to build on that site although in the Mexican barrio. Next, the committee passed a motion to purchase additional lots around the Artesia site and to construct a new Mexican school there.

The board and its Advisory Committee had finally overcome the impasse that had impaired its progress on the school construction program and chose to ignore the Anglo citizens' objections. On 30 April 1929, at the regular board meeting, the committee from the Artesia district urged the board to reconsider its decision and to "select another site for the Artesia school." After considerable discussion, no change occurred in previous decisions.[36]

The new Artesia School, renamed the Fremont School and enrolling 475 children, opened in the 1929–30 school year. Logan enrolled 232, and Delhi 319, for a total of 1,026 Mexican children, or well above one quarter of the district's enrollment of 3,514.

By 1930 segregation had reached its ultimate form, and it rarely became a topic again for discussion at board meetings. Of more critical interest in the 1930s was the depression and district finances. Although massive repatriation drives reduced the Mexican population in some areas by a third, the Mexican population in Orange County remained fairly stable. In fact, the Mexican school population grew during the depression, and one researcher found an average increase of 16 pupils per Mexican school between 1930 and 1934.[37]

Segregation resulted from a mandatory attendance policy, not from a policy of neighborhood schools. Officials generally drew school districts so that Mexican children would attend only Mexican schools, and when an Anglo child happened to live in a Mexican district, school authorities routinely accepted requests for transfers. On the other hand, when Mexican youngsters lived outside of a Mexican district the school authorities would arrange for transfers to a Mexican school. The transfer of pupils to achieve segregation was commonly achieved through busing, an ironic commentary on current efforts at busing to achieve integration. Throughout the era of de jure segregation, any request by Mexican parents to transfer to Anglo schools were routinely denied. Thus, while the board offered a legal justification for segregation on the basis of language, age, or attendance, seldom did it accept these as criteria for transfer.

Mainly utilized in the agribusiness of the area, the Mexican community served an economic function that clung to them even as they left the fields and orchards and entered the classrooms. And this economic function persisted within and outside of the community, not because of a cultural affinity. Through the segregation period, schools operated only half a day during the walnut-picking season. Board policy limited schooling to half a day to satisfy both the minimal compulsory education laws and maximal agribusiness interests.

Child labor proved valuable to the area and the board felt some responsibility in supplying child labor. At the 13 September 1943 board meeting, the district attendance officer

> recommended that we follow . . . plan of a walnut session in the Mexican schools as this would permit these children to get their education and also to work five hours per day. He stated that unless otherwise directed he will continue our policy of not excusing students to work in the morning and of issuing no permits to students under fourteen of age, as provided by law. It was stated that if a father contracts for the whole family a work permit is not necessary for those under 14. It was the consensus that the above policy be followed and it was thought that such a plan would meet with approval of the growers. It was thought that they would furnish transportation for students with a supervisor who would receive $1.00 per hour for such supervision.[38]

In contrast to its willingness to organize the educational program to accommodate the labor needs of local growers, the board refused to provide free nourishment to needy children. On 12 February 1940, the board concluded "that the providing of food to underprivileged children is not an educational program," and announced "that they cannot supply food for underprivileged children."[39] Thus, segregation included more than just the separation of nationalities; broader economic and social issues also figured significantly.

THE FIGHT FOR DEMOCRACY IN EDUCATION: MENDEZ ET AL. V. WESTMINSTER BOARD OF EDUCATION

On 2 March 1945, Gonzalo Mendez, William Guzman, Frank Palomino, Thomas Estrada, and Lorenzo Ramirez, filed a class action suit against the Westminster, El Modena, Garden Grove, and Santa Ana school districts "to enjoin the application of alleged discriminatory rules, regulations, customs, and usages."[40] They filed the complaint "on behalf of their minor children, and . . . on behalf of 'some 5000' persons similarly affected, all of Mexican or Latin descent. . . ."[41] Events in Santa Ana and Westminster in 1943 leading to the filing of that petition illuminate the nature of that important episode in the history of the Chicano people. These events represent lessons in antidemocracy.

In 1943 returning Santa Ana veterans formed a civil rights group, the Latin American Organization, specifically to combat school segregation. One of the first actions taken by the LAO was confronting the Board of Education with requests for transfers.

On 25 October 1943, Mrs. Leonides Sanchez and Mrs. Frank Garcia appeared before the Santa Ana Board of Education to "protest the denial of a request to send their children" to the primarily Anglo Franklin School. According to the board minutes, the two "wished to have their children educated in an American School so that they would have all the advantages of American children and learn to speak English as Americans do." The mothers charged that "it is a matter of discrimination when Mexican children are forced to go to the Mexican School." Sanchez and Garcia stated that if the board did not grant the transfers, they would "send their children to school elsewhere."[42]

The board reaffirmed their stance. Superintendent J. A. Cranston, who had supervised the development of the segregated schools in 1913 and was still with the district, admitted that the board regularly granted transfers to Anglo children because "it would be educationally unsound to send them to a school made up entirely of Mexican children." However, the board saw little basis for transferring Mexican students out of Fremont School. Attendance officer Smith agreed that Anglo children regularly transferred, some thirty-four having transferred out of Fremont during the 1943 academic year, but the "present policy" aimed at diminishing transfers, not increasing them. Thus, if these families (the Garcias and Sanchezes) "continue to reside in the Fremont District they attend that school." The board also called in the Fremont principal, Mrs. Edith Gilbert, to back up the denial. She, like the superintendent, discussed the "positive side" of Fremont School. She mentioned that "the older girls are taught to do the cooking" in the cafeteria and Mexican "students are encouraged to speak English at all times, on the grounds as well as in the classroom." The board instructed the attendance officer not to grant the transfers, arguing that "if they (the boundaries) are moved for one family there will be a great many requests for transfer."[43]

Nevertheless, the Sanchez and Garcia request forced the board to reconsider its segregation policy. The board began a process of "studying on the problem of Mexican children" and focused its attention upon a seminar on intercultural education and Mexican children offered at the Claremont colleges.[44] Although prepared to make some token efforts at placating the Mexican community, the board did not propose to end de jure segregation. Events that followed shortly, forced the board into a noncompromising position, for the Mexican parents were not in a mood for tokens or compromises.

A year later the superintendent reported that Sanchez and Garcia enrolled their children in the Franklin School in spite of the board's ruling the previous year. The board "discovered that false addresses were filed in order that the children could so enroll." Quickly the board decided "that as soon as facts have been verified, the children will again be enrolled in their rightful district, Fremont."[45] The fight had barely begun when on 23 October, Charles Martin, the attorney representing Mr. and Mrs. William Guzman, parents of Billy Guzman, and other parents from the Fremont school district, among them Mr. Leonides Sanchez, Mr. Fuentes, and Mr. Reyes, appeared before the board to request permission to send young Billy Guzman to the Franklin School. The struggle had escalated from that of individual parents with the support of the LAO protesting before the board, to that of a legal representation prepared to carry forward a struggle on the basis of law.

The board did not capitulate without determined resistance. Its strategy did not change. It ultimately denied the request with its usual expressions of disbelief that anyone would refuse to send their child to Fremont. At first the board responded that it was in the process of "considering district boundary problems" and requested time to study Guzman's "problem" before coming to a final decision. Martin replied that his client would agree to a ninety-day period before approaching the board for the final decision. Three months passed without the slightest change in board policy.

Nearly concurrent with the conflict in Santa Ana, a parallel situation developed in Westminster, located about fifteen miles from Santa Ana. The families involved in both cases eventually joined their struggles to fight the antisegregation legal battle. It is instructive to review the series of events orchestrated by the Westminster parents.

In the small farming community of Westminster, Gonzalo and Felicitas Mendez experienced for the first time the denial of equal educational opportunity for their children. Rather than accepting segregation, they refused anything less than a democratic school system, and in the months and years that followed, they and their comrades fought the political power of Orange County. It was the Mendezes who gave their name to one of the most significant legal cases in the history of the Southwest, *Mendez et al.* v. *Westminster School District of Orange County.*

At the time they filed the suit, the Mendez family leased a sixty-acre farm owned by a Japanese family then interned in a concentration camp.[46] They raised asparagus, tomatoes, cabbage, green beans, peppers, and lettuce. Their venture proved moderately successful, and by the midforties, they had a work force of thirty people during peak season.

Gonzalo and Felicitas, children of migrant agricultural workers, grew up in that same setting. Gonzalo, a native of Mexico but raised in southern California, had earned the reputation of "champion" orange picker in his youth, and he attended grammar school in Westminster when that town did not yet have a segregated school system. Felicitas, a native of Hongos, Puerto Rico, came to the United States when Arizona farm agents recruited her family to work on the cotton farms of the Salt River Valley. Like all migrant families, they worked in several different places until they settled down in Orange County as agricultural workers. By dint of several years' hard work, they managed to do well enough and had become respected and popular figures in the *colonia*. In the early forties, they decided to lease a farm in nearby Westminster; this meant that their children would enroll in the Westminster school.

On the first day of the 1944 school year, the three Mendez children were taken by their aunt Soledad Vidaurri to the nearest school, the Westminster Elementary School, to enroll them. Ironically, Gonzalo had attended years before, but by the 1940s, the school admitted only Anglos. Soledad's own children had gained admission and attended that school but only because, as she later found out, of their light complexions and their last name, Vidaurri, which was thought to be French. However, the school denied admission to the Mendez children on the grounds of language deficiency, although their cousins also Mexicans, were allowed to attend.

Furious because the school sent away her two nephews and niece, Soledad immediately withdrew her own children and returned to the farmhouse and informed Gonzalo and Felicitas about what had occurred. The Mendez approved of her action, but instead of trying only to gain admission for their children, they decided upon organizing a local group of parents to petition the board to desegregate the schools. Thus, on 8 September 1944, the group sent a letter to the clerk asking an end to segregation. The petition read:

Dear Sir,

We the undersigned parents of whom about one-half are American born, respectively call to your attention to the fact of the segregation of American children of Mexican descent is being made at Westminster in that the American children of non-Mexican descent are made to attend Westminster Grammar School on W. 17th Street at Westminster and the American children of Mexican extraction are made to attend Hoover School on Olive Street and Maple Street. Children from one district are made to attend the school in the other district and we believe that this situation is not conducive to the best interests of the children nor friendliness either among the children or their parents involved nor the eventual thorough Americanization of our children. It would appear that there is racial discrimination and we do not believe that there is any necessity for it and would respectfully request that you make an investigation of this matter and bring about an adjustment, doing away with the segregation above referred to. Some of our children are soldiers in the war, all are American born and it does not appear fair nor just that our children should be segregated as a class.[47]

In effect, the superintendent responded by arguing that Mexican children belonged in the Mexican school; however, he continued, in this case he would make an "exception" and offer special enrollment for the Mendez children. Gonzalo and Felicitas rejected the idea of an "exception," and argued that since their children should be regularly enrolled, they would keep them out of school until the board allowed for such. The district made its last attempt at compromise, but this effort also failed, thus prompting the Mendezes' decision to use the courts not only to gain admission, but to eliminate the practice of "Mexican schools."

Although Gonzalo and Felicitas had at that point decided on a legal course of action, they had no one in mind to represent them. Upon the suggestion of their produce truck driver, Henry Rivera, Gonzalo learned of an attorney, David Marcus. Rivera mentioned that Marcus had done effective work in the interests of the Mexican community and convinced Gonzalo to meet with him. Having won the court battle to desegregate the San Bernardino public parks and pools and handled legal matters for the Mexican consulates in Los Angeles and San Diego, Marcus had experience in desegregation cases.[48] In the attorney's Los Angeles office they met to discuss the issue. Marcus expressed that their chances for winning an injunction against segregation appeared very good. They agreed upon the strategy and the terms, and several years of dedication and commitment to the cause of desegregation followed.

On 2 March 1945, the Guzman family of Santa Ana and their friends Gonzalo and Felicitas Mendez and with Mexican parents of Garden Grove and El Modena school districts filed suit in the Ninth Federal District Court seeking an immediate injunction against the segregation of Mexican schoolchildren. Gonzalo Mendez practically became Marcus's assistant, driving him throughout the county to gather evidence and supportive data, and to interview individuals. Gonzalo threw himself so completely into the cause that he left the farm for Felicitas to administer for over one year. She not only ran the farm well, but it became more prosperous than ever. Thus, both dedicated themselves to a long struggle.

In addition to her work on the farm, Felicitas also organized in the community in order to gather support for the cause. She initiated meetings with the local parents, which eventually developed into an educational support group known as the *Asociacion de Padres de Ninos Mexico-Americanos*. For nearly a year the organization provided support of a moral nature, for it had no organizational experience nor funds to speak of. It served an important purpose in that it conveyed to the school officials the message that the Mexican community supported the efforts of the Mendezes, Guzmans, Palominos, and others. But it also expressed to the plaintiffs that they did not stand alone in their battle. However, one of the main functions of the group involved attending the trial to display a show of strength to the court. Since it consisted mostly of farm workers who did not have the funds to cover the cost of travel plus loss of work, Gonzalo and Felicitas agreed not only to cover their transportation costs, but also to reimburse them for their loss of pay. The Mendezes thus carried the burden of the lawyer's fee, compensation for their backers, and time and effort devoted to manage the legal battle. Their effort to a large extent, represented an individual struggle, yet they not only did it themselves. They also acted in the interests of the entire Mexican community. A contemporary reporter wrote that two principles motivated Gonzalo Mendez.

> One is that the purpose of the law suit is to benefit the whole Mexican community, not a mere handful of fortunate ones; and the other is that his little Sylvia, Gonzalo, and Geronimo . . . can never be good Americans if this insulting and painful segregation continues.[49]

Given the strength of their convictions, it should not appear surprising to find that the Mendezes contributed well over one year's time, labor, and income to cover the lawyer's fees and other expenses, such as reimbursing their supporters' lost wages. Well over one thousand dollars (a considerable sum at the time) came out of their pockets and made it possible to carry the case to its conclusion. In the end, their individual fight had far-reaching ramifications.

The *Mendez* suit claimed that segregation of Mexican children violated the Fourteenth Amendment in the absence of specific state laws that required or enabled the local school districts to mandate a Mexican school system. State education codes allowing or requiring school segregation applied only to "nonwhite" races, specifically Indian children (except Native American Indians), Chinese, Japanese, and Mongolian. The suit alleged that no legal "racial" status had been applied to Mexicans other than that they were members of the Caucasian race and therefore not subject to the discriminatory education codes. Consequently, the suit demanded that no grounds existed for the segregation of Mexican children and therefore its practice should end. The defendants, represented by the county counsel, Joel Ogle, countered that the federal courts had no jurisdiction over essentially a state matter. Furthermore, the district did not practice segregation of Mexican children on the basis of race or nationality, but on the basis of the educational needs of Mexican children, that is, special instruction in English and in American culture.[50] As such, no constitutional issues pertained to this case; moreover, argued Ogle, segregation on the basis of race or nationality was constitutional as long as districts maintained separate but equal facilities for each race or nationality.

The essence of the *Mendez* case revolved around the charge that segregation operated "to deny or deprive equal protection of the laws" to English and non-English-speaking Mexican children. That argument impressed the presiding judge, Paul J. McCormick, and on 18 February 1946, he issued an injunction prohibiting the segregation of Mexican children. McCormick allowed that the federal court had jurisdiction over the case since the state of California did not have legislation establishing segregated Mexican schools.[51]

The defendants raised the separate but equal doctrine, thereby obliging McCormick to address the Plessy doctrine, that is, separate did not imply inequality. In his decision, he responded to Ogle's contentions by stating that "the paramount requisite in the American system of public education is social equality. It must be open to all children by unified school association regardless of lineage." In so stating, the judge broke with Plessy and clearly defined a distinction between physical equality (facilities) and social equality. In this case, separate but equal facilities were unconstitutional because it created a social inequality. Thus, rather than acting as a protection for the practice of segregation, the Fourteenth Amendment served to repeal segregation.

Moreover, McCormick contended that no evidence existed that showed segregation aided in the development of English proficiency, that on the contrary, evidence demonstrated that segregation retarded language and cultural assimilation. Consequently, the segregation of Mexican children had no legal or educational justification.[52]

The court's decision countered each point made by the defense. Nevertheless, the four school districts decided to appeal to the United States Circuit Court of Appeals in San Francisco, Joel Ogle again representing the districts. On 14 April 1947, the seven judges of the appellate court unanimously upheld the Ninth District Court decision.

Mendez immediately gained widespread attention from legal scholars who quickly recognized the historical significance of the court decision. An article in the *Columbia Law Review* stated that in the past "so long as equal facilities were made available to both groups," no constitutional issues existed to be raised. However, the article continued,

> The courts in the [Mendez] case breaks sharply with this approach and finds that the Fourteenth Amendment requires "social equality" rather than "equal facilities."[53]

> Another analyst commented in the *Yale Law Journal* that the Mendez decision

> has questioned the basic assumption of the Plessy Doctrine. . . . Modern sociological and psychological studies lend much support to the District court's views. A dual school system even if "equal facilities" were provided does imply social inferiority.[54]

Judge McCormick's ruling had an immediate effect upon the Mexican community and upon the Board of Education. Protests against segregation became much stronger, as evidenced by the visit to the Santa Ana board by Hector Tarango of the Latin American Organization, along with Fred Ross, a "field worker for the American Council on Race Relations." The minutes portrayed the pair as "belligerent and antagonistic . . . concerning the matter of the Mexican-American children." Ross informed the board that "he had instructed the Mexican children to go to the school of their choice on the opening day of school and if they were not admitted, the Board of Education would be cited for contempt." The board discussed the strategy now spoken of openly by the organized Mexican community and discovered that a number of Mexican children had enrolled at the all-Anglo McKinley school but were sent back to their former school. The board "feared that they might have been sent [to McKinley] purposely to see what action the schools would take."[55]

The action the school districts decided upon represented tokenism in its narrowest form, a favorite tactic of segregationist boards in the fifties and sixties. Rather than dismantling segregated schools, the Santa Ana board agreed to meet with community representatives to discuss an "amicable solution." It agreed to allow transfers of Mexican children out of their district "in the same proportion as Anglo-Americans are transferred out of their district." However, the board imposed discriminatory restrictions:

> 1.That they [Mexican community] understand that such transfer would not be granted into a class or school which is already filled to reasonable capacity.
>
> 2.That the Mexican-Americans impress upon their group the necessity for a continuous emphasis upon those things which will make the Mexican-Americans socially acceptable in transfer.
>
> 3.That the Mexican-Americans continue their training in such a manner as to continuously foster good relationships in this adjustment.[56]

Thus, the Santa Ana board would not give up segregation as a policy, but it did begin a policy of token reforms. Not long after the decision to grant token transfers in order to maintain segregation, the appellate court upheld the McCormick ruling. The board knew that it could no longer sustain segregation nor tokenism against the organized protestations of the community and court rulings. Shortly before the appellate court ruled, the Santa Ana LAO formed a League of United Latin American Citizens chapter, acting as an umbrella organization in the desegregation struggle throughout the county. Thus the common demand for integrated schooling generated a political mobilization, which eventually reshaped the political balance of power.

On 5 June 1947, the board voted to inform the county counsel, Joel Ogle, that it "does not wish to appeal [further] the Mexican segregation case."[57]

On the opening day of the next school year, 1947–48, the board enforced a policy allowing Mexican-American transfers, and the formerly all-Anglo Franklin School became 50 percent Mexican and 50 percent Anglo.[58] Shortly before the appellate ruling, the legislature of the state of California struck down the educational codes that legally required the segregation of Indian and Asian children. Thus, *Mendez* reverberated beyond the confines of Orange County. Segregation, if it continued to exist, would be de facto; the era of de jure segregation, however, had ended in California.

The *Mendez* case inspired renewed antisegregation efforts by the GI Forum and the League of United Latin American Citizens in Arizona and Texas. Their struggles resulted in legal decisions enjoining school districts from segregating Mexican children. Some twenty Mexican parents in Bastrop, Texas, allied themselves with the LULAC and successfully carried out a legal battle to terminate segregation in the *Delgado* v. *Bastrop* case. The *Delgado* decision reaffirmed *Mendez* in that it represented a "momentous victory" that "undermined the rigid segregation of the pre-1948 Texas school system."[59]

In face of this, the main question remains squarely in focus: Did the termination of de jure segregation of Mexican children substantially alter the educational practices of schools attended by Mexican children? The answer is yes and no. Yes in that legal segregation ended, which in itself marked a substantial change and a political victory for the Mexican community. On the other hand, schooling for Mexican children continued to come under the significant influence of pseudoscientific intelligence testing, with its heavy tracking into slow learner, vocational, and EMR (Educationally Mentally Retarded) classes. Coercive accultur-ationist objectives continued to dominate education, and high dropout rates continued to plague the Mexican community.

Although Mexican schools no longer operated, there still existed many schools with a predominantly Mexican enrollment and administrators and teachers perceived these institutions as Mexican schools. A large number of school districts in Texas continued a form of Mexican schools via bureaucratic impediments as well as the subterfuge of "free choice"— that is, Mexican parents had the choice of either sending their child to the local, or nearby, school (the old Mexican school), or to the distant integrated (or old Anglo school). Rarely did school districts exchange students so as to integrate both schools. Usually these districts achieved integration only if Mexican parents sent their children to the old Anglo school. Quite often they achieved integration by closing down the old Mexican school, a practice seldom applied to the old Anglo school. Thus, as de jure segregation terminated, a variation on the old theme of segre-gation and discrimination appeared.[60] Much of the old internal system remained intact, such as tracking and the emphasis on vocational educa-tion. However, the official Mexican school eventually became a distant figure in the history of the Mexican people in the United States.

Not until the 1960s with the Chicano Movement, did inequality and cultural oppression through institutionalized techniques come under direct attack. In Texas, segregation resurfaced as an issue in the midsix-ties, as the LULAC and MALDEF (Mexican American Legal Defense Fund) took up the campaign to legally enforce the court decisions of twenty years before. Eventually that struggle evolved into the campaign for bilingual education as the fundamental tool to overcome inequality in education. Nevertheless, the desegregation campaign of the forties and fifties stands out as a significant chapter in the Chicano struggle for democracy, thus earning consideration as a precursor to the Chicano Movement of the sixties.[61]

THE EDUCATION OF CHICANO CHILDREN

CONTINUITY AND CHANGE

Most historical accounts of the Chicano educational experience tend to blend the various aspects of this history into a single, unilinear, and unbroken process. In this study, I have taken the opposite approach by separating the segments composing this history and by analyzing them as particular entities, which together formed a single educational process. I have also looked at the changes occurring over time, the causes of these changes, and their consequences for the Mexican community.

I have consistently related the educational process to the political and economic institutions at large by viewing education as a political institution with an economic function to fulfill. Thus, segregation grew out of an undemocratic political decision-making process, which reproduced a socioeconomic bifurcation in society. However, the mere segregation of children by itself could never lead to these consequences; it needed certain techniques to accomplish its politico-economic goal. Americanization, testing, tracking into vocational education, and slow-learner and mentally retarded classes, provided the internal machinery that made segregation an effective tool.

Fashioned by the emerging social scientists and reformers in the early period of the century, various theoretical constructions legitimized the use of these educational techniques. These ideas generally coincided with the manner in which wealth, power, capital, and labor was divided in society. The social function of one key institution appearing in this century, mass compulsory education, to a large extent, originated in social science thought. The general application of the functionalist theory of the organic society established the overall guidelines for the educational establishment. The universal use of IQ testing, for example, and its educational consequences, had their roots in the social science concept of intelligence, which corresponded with organic theory. Americanization was extensively applied, and it was based on assimilation theory, which also was linked closely with organic theory. Consequently, in order to understand the nature of the segregated schooling period, the "hidden" aspect, social science theory, must be appreciated for its significance upon educational practice in the Mexican community.

In addition, I analyzed the noneducation of a significant element of the Mexican community, migrant children. In this instance, a common practice unfolded that deliberately denied migrant children a constitutional right to equal educational opportunity, even if such involved a segregated school. Consequently, the segregated period in Chicano educational history contained at least two widely divergent experiences from compulsory noneducation to compulsory education (with variations between them). This division generally corresponded to the two main economic experiences, the rural agricultural and urban industrial employment settings.

Aimed at eliminating a nonmodern culture and substituting it with the culture of the American middle class, Americanization also appeared as a significant activity in the Mexican school. In general, Americanization placed value judgments upon virtually all things Mexican. Thus, language, religion, dress, recreational activities, family traditions, and home life-style, constituted social as well as political problems that needed to be either eliminated or reconstructed upon a new foundation. However, such a task could not be completed only in the school room, and only among youths. Consequently, the main target of Americanization included both girls and women—the future and current mother and homemaker. They faced isolation in special Americanization programs geared toward producing an agent for the Americanization of future generations.

While the overall objective of the segregated school concerned the Americanization of the Mexican community, the more successful practice involved that of reproducing the class character of the Mexican community through the use of testing and tracking. Based upon prevalent social science and educational theory, schools slotted students upon a hierarchical scale, from superior intelligence to inferior intelligence. Their educational program reflected this hierarchy, and thus superior students received an academic preparation, while the inferior students received a preparation for manual vocations. In such an educational program, schools commonly slotted Mexicans en masse into the slow and inferior classes and based this practice upon the uncritical application of IQ tests for predictive purposes. To no surprise, therefore, the Mexican school became commonly known as the industrial school of the district. Within this setting, boys and girls received separate types of training. The former generally received traditional male training for unskilled or semiskilled occupations, while the latter received preparation for becoming a homemaker, mother, wife, or an employee in an occupation related to her domestic role, such as seamstress, laundry worker, and waitress. By the end of the segregation period, an unwritten tradition existed among educators that viewed Mexican children as best suited by "temperament" or "IQ" for vocational education.

The practice of segregation and its programs insured that the political and economic relationship between the Mexican and Anglo community would not only remain, but that it would also gain strength. However, there was a price to be paid for segregating Mexican from Anglo children: as adults they would remain separate and lack the political integration necessary for social stability. Thus, a serious contradiction in the reproduction of the dominant-subordinate relationship existed. This contradiction was manifested in bold relief at the eve of World War II when the antagonisms between minorities and nonminorities become potentially explosive areas threatening wartime solidarity. Consequently, the federal government launched national reform programs, such as intercultural and inter-American education, to ameliorate minority-nonminority relations and to mobilize society for war.

The method employed in this reform program was education. If the two sides could interact, learn of each other, and become accustomed to one another, then antagonisms would melt away. In addition, inter-American education encompassed both the Southwest and all of Latin America. The proponents of this type of education viewed the amelioration of Anglo-Mexican relations in the Southwest as indispensable to the realization of U.S. foreign policy objectives in the hemisphere. Essentially, policymakers in Washington, along with social scientists and many educators, opposed segregation (although accepting of the teaching methods within the segregated school) because it fostered antagonisms, created separatism, retarded assimilation, and hindered the wartime solidarity effort. Lastly, Latin perceptions of Anglo-Mexican relations in the United States greatly influenced the ability of the United States to realize policy objectives in Latin America.

Consequently, in such a climate certain reforms became acceptable and even mandatory. The termination of segregation of Mexican children had become the key objective of reform through a campaign directed from Washington by the Office of Inter-American Affairs and led by Nelson Rockefeller.

Coincident with this reform atmosphere, a maturing political awareness within the Mexican community manifested itself in numerous actions opposing segregation. Local community political organizations also appeared, which began to contend for political decision-making power, eventually extending to statewide and regional bases. Within a relatively short period of time, a generation of Mexican-American activists made their presence felt. The combination of the minority's political thrust and the government-sponsored reform campaign made the termination of de jure segregation inevitable. However, it is crucial that recognition be given to the role played by the international factor appearing in cold war aspects as well as national liberation movements. To a large extent the international factor emanated from the interrelationship between the political actions of U.S. minorities and of dominated peoples in underdeveloped areas of the world. Thus, a wide number of separate political actions on a local level created an international pattern having the potential to disrupt U.S. foreign policy objectives.

The development and maintenance of the de jure segregation of Mexican children involved a political relationship, especially a relationship of domination. Eventually, however, the subordinate community gathered itself and began a process first of balancing and eventually emerging as the politically dominant actor. This evolution of political subordination to political dominance (in this instance, limited to the struggle to desegregate) could not occur without certain favorable external conditions that gave the subordinate group added and decisive leverage. It is probably true, therefore, that at least since World War II, no significant minority democratic struggle in the United States can exist in isolation and must touch on national and, therefore, international issues.

Such a perspective leads to the conclusion that one cannot separate the education of the Mexican-American people, and of its political relationship to the dominant community, from the international relationship binding the destinies of Mexico to the United States. The debate over bilingual education, for example, raises an international, as well as national question. Americanization of Mexican immigrants remains a goal of the educational process. In a recent testimony before a congressional committee, Colorado Governor Richard D. Lamm warned of "perpetual tension and strife" if Latino immigrants "do not assimilate into American life."[1] Such provides an example of the continued concern over the assimilation of Mexicans. In another instance, the Texas legislature voted in 1975 to deny the right to an education for the children of undocumented workers. The courts, however, struck down that legislation in 1980. Nevertheless, the general educational issue for the Mexican-American community, whether it is bilingualism, Americanization, or mandatory exclusion, continues inseparable from the general migration question.

The continued inequality in educational outcomes distinguishing Mexican from Anglo communities remains, to a large extent, a lingering consequence of an historical relationship between a developed and underdeveloped nation. This does not mean that no educational improvement can be expected for the Mexican-American community until Mexico emerges as a developed country. It is to say, however, that a number of major problems confronting the Mexican-American community stem from the ties binding this immigrant community to the vicissitudes of an international relationship. As a subordinate and dependent nation, Mexico cannot exist independently of the economic power of the United States. Consequently, continued and massive migration, the major consequence of this international tie, maintains, reproduces, and deepens a long history of socioeconomic inequality separating the Anglo from the Mexican-American community. The educational process tends to integrate this segmentation into its structure and thereby maintains, rather than alters, this socioeconomic relationship. Education in this society, as in any society, tends toward reflecting the social relationships imbedded in society.

ENDNOTES

PREFACE

1. Moises Gonzalez Navarro, *Historia Moderna de Mexico, El Porfiriato*, vol. 4 (Mexico City: Editorial Hermes, 1957), p. 25.

2. Robert N. McClean, *That Mexican as He Really Is, North and South of the Rio Grande* (New York: Home Missions Council, 1930), p. 25.

3. Carey McWilliams, *North From Mexico: The Spanish Speaking People of the United States* (Philadelphia: J. P. Lippincott, 1949), p. 206.

4. Frederick Simpich, "The Little Brown Brother Treks North," *The Independent*, 116 (1924): 239.

5. Santa Ana Board of Education, minutes, 19 March 1928, p. 116.

6. Interview with Fred Aguirre, Placentia, California, 17 September 1987.

7. Suzanne Daley, "Panel urges U.S. to push for proficiency in English," *Santa Ana Register*, 6 May 1983. The Twentieth Century Fund was composed of "governors, corporate leaders and other prominent figures who make up the National Task Force on Education and Economic Growth."

8. "Unassimilated Illegal Immigrants Imperil Society, Lamm Tells Panel," *Los Angeles Times*, 30 May 1986.

9. On the social consequences of NAFTA see David Bacon, "How US Policies Fueled Mexico's Great Migration," *The Nation*, 4 January 2012.

10. Ira Mehlman, "Tax Ledgers Will Never Balance," *Los Angeles Times*, 9 August 1994.

11. Ramon McLeod, "Study finds immigrants receive more welfare benefits," *Orange County Register*, 8 April 1995.

12. Patrick J. McDonnell, "Immigration Study Urges New Curbs and Criteria," *Los Angeles Times*, 15 September 1997.

13. Marion Lloyd, "Mexican Farms Go to Seed under NAFTA," *Orange County Register*, 1 December 2002.

14. Victor Quintana, "Why the Mexican Rural Sector Can't Take it Anymore," in Gilbert Gonzalez, et al., eds., *Labor, Versus Empire: Race, Gender and Migration* (New York: Routledge, 2004), p. 256; Peter S. Goodman, "In Mexico, 'People Do Really Want to Stay': Chicken Farmers Fear U.S. Exports Will Send More Workers North for Jobs," *Washington Post*, 7 January 2007.

15. John Warnock, "Who Benefits from the Free Trade Agreements?" *Z Magazine*, 23 April 2001. Warnock is a retired political economist at Regina University, Canada.

16. Maria A. Jimenez, "Humanitarian Crisis: Migrant Deaths at the U.S.-Mexico Border," ACLU of San Diego and Imperial Counties, 1 October 2009, p. 8.

17. Carol Masciola, Augustine Gurza and Jeff Kramer, "Migrant-camp attack stirs fear, anger," *Orange County Register*, 15 August 1994.

18. Nancy Cleeland, "Immigration Foes Forming Joint Front," *Los Angeles Times*, 11 September 1997.

19. Tom Gorman, "Up in Arms at Mexico Border," *Los Angeles Times*, 8 December 2002.

20. Terry McCarthy, "Stalking on Day Laborers," *Time*, 28 November 2005.

21. "Prop. 187 Approved in California," *Migration News*, December 1994, Vol. 1, no. 11.

22. "Va. Considers Ban on Illegal Immigrants at Colleges," *Los Angeles Times*, 6 February 2004.

23. Warren Vieth, GOP Faction Wants to Change 'Birthright Citizenship' Policy," *Los Angeles Times*, 10 December 2005.

24. David Kelly, "Colorado Activists Push Immigration Initiative," *Los Angeles Times*, 13 March 2005.

25. Ananda Shorey, "Arizona to Deny Some Benefits to Illegals," Washingtonpost.com, accessed December 22, 2004.

26. See Devin Burghart and Leonard Zeskind, Beyond Fair: The Decline of the Established Anti-Immigrant Organizations and the Rise of Tea Party Nativism, Special Report. Kansas City: Institute for Research and Education on Human Rights.

27. Alia Beard Rau, "ACLU: Pearce emails prove SB1070 was racially motivated," *The Arizona Republic*, 19 July 2012.

28. Ann Morese, "Arizona's Immigration Enforcement Laws," National Conference of State Legislatures, 28 July 2011. The Colorado legislature also brought forward a similar, if not identical law. See also David Kelly, "Colorado Activists Push Immigration Initiative," *Los Angeles Times*, 13 March 2005.

29. Jerry Gonzalez, "HB 87, Georgia's Arizona-Style Law, Is Not About Race?" NewsTaco.com, 16 September 2011.

30. "2,500 protesters rally for repeal of immigration law," Montgomeryadvertiser.com, http://www.montgomeryadvertiser.com/fdp/?/unique=12348502107. Greg Asbed and Sean Sellers, "The High Cost of Immigration Laws," *The Nation*, 11 October 2011.

31. Julianne Hing, "5 Ways Alabama's New Anti-Immigrant Law is Even Worse than Arizona's SB 1070," *AlterNet*, 24 June 2011.

32. Pamela Constable, "Alabama Law Drives Out Illegal Immigrants, With Unexpected Consequences," *The Washington Post,* 18 June 2012.

33. Pili Tobar, "Ten Things to Know About Alabama's New Immigration Law," *America's Voice,* 18 October 2011.

34. Julia Preston, "Immigration Ruling Leaves Issues Unresolved," *New York Times,* 26 June 2012.

35. Devin Burghart and Leonard Zeskind, op. cit.

36. Miguel Perez, "The Latino Clock is Irreversible," *North County Times,* 2 September 2011.

37. "Bilingual Material in Libraries Draws Some Criticism," *New York Times,* 5 September 2005.

38. Patrick J. Buchanan, *State of Emergency: The Third World Invasion and Conquest of America* (New York: St. Martins Press, 2006).

39. Samuel P. Huntington, "The Hispanic Challenge," *Foreign Policy* (May-June 2004).

40. Quoted in Patrick Buchanan, op cit, 136.

41. Damien Cave, "American Children, Now Struggling to Adjust to Life in Mexico," *New York Times,* 16 June 2012.

42. Adriana Gomez Licon, "US-Citizen Children of Returned Mexican Migrants Lose Right to School, Health Care in Mexico," *Associated Press,* 18 July 2012.

43. Seth Freed Wessler, "Thousands of Kids Lost from Parents in U.S. Deportation System," *ColorLines,* 2 November 2011.

44. Alberto Arce, "Deportation Stay Comes Late for Some Immigrants," *Orange County Register,* 18 June 2012.

45. "Immigration Change to Ease Family Separations," Julia Preston, *New York Times,* 2 January 2013.

46. See Juan Gonzalez, *Harvest of Empire: A History of Latinos in America* (New York: Penguin Books, 2000); Gilbert Gonzalez and Raul Fernandez, *A Century of Chicano History: Empire, Nations and Migration* (New York: Routledge, 2003); and David Bacon, "How US Policies Fueled Mexico's Great Migration," *The Nation*, 4 January 2012.

47. Eduardo Porter, "Who Will Work the Farms?" *New York Times*, 23 March 2006.

48. Jesse McKinley and Julia Preston, "Farmers Oppose G.O.P. Bill on Immigration," *New York Times*, 30 July 2011; on a new contract labor program see: Julia Preston, "Lawmaker Offers Plan to Lure Migrant Farm Workers," *New York Times*, 8 September 2011.

49. Christopher Goffard, Esmeralda Bermudez and Melissa Leu, "Elation and Uncertainty," *Los Angeles Times*, 16 June 2012; also see Julia Preston and John H. Cushman, Jr., "Obama to Permit Young Migrants to Remain in U.S.," *New York Times*, 16 June 2012.

50. Christopher Goffard, op cit.

51. Kathleen Hennesey, "As the Rich-Poor Gap Widens, So Does the Debate About What it Means," *Los Angeles Times*, 29 November 2011.

52. Joseph E. Stiglitz, "Inequality of the 1%, by the 1%, for the 1%," *Vanity Fair*, May 2011.

53. Jeffery Passel and D'Vera Cohn, "Unauthorized Immigrant Population: National and State Trends," PEW Hispanic Center, 1 February 2011.

54. Anthony Cody, "Confronting the Inequality Juggernaut: A Q&A with Jonathan Kozol," *Teacher Blogs*, 18 July 2011.

55. Dan Barry, "Legacy of School Segregation Endures, Separate but Legal," *New York Times*, 30 September 2007.

56. Julian Weinglass, "For Equality's Sake, the SAT should be Abolished," *Los Angeles Times*, 24 January 2000.

57. Cody, op cit.

58. Sabrina Tavernise, "Education Gap Grows Between Rich and Poor, Studies Say," *New York Times*, 9 February 2012.

59. Kayla Webley, "The Achievement Gap: Why Hispanic Students Are Still Behind," *Time*, 23 June 2011.

60. Stephan Caesar and Teresa Watanabe, "Education Takes a Beating Nationwide," *Los Angeles Times*, 31 July 2011.

61. Jennifer Medina, "California Cuts Threaten the Status of Universities," *New York Times*, 1 June 2012.

62. Walter Hamilton, "Student Loan Blues: More Americans Can't Get on with Their Lives Because They're Paying for College after Graduation," *Los Angeles Times*, 13 May 2012.

63. Shannon Bond and Matt Kennard, "Funding Woes Sap Quality of US Education," *Financial Times*, 28 September 2011.

64. Ibid.

65. Walter Hamilton, op. cit.

66. "Education: Borrowing by students on the rise," *Los Angeles Times*, 18 July 2012.

67. Tamar Lewin, "College May Become Unaffordable for Most in U.S.," *New York Times*, 3 December 2008.

68. "Wealth Gaps Rise to Record Highs Between Whites, Blacks and Hispanics," Pew Research Center, Social and Demographic Trends, 26 July 2011, p. 1. "Household wealth is the accumulated sum of assets (houses, cars, savings and checking accounts, stocks and mutual funds, retirement accounts, etc.) minus the sum of debt (mortgages, auto loans, credit card debt, etc.)," p. 4.

69. Eric Kelderman, "As State Funds Dry Up, Many Community Colleges Rely More on Tuition Than on Taxes to Get By," *The Chronicle of Higher Education*, 6 February 2011.

70. Tamar Lewin, "College Costs Keep Rising, Report Says," *New York Times*, 21 October 2009.

71. David Moltz, " 'Triage' Funding for Community Colleges," *Inside Higher Ed*, 31 March 2011.

72. Carla Rivera, "California Community Colleges to Slash Enrollment, Classes," *Los Angeles Times*, 31 March 2011.

73. Lee Romney, "Report finds City College of San Francisco riddled with problems," *Los Angeles Times*, 15 July 2012.

74. Carla Rivera, "Summer-School Blues for College Students," *Los Angeles Times*, 19 June 2012.

75. Glendale Community College. http://www.glendale.edu/index.aspx?page=167

76. Carla Rivera, "Santa Monica College students protest summer fees," *Los Angeles Times*, 4 April 2012.

77. Carla Rivera, "Santa Monica to offer two-tier course pricing," *Los Angeles Times*, 14 March 2012.

78. "Students Pepper-Sprayed at Santa Monica College Protest," *Los Angeles Times*, 3 April 2012.

79. Coalition of the Academic Workforce, A Portrait of Part-Time Faculty Members: A Summary of Findings on Part-Time faculty Respondents to the Coalition on Academic Workforce Survey of Contingent Faculty Members and Instructors (2012), p. 5.

80. Karen Fischer, "Admissions Offers to Foreign Students at U.S. Graduate Schools Climb at Faster Pace," *The Chronicle of Higher Education*, 16 August 2011.

81. Stephanie Siek, "The Dismantling of Mexican American Studies in Tucson Schools," CNN, 22 January 2012.

82. Ibid.

83. Julianne Hing, "Tucsons Ousted Mexican American Studies Director Speaks—The Fight's Not Over," *ColorLines*, 8 May 2012.

Introduction: Background to Segregation

1. Robert F. Drinan, "The Administration and Civil Rights: The First Thousand Days," *America*, 24 September 1983.

2. James Weinstein, *The Corporate Ideal in the Liberal State* (Boston: Beacon, 1968), xiv.

3. Clarence Karier, *Shaping the American Educational State, 1900 to the Present* (New York: Free Press, 1975), pp. 8, 9.

4. Gilbert G. Gonzalez, *Progressive Education: A Marxist Interpretation* (Minneapolis, Minn.: Marxist Educational Press, 1982). See also Meyer Weinberg, *A Chance to Learn: A History of Race and Education in the United States* (Cambridge: Cambridge University Press, 1979); and James Weinstein, *The Corporate Ideal in the Liberal State, 1900–1918* (Boston: Beacon, 1968).

5. See Gonzalez, *Progressive Education*. See also "Public Education and Its Function within the Chicano Communities, 1910–1930" (Ph.D. diss., University of California, Los Angeles, 1974).

6. See Karier, *Shaping the American Educational State*, p. 5. "A preponderance of evidence seems to indicate that the major social philosophy of many of the corporate and educational leaders (during the Progressive reform era) was largely pragmatic, reflecting a good deal of John Dewey's instrumentalism." See also Gonzalez, *Progressive Education*.

7. Leo Grebler, Joan W. Moore, and Ralph C. Guzman, *The Mexican American People* (New York: Free Press, 1970), p. 64.

8. Annie S. Reynolds, *The Education of Spanish-Speaking Children in Five Southwestern States,* United States Department of the Interior Office of Education Bulletin no. 11 (Washington, D.C.: U.S. Government Printing Office), p. 7.

9. Jose Hernandez Alvarez, "A Demographic Profile of the Mexican Immigration to the United States, 1910–1950," *Journal of Inter-American Studies* 8 (July 1966): 488.

10. "Increase of Mexican Labor in Certain Industries in the United States," *Monthly Labor Review* 37 (July 1933): 82.

11. Mario Barrera, *Race and Class in the Southwest* (Notre Dame, Ind.: University of Notre Dame Press, 1979), p. 77.

12. Ibid., p. 78.

13. Fuller Roden, "Occupation of the Mexican Born Population of Texas, New Mexico, and Arizona," *American Statistical Association Journal* 23 (March 1928): 145.

14. Examples of racial stereotyping abound in the literature of the period. For example,

Their conversation shows an apathy and a lack of expectation that anyone will understand them. They worship and imitate authority. A certain group loyalty exists but is not coherent. In fact, they desire nothing so much as to be let alone to indulge in a liberty that often becomes license after they take their first drink. . . . The chief amusements of the young men are smoking, drinking and sex. . . . The above is just a hint of the real problem of a Mexican town.

Jay Newton Holliday, "A Study of Non-Attendance in Miguel Hidalgo School of Brawley, California" (Master's thesis, University of Southern California, 1935)

Other works containing similar views are Merton E. Hill, *The Develop-ment of an Americanization Program* (Ontario, Calif.: Board of Trustees of the Chaffey Union High School and the Chaffey Junior College, 1928; Kimball Young, *Mental Differences in Certain Immigrant Groups,* Univer-sity of Oregon Publication 1, no. 11 (1922); and Edward Everett Davis, *A Report on Illiteracy in Texas,* University of Texas Bulletin no. 2328 (July 1923).

15. T. Wilson Longmore and Homer L. Hitt, "A Demographic Analysis of First and Second Generation Mexican Population," *Southwestern Social Science Quarterly* 24 (September 1943): 145.

16. Ibid.

17. Paul S. Taylor, *An American-Mexican Frontier, Nueces County, Texas* (Chapel Hill: The University of North Carolina Press, 1934), p. 192.

18. As quoted in Mary M. Peters, "The Segregation of Mexican Amer-ican Children in the Elementary Schools of California. Its Legal and Administrative Aspects" (Master's thesis, University of California, Los Angeles, 1948), p. 37.

19. Guadalupe San Miguel, Jr., "From a Dual to a Tri-Partite School System," *Integrated Education* 17, nos. 5–6 (1980).

20. Studies that focus upon regional factors include Ward Leis, "The Status of Education for Mexican Children in Four Border States" (Master's thesis, University of Southern California, 1934), pp. 23–24; and Charles Wollenberg, *California Historical Quarterly* 53, no. 4 (1979); also, Thomas P. Carter and Roberto D. Segura, *Mexican Americans in the Schools: A Decade of Change* (New York: College Entrance Board, 1979); and Irving G. Hendrick, *The Education of Non-Whites in California, 1849–1970* (San Francisco, Calif.: R & E Research Associates, Inc., 1977).

21. Gonzalez, "System of Public Education and its Function within the Chicano Communities," (Ph.D. diss., University of California, Los Angeles, 1974).

22. See Hill, *Development of an Americanization Program;* also Helen Walker, "The Conflict of Cultures in First Generation Mexicans in Santa Ana, California" (Master's thesis, University of Southern California, 1928).

23. See Charles Wollenberg, "Mendez vs. Westminster: Race, Nationality and Segregation in California Schools"; also, Gonzalez, "Racism, Education and the Mexican Community in Los Angeles, 1920–1930," *Societas* 4, no. 1 (1974).

24. Charles Clifford Carpenter, "A Study of Segregation versus Non-Segregation of Mexican Children" (Master's thesis, University of Southern California, 1935), p. 152.

25. Gonzalez, "System of Public Education." Virgil E. Strickland and George Sanchez summarized a survey of ten school systems, and found, in part, that the "physical facilities, equipment and instructional materials in the schools for Spanish-name children were found to be generally inferior and inadequate as compared to those existing in the Anglo schools." As quoted in Strickland and Sanchez, "Spanish-Name Spells Discrimination," *The Nation's Schools* (January 1948): 23.

26. Katherine Hollier Meguire, "Educating the Mexican Child in the Elementary School" (Master's thesis, University of Southern California, 1938), p. 64.

27. Pauline R. Kibbe, *Latin Americans in Texas* (Albuquerque: University of New Mexico Press, 1946), pp. 98–99.

28. Meyer Weinberg, *A Chance to Learn. A History of Race and Education in the United States* (Cambridge: Cambridge University Press, 1977), p. 166.

29. California Education Code Sections 8003 and 8004 provided the basis for "separate schools for Indian children, excepting children who are wards of the United States Government and children of all other Indians who are descendants of the original American Indians of the

United States, and for children of Chinese, Japanese or Mongolian parentage," and "when separate schools were established . . . the Indian children or children of Chinese, Japanese or Mongolian parentage shall not be admitted to any other school." As quoted in Charles Wollenberg, "Mendez vs. Westminster." Ibid., p. 318.

30. Strickland and Sanchez, "Spanish-Name Spells Discrimination," p. 22.

31. Grace C. Stanley, "Special Schools for Mexicans," *The Survey* 45 (15 September 1920): 714.

32. Carpenter, "Segregation versus Non-Segregation," p. 1.

33. Arizona State Department of Education. *Course of Study for Elementary Schools of Arizona,* Bulletin no. 13 (1939), p. 26.

34. Hill, "Development of an Americanization Program," p. 107.

35. Gladine Bowers, "Mexican Education in East Donna," *Texas Outlook* 15, no. 3 (1931): 30.

36. Stanley, "Special Schools for Mexicans," p. 715.

37. "Defense Opens in Desegregation Case," *Fullerton Daily News,* 11 July 1945.

38. "Dismissal of Segregation Charges Denied," *Orange Daily News,* 11 July 1945.

39. Stanley, "Special Schools for Mexicans," p. 714.

40. Emma Raybold, "Brotherization," *Los Angeles School Journal* 8, no. 9 (2 November 1925): 19.

41. Marguerite W. Hill, "A Proposed Guidance Program for Mexican Youth in the Junior High School" (Master's thesis, Claremont College, 1945), p. 65.

42. Florence Gordon Mason, "A Case Study of Thirty Adolescent Mexican Girls and Their Social Conflicts and Adjustments Within the School" (Master's thesis, University of Southern California, 1929), p. 6; also, Laura Lucille Lyon, "Investigation of the Program for the Adjustment of Mexican Girls to the High Schools of the San Fernando Valley" (Master's thesis, University of Southern California, 1933), pp. 34–37.

43. C. C. Trillingham and Marie M. Hughes, "A Good Neighbor Policy for Los Angeles County," *California Journal of Secondary Education* 18, no. 6 (October 1943): 343.

44. Hill, "Development of an Americanization Program," p. 106.

45. State of California. *Thirty-First Biennial Report of the Superintendent of Public Instruction* (Sacramento: California State Printing Office, 1924), p. 52.

46. Ibid.

47. Ibid.

48. See Francisco Balderrama, *In Defense of La Raza: The Los Angeles Mexican Consulate and the Mexican Community, 1929 to 1936* (Tucson: University of Arizona Press, 1982), pp. 55–72.

49. Stan Oftelie, "Murder Trial Obscured 1946 O.C. Integration Landmark," *Santa Ana Register,* 22 August 1976.

50. Lester H. Phillips, "Segregation in Education: A California Case Study," *Phylon,* no. 4 (1949): 407.

51. Jorge C. Rangel and Carlos M. Alcala in "Project Report: De Jure Segregation of Chicanos in Texas Schools," *Harvard Civil Rights-Civil Liberties Review* 7 (March 1972): 315, and Oscar Uribe, in "The Impact of 25 Years of School Desegregation on Hispanic Students," *Agenda: A Journal of Hispanic Issues* 10, no. 5 (September-October 1980): 18, pointed

out that de facto segregation in the Southwest remained widespread and today is on the increase.

Chapter 1. Culture, Language, and the Americanization of Mexican Children

1. Joseph Hraba, *American Ethnicity* (Ithaca, N.Y.: F. E. Peacock Publishers, Inc., 1979), pp. 32–33.

2. Charles H. Cooley, *Social Process* (New York: Scribner, 1926), p. 26.

3. Hraba, *American Ethnicity,* pp. 76–83.

4. Florian Znaniecki, "On Social Roles and Social Circles," in Marcello Truzzi, *Sociology: The Classic Statements* (New York: Random, 1971), p. 113.

5. Fred Wacker, *Ethnicity, Pluralism, and Race* (Westport, Conn.: Greenwood, 1983), p. 44.

6. Ralph H. Turner, Introduction to *Robert E. Park on Social Control and Collective Behavior,* edited by Ralph H. Turner (Chicago: University of Chicago Press, 1967), p. xi.

7. Morris Janowitz, *W. I. Thomas on Social Organization and Social Personality* (Chicago: University of Chicago Press, 1966), p. xlvii.

8. R. E. Park and E. W. Burgess, "Competition, Conflict, Accommodation, and Assimilation," in Truzzi, *Sociology,* p. 126.

9. Hraba, *American Ethnicity,* pp. 31–33.

Profound changes had been taking place in nineteenth-century Europe. Many countries there were being transformed from agrarian societies, with simple divisions of labor and largely rural populations, into industrial societies, with complex divisions of labor and growing urban populations. . . . Social evolutionists envisioned a transformation of the medieval bonds of blood and place, the basis of peasant life, into individual anonymity and rationally calculated human exchange in modern society. Modern people would relate to each other as commodities in marketplaces, each trying to maximize individual profit. Impersonal bureaucracy, as a symbol of this change, would replace the communal organization of life. Assimilationists read this legacy as reason for the eventual demise of ethnicity in modern American society.

10. See Mario Garcia, "The Americanization of the Mexican Immigrant," *Journal of Ethnic Studies* 6, no. 2 (1978).

11. Park and Burgess, *Introduction to the Science of Sociology* (Chicago: University of Chicago Press, 1969), p. 757.

12. Ibid., p. 128.

13. David Ward, *Cities and Immigrants: A Geography of Change in Nineteenth Century America* (New York: Oxford University Press, 1971), p. 51.

14. See Wacker, *Ethnicity, Pluralism, and Race,* pp. 16–17.

15. Ibid.

16. Hraba, *American Ethnicity,* p. 36.

17. W. I. Thomas, "Assimilation and Old World Traits Transplanted," in Janowitz, *W. I. Thomas,* p. 198.

18. Quoted by Thomas, "Assimilation and Old World Traits Transplanted," p. 204.

19. Maxine Sellers, "The Education of the Immigrant Woman, 1900–1915," *Journal of Urban History* 6, no. 3 (1978).

20. Ricardo Romo, *History of a Barrio in East Los Angeles* (Austin: University of Texas Press, 1984).

21. Garcia, "Americanization of the Mexican Immigrant."

22. Susan B. Dorsey, "Mrs. Pierce and Mrs. Dorsey Discuss Matters Before the Principal's Club," *Los Angeles School Journal* 6, no. 25 (5 March 1923): 59.

23. Merton E. Hill, *The Development of an Americanization Program* (Ontario, Calif.: Board of Trustees, Chaffey Union High School and Chaffey Junior College, 1928), p. 5.

24. Jessie Hayden, "The La Habra Experiment in Mexican Social Education" (Master's thesis, Claremont Colleges, Claremont, California, 1934), p. 191.

25. See Charles Clifford Carpenter, "A Study of Segregation versus Non-Segregation of Mexican Children" (Master's thesis, University of Southern California, 1935), p. 152.

Considering the above facts, (1) because of the great social differences of the two races, (2) because of a higher percentage of contagious diseases, (3) because of a higher percentage of undesirable behavior characteristics, (4) because of much slower progress in school, and (5) because of their much lower moral standard, it would seem best that:

Wherever numbers permit, Mexican children be segregated, and that teachers especially qualified be placed in charge of Mexican groups.

A special course of study be prepared to meet the needs of Mexican children.

26. Hayden, "The La Habra Experiment," p. 27.

27. Ibid.

28. H. F. Bradford, "The Mexican Child in Our American Schools," *Arizona Teacher Parent* 27 (March 1939): 199.

29. Leonard John Vandenbergh, "The Mexican Problem in the Schools," *Los Angeles School Publications* 11, no. 34 (14 May 1928).

30. E. E. Davis, *A Report on Illiteracy in Texas,* University of Texas Bulletin no. 2328 (Austin: University of Texas Press, 1923), p. 30.

31. James Kilbourne Harris, "A Sociological Study of a Mexican School in San Antonio, Texas" (Master's thesis, University of Texas, Austin, 1927), p. 13.

32. Lucy Claire Hoard, *Teaching English to the Spanish-Speaking Child in the Primary Grades* (El Paso: El Paso Public Schools, 1936), p. 9.

33. Simon Ludwig Treff, "The Education of Mexican Children in Orange County" (Master's thesis, University of Southern California, 1934), p. 1.

34. Katherine Hollier Meguire, "Educating the Mexican Child in the Elementary School" (Master's thesis, University of Southern California, 1938), p. 8.

35. Vera A. Chase, *Course of Study for Elementary Schools of Arizona.* State Department of Education Bulletin no. 13 (Phoenix: State Department of Education, 1939), p. 9.

36. Ibid., p. 10.

37. Ibid., p. 12.

38. Ibid., p. 13.

39. Betty Gould, "Methods of Teaching Mexicans" (Master's thesis, Los Angeles: University of Southern California, 1932), pp. 79–86.

40. Ibid., p. 57.

41. California Department of Education, *A Guide for Teachers of Beginning Non-English Speaking Children* Bulletin no. 8 (1932), p. 29.

42. Ibid.

43. Annie S. Reynolds, *The Education of Spanish-Speaking Children in Five Southwestern States* (Washington, D.C.: U.S. Department of the Interior, Office of Education), p. 22.

44. See, for example, Gould, "Methods of Teaching Mexicans," pp. 93–96.

45. "Education of Foreign Language Groups," *California Journal of Elementary Education* 5, no. 2 (November 1936): 67.

46. Herschel T. Manuel, *The Education of Mexican and Spanish Speaking Children in Texas* (Austin: University of Texas, 1930), p. 150.

47. Elma A. Neal, "Adapting the Curriculum to Non-English Speaking Children," *Elementary English Review* 8 (September 1929): 183.

48. Ruby Baughman, "Elementary Education for Adults," *The Annals of the American Academy* (1920): 161.

49. Laura Frances Murphy, "An Experiment in Americanization," *Texas Outlook* 23, no. 11 (November 1939): 23.

50. Chase, in *Course of Study for Elementary Schools of Arizona,* states, "If immigrant parents make no decided effort to learn and use English in their daily life, it is probable that they cling to the customs and traditions of their native land. Whenever this is true it has a deep significance in all educational problems concerning their children."

51. Manuel, *Education of Mexican and Spanish-Speaking Children in Texas,* pp. 126–27.

52. Ibid., p. 127.

53. "Neighborhood Schools," *Los Angeles School Journal* 10 no. 28 (21 March 1927): 14; also see Vandenbergh, "Mexican Problem in the Schools," p. 15.

54. Edith M. Bates, "The Non-Curricular Child in the Junior High School," *Los Angeles School Journal* 11, no. 3 (26 September 1927): 23;

also, Harry M. Shafer, "Americanization in the Los Angeles Schools," *Los Angeles School Journal* 7, no. 34 (12 May 1924): 31; and Mary Cunliffe Trautwein, "A History of the Development of Schools of Foreign-Born Adults in Los Angeles" (Master's thesis, Los Angeles: University of Southern California, 1928), p. 98.

55. Junius Meriam, *Learning English Incidentally: A Study of Bilingual Children.* Project in Research in Universities Bulletin, no. 15 (Washington, D.C.: Government Printing Office, 1938), pp. 14–15.

56. Laura Frances Murphy, "An Experiment in Americanization": 23.

57. Ibid.

58. J. T. Taylor, "The Americanization of Harlingen's Mexican School Population," *The Texas Outlook* 28 (September 1934): 38.

59. Ibid.

60. Arizona State Board of Education. *Course of Study for Elementary Schools for Arizona: Instruction of Bilingual Children,* Bulletin no. 13 (1939), p. 26.

61. Ibid.

62. Ibid., p. 42.

63. Pauline Jeidy, "First Grade Mexican-American Children in Ventura County," *California Journal of Elementary Education,* 15, nos. 3–4 (February-May 1947), pp. 200–201.

64. Gladine Bowers, "Mexican Education in East Donna," *Texas Outlook* 15, no. 3 (1931): 29.

65. California Department of Education, *Guide for Teachers,* p. 24.

66. Ibid., p. 2.

67. Ibid. See also "A Course in English for Non-English-Speaking Pupils," *State Department of Education Bulletin* 7, no. 3 (March 1932): 24.

Teach the words *hands, face, hair;* then one or two at a time introduce the words *water, wash, clean, dirty, soap.* Make clear the meaning of these words by a dramatization with a pan of water and the actual washing of dirty hands and a dirty face. Show thus the meaning of *clean.* Introduce the use of *soap* in this way: Talk much about "clean face," "clean hands," "clean hair." Begin early morning inspection of each child to impress the value of clean hands, face, etc. This appeals to the child's pride and slowly but surely produces desirable results.

68. Ibid.

CHAPTER 2. THE AMERICANIZATION OF THE MEXICAN FAMILY

1. Harry M. Shafer, "Americanization in the Los Angeles Schools," *Los Angeles School Journal* 7, no. 34 (17 May 1924): 31.

2. Maxine Seller, "The Education of the Immigrant Woman, 1900–1935," *Journal of Urban History* 6, no. 3 (1978).

3. Richard Griswold del Castillo, *La Familia: Chicano Families in the Urban Southwest, 1848 to the Present* (Notre Dame: University of Notre Dame Press, 1984).

4. Ricardo Romo, *History of a Barrio, East Los Angeles* (Austin: University of Texas Press, 1983).

5. Seller, "Education of the Immigrant Woman."

6. *The Course of Study for Elementary Schools of Arizona. Instruction of Bilingual Children,* Bulletin no. 13 (Phoenix: State Department of Education, 1939), p. 59.

7. Merton E. Hill, *The Development of an Americanization Program* (Ontario, Calif.: Union High School District, 1928), p. 75.

8. Pearl Idelia Ellis, *Americanization through Homemaking* (Los Angeles: Wetzel Publishing Co.), p. 3.

9. Ibid., p. 31.

10. Ibid., p. 6.

11. John E. Branigan, "Education of Overage Mexican Children," *Sierra Educational News* 12 (December 1929): p. 39.

12. Ibid.

13. Gladine Bowers, "Mexican Education in East Donna," *Texas Outlook* 15, no. 3 (March 1931): 29–30.

14. *Los Angeles School Journal* 10, no. 22 (7 February 1927): 58.

15. Ibid., p. 13.

16. Laura Lucille Lyon, "Investigation of the Program For the Adjustment of Mexican Girls to the High Schools of the San Fernando Valley" (Master's thesis, University of Southern California, 1933), p. 8.

17. Ibid., p. 49.

18. Ellis, *Americanization through Homemaking,* p. 15.

19. Ibid., p. 35.

20. Katherine Hollier Meguire, "Educating the Mexican Child in the Elementary School" (Master's thesis, University of Southern California, 1938), p. 122.

21. Ibid., pp. 117–18.

22. Ibid., p. 33.

23. Ibid., p. 41.

24. Hazel Peck Bishop, "A Case Study of the Improvement of Mexican Homes through Instruction in Homemaking" (Master's thesis, University of Southern California), p. 87.

25. Bishop, "Case Study," p. 91. This southern California teacher stated:

The fact that the Mexican girl marries young and becomes the mother in the home at the age the American girl is in high school means that the junior high school is trusted with her education for homemaker. For this reason, it seems to me that all or most of her junior high school training should be directed toward making her a better wife, mother and homemaker.

26. Amber Warburton, Helen Wood, and Marian Crane, M.D., *The Work and Welfare of Children of Agricultural Laborers in Hidalgo County, Texas,* U.S. Department of Labor, Children's Bureau Publication 298 (Washington, D.C.: U.S. Government Printing Office, 1943), p. 33.

27. Frances W. Doyle, "Questions on the Education of Mentally Retarded Minors in California," *California Department of Education Bulletin* 14, no. 1 (January 1950): 21.

28. Lyon, "Adjustment of Mexican Girls," p. 30.

29. Ibid., p. 31.

30. Ibid.

31. Ibid., p. 35.

32. Ibid., p. 54.

33. Grace Elizabeth Reeves, "Adult Mexican Education in the United States" (Master's thesis, Claremont Colleges, Claremont, California, 1929), pp. 21–22.

34. Ibid.

35. Ibid., p. 23.

36. Mary Cunliffe Trautwein, "A History of the Development of Schools for Foreign Born Adults in Los Angeles" (Master's thesis, University of Southern California, 1928), p. 58.

37. Ibid., p. 67.

38. Ruby Baughman, "Elementary Education for Adults," *Annals of the American Academy* 97 (January 1920): 103.

39. Beulah Amidon, "Home Teachers in the City," *Survey Graphic* (June 1926): 306.

40. Ibid.

41. Ibid.

42. Harry M. Shafer, "Americanization in the Los Angeles Schools," p. 31.

43. Alice Osborne McKenna, "Americanizing the Foreign Home," *Los Angeles School Journal* 9, no. 4 (28 September 1925): 13.

44. Vera Sturges, "Home Standards among Our Mexican Residents," *Los Angeles School Journal* 9, no. 4 (28 September 1925): 15.

45. *Course of Study for Elementary Schools of Arizona: Instruction of Bilingual Children,* Bulletin no. 13 (Phoenix: State Department of Education, 1939), p. 62.

46. Ibid.

47. Everett E. Davis, *A Report on Illiteracy in Texas,* University of Texas Bulletin no. 2328 (22 July 1923), p. 35.

48. Ibid., p. 50.

49. Anna Christine Lofstedt, "A Study of the Mexican Population in Pasadena, California" (Master's thesis, University of Southern California, 1922), Appendix A.

50. Ibid.

51. Reeves, "Adult Mexican Education," p. 43.

52. Ibid., p. 44.

53. Ibid., p. 48.

54. Ibid., p. 47.

55. Ibid., p. 49.

56. Ethel Richardson, "Doing the Things That Couldn't Be Done," *Survey Graphic* 56 (June 1926): 298.

57. Ibid., p. 299.

58. George B. Hodgkin, "Making the Labor Camp Pay," *California Citrograph* (August 1921): 354.

59. Ibid.

60. Ibid.

61. Ibid.

62. Ibid.

63. Baughman, "Elementary Education for Adults," p. 165.

64. Ibid.

65. Hodgkin, "Making the Labor Camp Pay," p. 354.

66. Ibid.

67. Ibid.

68. Ibid.

69. Ibid.

70. Ibid.

71. Mary S. Gibson, "Schools for the Whole Family," *Survey Graphic* 56 (June 1926): 303.

72. Ibid.

73. Interview with Arietta Kelly by B. E. Schmidt. California State University, Fullerton. Oral History Library Tape no. 48.

74. Reeves, "Adult Mexican Education," p. 45.

75. Interview with Arietta B. Kelly, California State College Fullerton Oral History Program. Oral History Tape no. 48. (Kelly's views on the strike were identical to those of the management; she had no problem in taking the side opposing her clientele.)

76. *The Thirty-Fourth Biennial Report of the California State Department of Education* (Sacramento: California State Printing Office, 1933), p. 68.

77. Merton E. Hill, *Development of An Americanization Program,* p. 10.

78. Ibid., p. 11.

79. Ibid.

80. Ibid., p. 12.

81. Jessie Hayden, "The La Habra Experiment in Mexican Social Education" (Master's thesis, Claremont Colleges, Claremont, Calif., 1934).

82. California State Department of Education, *Biennial Report* (1931–1932), p. 68.

83. See, for example, Stephen Jay Gould, *The Mismeasure of Man* (New York: Norton, 1981).

CHAPTER 3. INTELLIGENCE TESTING AND THE MEXICAN CHILD

1. Lewis Terman, "Intelligence and Its Measurement: A Symposium," *Journal of Educational Psychology* 12, no. 3 (March 1921). An interesting and informative review of the nature versus nurture debate is contained in Nicholas Pastore, *The Nature-Nurture Controversy* (New York: King's Crown Press, 1949). The nature advocates were generally conservative and avowedly antidemocratic. William Bateson, "a leading figure in the development of modern genetics," wrote, for example, the following:

The essential difference between the ideals of democracy and those which biological observation teaches us to be sound, is this: democracy regards class distinction as evil; we perceive it to be essential. It is the heterogeneity of modern man which has given him his control of the forces of nature. The maintenance of that heterogeneity, that differentiation of members, is a condition of progress. The aim of social reform must not be to abolish class, but to provide that each individual shall so far as possible get into the right class and stay there, and usually his children after him.

As quoted in Pastore, *Nature-Nurture Controversy,* p. 44.

2. Terman, *Intelligence Tests and School Reorganization* (Yonkers-on-Hudson, N.Y.: World Book Co., 1922), p. 13.

3. Gilbert G. Gonzalez, *Progressive Education: A Marxist Interpretation* (Minneapolis: Marxist Educational Press, 1982). See chap. 5, "The Rise of Intelligence Testing"; James K. Lawler, "IQ Theory and the Concept of Intelligence" in Marvin J. Berlowitz and Frank E. Chapman, eds., *The United States Educational System: Marxist Approaches* (Minneapolis: Marxist Educational Press, 1980); and Stephen J. Gould, *The Mismeasure of Man* (New York: Norton, 1981).

4. George I. Sanchez, "Group Differences and Spanish-Speaking Children—A Critical Review," *Journal of Applied Psychology* 16, (October 1932): 550.

5. Alfred Binet and Thomas Simon, *The Development of Intelligence in Children,* trans. Elizabeth S. Kite (Vineland, N.J.: Vineland School, 1916), p. 262.

6. Edward Lee Russell and Thomas Frederic Humiston, "Mental Ability in Children of White and Mexican Parentage," *California Journal of Elementary Education* 2, no. 4 (May 1934): 239.

7. Ibid.

8. Franklin C. Paschal and Louis R. Sullivan, "Racial Differences in the Mental and Physical Development of Mexican Children," *Comparative Psychology Monographs* 3, no. 4 (1925): 73.

9. Kimball Young, "Mental Differences in Certain Immigrant Groups," University of Oregon Publication 1, no. 11 (July 1922), p. 5.

10. Ibid., p. 3. Young's introductory statement to his 1922 study is a good example of what basically was a hollow genuflection to scientific objectivity.

The incentive to this study grew out of an attempt to discover if possible some of the causes of the difficulty in the education of children of South European ancestry in our public and further to see if a study of these children of immigrants might not throw some light on the larger question of adult immigration. The purposes of this research include: 1) to investigate by psychological tests and other measures the mental capacity of the South Italian, Portuguese and Spanish-Mexican children in certain public schools, and 2) to discover whether their inability to master the traditional American education is due: (a) to their alleged language handicap, or (b) to the lack of native mental endowment (as compared to that of "American" children of North European ancestry) which prevents their acquisition of the content of our curricula.

11. Helen L. Koch and Rietta Simmons, "A Study of Test Performance of American, Mexican, and Negro Children," *Psychological Monographs* 35, no. 5 (1928): 1. Simmons and Koch in the introduction to their 1928 publication stated,

At the present stage of the development of intelligence testing, one needs to be cautious in evaluating and interpreting tests. Our intelligence tests are apt to measure the influence of environmental factors as well as "innate abilities." Health, home conditions, school attendance, interest, cultural traditions, etc., are determining factors in intelligence test performance. When comparisons are to be made, furthermore, between different racial, national, and socio-economic groups, the problem is complex indeed. There are here not only a vast complex of associated factors to be taken into account, but also the variation of these factors from group to group.

12. Young, "Mental Differences," p. 8.

13. Thomas R. Garth, "A Comparison of the Intelligence of Mexican and Mixed and Full-Blood Indian Children," *Psychological Review* 33: 388–89. In a paper read before the American Psychological Association in 1922 he said,

In all experimental studies . . . it is the obligation of the experimenter to endeavor to measure the behavior of such somatic tendencies producing mind as may be alone due to tendencies peculiar to racial germ cells and not to environmental influences alone. If he was not able after strenuous effort to control all other factors so that the result may be said to be a measure of behavior due to the influence of germ plasm, no desire on his part to make a clean-cut statement should induce him to hasten to draw conclusions relative to race differences.

14. Thomas R. Garth, *Race Psychology: A Study of Racial Mental Differences* (New York: McGraw-Hill, 1931), p. vii.

15. Ibid.

16. O. K. Garretson, "A Study of the Causes of Retardation among Mexican Children in a Small Public School System in Arizona," *Journal of Educational Psychology* 19 (1928): 1.

17. See Mark Reisler, *By the Sweat of Their Brow* (Westport, Conn.: Greenwood, 1978).

18. Garretson, "Causes of Retardation," p. 40.

19. Thomas R. Garth, "The Industrial Psychology of the Immigrant Mexican," *Industrial Psychology Monthly* 1 (March 1926): 183.

20. Ellen Alice McAnulty, "Distribution of Intelligence in the Los Angeles Elementary Schools," *Los Angeles Educational Research Bulletin* 8 (March 1923): 91.

21. Garretson, "Causes of Retardation," p. 32.

22. Florence L. Goodenough, "Racial Differences in the Intelligence of School Children," *Journal of Experimental Psychology* 9 (1928): 395.

23. Paschal and Sullivan, "Racial Differences," p. 6.

24. Ibid., p. 6.

25. Ibid., pp. 12–13.

26. Ibid.

27. B. F. Haught, "The Language Difficulty of Spanish-American Children," *Journal of Applied Psychology* 15 (February 1931): 92.

28. Ibid., pp. 92–95.

29. Goodenough, "Racial Differences," p. 393.

30. Haught, "Language Difficulty," p. 95.

31. Ibid.

32. Garretson, "Causes of Retardation," p. 34.

33. Delmet, "Mental and Scholastic Abilities," p. 278.

34. Leo M. Gamble, "The Mexican: An Educational Asset or an Educational Liability?" *Los Angeles City Schools Educational Research Bulletin* 5 (December 1925): 10.

35. Walter S. Neff, "Socio-economic Status and Intelligence: A Critical Survey," *Psychological Bulletin* 35, no. 10 (December 1938): 752.

36. Sanchez, "Bilingualism and Mental Measures: A Word of Caution," *Journal of Applied Psychology* 18 (1934): 766.

37. Frank Boas, *Race and Democratic Society* (New York: J. J. Augustin, 1946), p. 19.

38. Boas, *Race, Language, and Culture* (New York: Macmillan, 1940), p. 45.

39. Ibid., p. 26.

40. Ibid., p. 34.

41. Natalie T. Darcy, "A Review of the Literature on the Effects of Bilingualism Upon the Measurement of Intelligence," *Journal of Genetic Psychology* 82 (March 1953): 51–52.

42. Sanchez, "Bilingual and Mental Measures," pp. 770–71.

43. Ibid., p. 771.

44. Hilding Carlson and Norman Henderson, "The Intelligence of American Children of Mexican Parentage," *Journal of Abnormal and Social Psychology* 45 (April 1950): 551.

45. Raymond B. Cattell, "A Culture-Free Intelligence Test I," *Journal of Educational Psychology* 31, no. 3 (March 1940): 161–63.

CHAPTER 4. TRAINING FOR OCCUPATIONAL EFFICIENCY: VOCATIONAL EDUCATION

1. Gilbert G. Gonzalez, "Racism, Education, and the Mexican Community in Los Angeles, 1920–1930," *Societas* 4, no. 4 (1974).

2. Gonzalez, *Progressive Education: A Marxist Critique* (Minneapolis: Marxist Educational Press, 1982), pp. 127–138.

3. California State Department of Education. *Vocational Education in California,* Bulletin of the California State Department of Education 14, no. 4 (October 1945), p. 7.

4. Ibid., p. 15.

5. See Gonzalez, "Racism, Education and the Mexican Community in Los Angeles."

6. Ibid., p. 98.

7. Ibid.

8. *Los Angeles' Educational Research Bulletin* 5, no. 10 (June 1926), p. 4.

9. See Gonzalez, "Educational Reform in Los Angeles and the Mexican Community," *Explorations in Ethnic Studies* 5 (July 1982).

10. *Los Angeles' High School Research Bulletin* 7, no. 5 (11 December 1922), p. 4.

11. *Los Angeles' Educational Research Bulletin* 4, no. 2 (25 January 1925).

12. Kimball Young, "Mental Differences in Certain Immigrant Groups," *University of Oregon Publications* 1, no. 11 (July 1922).

13. Ibid., p. 20.

14. Ibid., p. 64.

15. Ibid., p. 67.

16. Ibid.

17. Ibid.

18. Ibid.

19. Ibid.

20. Annie S. Reynolds, "The Education of Spanish-Speaking Children in Five Southwestern States," *United States Office of Education Bulletin,* no. 11 (1933).

21. Gonzalez, "Racism, Education, and the Mexican Community."

22. *Los Angeles' Educational Research Bulletin* 4, no. 2 (15 January 1925), p. 1.

23. Ibid., p. 7.

24. *Los Angeles' Educational Research Bulletin* 4, no. 5 (15 April 1925), p. 7.

25. G. Stanley, "Special Schools for Mexicans," *The Survey* (15 September 1920): 715.

26. Ibid.

27. Harry M. Shafer, "Tendencies in Immigrant Education," *Los Angeles School Journal* 9, no. 5 (5 October 1925): 10.

28. Ibid.

29. H. Frank Bradford, "The Mexican Child in Our American Schools," *Arizona Teacher Parent* 27 (1939): 199.

30. "The San Fernando School," *Los Angeles School Journal* 6 (4 June 1923): 23. At Lincoln High in Los Angeles, incoming Mexican students from the junior highs were regularly placed in slow-learner classes, where vocational work was emphasized. In 1939 the principal at Lincoln

High, Ethel Percy Andrus, considered such emphasis a help for the Mexican student, and said that the school had

an obligation to be definitely realistic in our treatment of these under-privileged folk because very shortly these young adolescents are to be thrown, vocationally dependent, upon an adult world. Therefore, in our vocational shops the aim is not so much to prepare youth for a definite trade for which there may be little or no vocational placement, because of prejudice against race or color, but to provide him with a variety of skills and techniques which may be gladly accepted by small shops or among his own people.

As quoted in Andrus, "Social Living Classes For the Underprivileged," *California Journal of Secondary Education* 14 (November 1939): 415.

31. Fred W. Ross to Mrs. Jean Trapnell, 9 February 1950, personal file.

32. Ward William Leis, "The Status of Education for Mexican Children in Four Border States" (Master's thesis, University of Southern California, 1931), p. 51.

33. Leis, "Status of Education," p. 72.

34. Harold J. Jones, "All Mexican School," *Sierra Educational News* 36 (1940): 17.

35. C. R. Tupper, "The Use of Intelligence Tests in the Schools of a Small City" in Lewis Terman, ed., *Intelligence Tests and School Reorganization* (Yonkers-on-Hudson, N.Y.: World Book Co., 1922), pp. 97–98.

36. Isabel Work Cromack, "Latin-Americans: A Minority Group in the Austin Public Schools" (Master's thesis, University of Texas, Austin, 1949), p. 26.

37. State Department of Education Bulletin, *A Course in English for Non-English Speaking Pupils* 8, no. 3 (March 1932), Austin, Texas, p. 46.

38. Merton E. Hill, *The Development of an Americanization Program* (Ontario, Calif.: The Board of Trustees of the Chaffey Union High School and the Chaffey Junior College, 1928).

39. Ibid., p. 110.

40. *Los Angeles Educational Research Bulletin* 6 (14 June 1926): 3.

41. State of California, Department of Education Bulletin. *Occupational Trends in California with Implications for Vocational Education,* no. 10 (15 May 1937), p. 5.

42. *Los Angeles School Journal* 5 (16 January 1922): 16.

43. *Los Angeles School Journal* 9 (15 February 1926): 41.

44. Ibid.

45. "The Junior Schools Organization and Administration," *San Antonio Public Schools Bulletin* 1, no. 1 (February 1924): 59.

46. G. A. Works, *Texas Educational Survey Report* 8 Austin: Texas Educational Survey Commission (1925): 143.

47. "Vocational Education," *Texas Educational Survey Commission Report* 7, Austin: Texas Educational Survey Commission (1924): 108.

48. "The Junior Schools Organization and Administration," *San Antonio Public Schools Bulletin,* p. 57.

49. Ibid.

50. "The Public Schools of San Antonio," *San Antonio Public Schools Bulletin* 2, no. 1 (1924), 70.

51. Los Angeles City Schools. *Schools and Classes For Exceptional Children: The Child With a Problem.* Los Angeles School Publication, no. 373 (1941), p. 20.

52. Ibid.

53. Los Angeles City School District, *Manual for Development Schools and Rooms* (September 1924), p. 9.

54. Ibid., pp. 11–12.

55. Los Angeles City Schools, *Schools and Classes for Exceptional Children,* p. 9.

56. Ibid., p. 12.

57. Ibid.

58. Los Angeles City Schools, *Fourth Yearbook of the Division of Psychology and Educational Research,* Los Angeles City School District (1931), p. 114.

59. Ellen Alice McAnulty, "Distribution of Intelligence in the Los Angeles Elementary Schools," *Los Angeles Educational Research Bulletin* 8, no. 7 (March 1929): 6–7.

60. Ibid.

61. Ibid.

62. Ibid., p. 116.

63. Ibid., pp. 115–16.

64. Los Angeles City Schools. *Third Yearbook of the Department of Psychology and Educational Research,* Los Angeles City School District School Publication, no. 185 (1929), p. 87.

65. Bradford, "Mexican Child," p. 199.

CHAPTER 5. THE EDUCATION OF MIGRANT CHILDREN

1. Examples of the neglect of historical analysis of Mexican migrant education include Thomas P. Carter and Roberto D. Segura, *Mexican Americans in School: A Decade of Change* (New York: College Entrance

Examination Board, 1979); Meyer Weinberg, *A Chance to Learn: A History of Race and Education in the United States* (Cambridge: Cambridge University Press, 1977), chap. 4, "Mexican American Children: The Neighbors Within"; also, Gilbert G. Gonzalez, "The System of Public Education and Its Function Within the Chicano Community, 1920–1940" (Ph.D. diss., University of California, Los Angeles, 1974).

2. James Kilbourne Harris, "A Sociological Study of a Mexican School in San Antonio, Texas" (Master's thesis, University of Texas, Austin, 1927), p. 35.

3. Gilbert G. Gonzalez, "Segregation in a Southern California City: The Legacy of Expansionism and the American Southwest," *The Western Historical Quarterly* 16, no. 1 (1985): 63.

4. See Carey McWilliams, *Ill Fares the Land* (New York: Barnes & Noble, 1942), pp. 299–329; and Mark Reisler, *By the Sweat of Their Brow* (Westport, Conn.: Greenwood Press, 1976), p. 4. On the subject of land tenure, Acuna writes that

farm monopolization in California reached high levels by the end of the 1920's with 37 percent of all large-scale farms in the United States operating in that state and 2.1 percent of California farms producing 28.5 percent of all United States agricultural products. However, the data on the concentration of production and ownership do not accurately reflect the degree of control within agriculture by relatively few farming enterprises, or by an association of enterprises. For example, only 7 percent of California farms employed 66 percent of all workers; 10 percent of all farms received 53 percent of all farm income. These same few farming enterprises also organized associations, such as the California Farm Bureau Federation, to extend their influence and control over legislation, wages, labor recruitment and distribution, prices, and production.

As quoted in Rodolfo Acuna, *Occupied America* (New York: Harper, 1981), pp. 207–14.

5. Reisler, *By the Sweat of Their Brow*, p. 87.

6. McWilliams, *Ill Fares the Land*, p. 230.

7. Ibid., p. 234.

8. Pauline Kibbe wrote in 1946:

Generally speaking, the Latin American migratory worker going into West Texas is regarded as a necessary evil, nothing more nor less than an avoidable adjunct to the harvest season. Judging by the treatment that has been accorded him in that section of the State, one might assume that he is not a human being at all, but a species of farm implement that comes mysteriously and spontaneously into being coincident with the maturing of the cotton, that requires no upkeep or special consideration during the period of its usefulness needs no protection from the elements, and when the crop has been harvested, vanishes into the limbo of forgotten things—until the next harvest season rolls around.

As quoted in Kibbe, *Latin Americans in Texas* (Albuquerque: University of New Mexico Press, 1946), p. 176.

9. Ibid., p. 174.

10. McWilliams, *Ill Fares the Land*, p. 239. McWilliams wrote:

Labor standards are simply non-existent in Texas nor is there any agency, governmental or otherwise, that can bolster up wage rates. With such an abundance of cheap labor, growers have naturally eliminated sharecroppers and tenants. . . . An official of a growers' organization told the [Texas State Employment Service] in 1938 that his group wanted a surplus for the season. "This," he said, "was quite beneficial in keeping the cost of harvesting at a minimum."

11. Ibid., p. 244.

12. Paul S. Taylor, *Mexican Labor in the United States. Dimmit County, Winter Garden District, South Texas,* University of California Publications 6, no. 5 (Berkeley: University of California Press), p. 372.

13. Seldon C. Menefee, *Mexican Migratory Workers of South Texas* (Washington, D.C.: U.S. Government Printing Office, 1941), p. 44.

14. Gilbert Ennis Hall, "Some Legal Aspects of the Education of Spanish-Speaking Children in Texas" (Master's thesis, University of Texas, Austin, 1947), p. 75.

15. Amber A. Warburton, Helen Wood, and Marian M. Crane, M.D., "The Work and Welfare of Agricultural Laborers in Hidalgo County, Texas," U.S. Department of Labor Children's Bureau Publication 298 (Washington, D.C.: U.S. Government Printing Office, 1943), p. 31.

16. Ibid., p. 31.

17. Herschel T. Manuel, "The Education of Mexican and Spanish-Speaking Children in Texas" (Austin: University of Texas, 1930) p. 72.

18. Ibid.

19. Ibid.

20. Ibid., pp. 76–77.

21. Warburton, Wood, and Crane, "Work and Welfare," p. 33.

22. Ibid., p. 35.

23. Ibid., p. 36.

24. Ibid., p. 37.

25. Menefee, *Mexican Migratory Workers,* p. xv.

26. McWilliams, *Ill Fares the Land,* p. 256.

27. Gilbert, "Some Legal Aspects," pp. 63–64.

28. Kibbe, *Latin Americans,* p. 93.

29. Ibid., pp. 94–95.

30. Herbert Phillips, "The School Follows the Child," *The Survey* 66, no. 2 (September 1931): 495.

31. State of California Superintendent of Public Instruction, Biennial Report for the School Years Ending 30 June 1923 and 30 June 1924 (Sacramento: California State Printing Office, 1924), p. 35.

32. Ibid.

33. Edna B. McCrae and W. K. Cobb, "The Education of Migrant Children in Ventura County," *The Western Journal of Education* 35, no. 12 (December 1929): 9.

34. Lillian B. Hill, "Study of Migratory Schools in California," *The Western Journal of Education* 37, no. 1 (January 1931): 9.

35. Herman A. Buckner, "A Study of Pupil Elimination and Failure Among Mexicans" (Master's thesis, University of Southern California, 1935), p. 31.

36. "Child Labor: Migratory Child Workers in California and Elsewhere." A summary of two papers delivered by George B. Mangold and William B. Hill, *Monthly Labor Review* 24, (September 1929): 557.

37. Cobb, "Retardation in Elementary Schools," p. 103.

38. Ibid., p. 14.

39. Ibid., p. 105.

40. Joy Newton Holliday, "A Study of Non-Attendance in Miguel Hidalgo School of Brawley, California" (Master's thesis, University of Southern California, 1935); Hogan, "A Study of the School Progress"; Cobb, "Retardation in Elementary Schools"; also, Bertha S. Underhill, "A Study of 132 Families in California Cotton Camps With Reference to

Availability of Medical Care," mimeographed (California State Department of Social Welfare, Division of Child Welfare Services, 1938).

41. Frank M. Wright, "A Survey of the El Monte School District," p. 32. See also Simon Ludwig Treff, "The Education of Mexican Children in Orange County" (Master's thesis, University of Southern California, 1934), pp. 31–33.

42. Ward William Leis, "The Status of Education for Mexican Children in Four Border States" (Master's thesis, University of Southern California, 1931), p. 41.

43. Paul S. Taylor, *Mexican Labor in the United States, Valley of the South Platte, Colorado,* University of California Publications in Economics 6, no. 2 (Berkeley: University of California Press, 1929), p. 115.

44. Ibid., p. 131.

45. Ibid., p. 132.

46. Seldon C. Menefee, *Mexican Migratory Workers of South Texas* (Washington, D.C.: U.S. Government Printing Office, 1941), p. x.

47. Ibid., p. 139.

48. Charles S. Gibbons and Howard M. Bell, *Children Working on Farms in Certain Sectors of the Western Slope of Colorado* (New York: National Child Labor Committee, 1925), pp. 30, 46.

49. Ibid., p. 41.

50. McWilliams, *Ill Fares the Land,* p. 124.

51. Bertram Mautner and W. Lewis Abbot, *Child Labor in Agriculture and Farm Life in the Arkansas Valley of Colorado,* Colorado College Publication, General Series, no. 164 (Colorado Springs: 1929), p. 29.

52. Ibid., p. 118.

53. Ibid., p. 146.

54. Taylor, *Mexican Labor in the United States*, p. 197.

55. Ibid., p. 155.

56. Ibid., p. 183.

57. Gibbons and Bell, *Children Working on Farms*, pp. 74–75, 83–84.

58. Ibid., p. 156.

59. Ibid., p. 158.

60. Menefee, *Mexican Migratory Workers*, p. 26.

61. Elizabeth S. Johnson, *Welfare of Families of Sugar Beet Laborers*, A Study of Child Labor and Its Relation to Family Work, Income, and Living Conditions in 1935, U.S. Department of Labor, Children's Bureau, no. 247 (Washington, D.C.: U.S. Government Printing Office, 1939).

62. Edgar G. Johnston, "The Education of Children of Spanish-Speaking Migrants in Michigan," *Michigan Academy of Science, Arts, and Letters* 32 (1946): 513.

63. Ibid., p. 514.

64. McWilliams, *Ill Fares the Land*, pp. 120–21.

65. Ibid., p. 119. McWilliams cited one study that demonstrated that after years of residence in Colorado, "Mexican sugar-beet workers remain sugar beet workers. . . . Since Mexican children are not receiving adequate educational opportunities, the inference is clear that they will tend to follow the same vocation as their parents."

CHAPTER 6. INTER-AMERICAN AND INTERCULTURAL EDUCATION

1. Joel Spring, *The Sorting Machine* (New York: McKay, 1976).

2. Rodolfo Acuna, *Occupied America* (New York: Harper, 1981).

3. Thomas P. Carter, *Mexican-Americans in the School* (New York: College Entrance Examination Board, 1979).

4. Meyer Weinberg, *Race and Class in American Education* (Cambridge: Cambridge University Press, 1977).

5. Charles Wollenberg, *All Deliberate Speed* (Berkeley: University of California Press, 1976), pp. 120–21.

6. Carey McWilliams, *North From Mexico* (New York: Greenwood, 1968), pp. 275–80.

7. J. Fred Rippy, "Historical Perspective" in James W. Wiggins and Helmut Schoeck, eds., *Foreign Aid Re-examined, A Critical Appraisal* (Washington, D.C.: Public Affairs Press, 1958).

8. Eugene Staley, *The Future of Underdeveloped Countries* (New York: Praeger, 1961).

9. See Gilbert G. Gonzalez, "Educational Reform and the University of Colombia," *Comparative Education* 17, no. 2 (1981); also, Gonzalez, "Imperial Reforms in the Neo-Colonies: The University of California's Basic Plan for Higher Education in Colombia," *Journal of Education* 164, no. 4 (1982).

10. Charles Frankel, *The Neglected Aspect of Foreign Affairs* (Washington, D.C.: The Brookings Institution, 1965), p. 25.

11. Phillip H. Coombs, *The Fourth Dimension of Foreign Policy: Educational and Cultural Affairs* (New York: Harper, 1964), pp. 26–27.

12. Nelson A. Rockefeller, "Education Is Removing Barriers," *Journal of Education* 127 (February 1944): 49.

13. Ibid., pp. 275–80.

14. Rockefeller, "Education Is Removing Barriers," p. 49.

15. Adolf A. Berle, Jr., "Race Discrimination and the Good Neighbor Policy" in R. M. McIver, *Discrimination and National Welfare* (New York: Harper, 1949), pp. 91–92.

16. Robin M. Williams, Jr., *The Reduction of Intergroup Tensions: A Survey of Research on Problems of Ethnic, Racial and Religious Group Relations* (New York: Social Science Research Council, 1947), p. 2, 3.

17. Paul S. Taylor, ". . . an End to the Beginnings. . . ," *Education for Cultural Unity,* Seventeenth Yearbook, California Elementary Schools Principals Association, Los Angeles (1945), p. 50.

18. Philip W. L. Cox, "Pan American Solidarity: Challenge and Solidarity," *The Educational Forum* 8 (May 1944): 417.

19. Talcott Parsons, "Racial and Religious Differences in Group Tensions" in Lyman Bryson, Louis Finkelstein, and Robert M. McIver, eds., *Approaches to National Unity,* Fifth Symposium of the Conference on Science, Philosophy and Religion in Their Relation to the Democratic Way of Life (New York: Harper, 1945), p. 195.

20. Ibid., p. 196.

21. Williams's book, *The Reduction of Intergroup Tensions,* is an excellent example of those works that stressed the control and domination of minority-nonminority relations. See also Bryson, Finkelstein, and McIver, *Approaches to National Unity.*

22. Joseph E. Weckles, "Spanish Speaking People in the United States Plans for Promoting Their Participation in the War Effort," *Interpreter Releases* 20, no. 10 (22 March 1943): 81–82.

23. Harold E. Davis, "Education Program for Spanish Speaking Americans," *World Affairs* 108 (1945): 44.

24. Ibid.

25. Ibid.

26. Ibid., p. 45.

27. Ibid.

28. Ibid.

29. Ibid. Davis suggested a program of vocational education that bore the trademarks of the future Alliance for Progress.

With proper occupational orientation, the latent productive capacity of their labor can be developed to a stage of increased efficiency through familiarity with the tools of the technological age. The first step, however, is to increase their productivity and usefulness at their present economic level by gradual improvement of agricultural systems, the development of varied handicrafts, and improvements in home life leading to the development of higher standards of living.

30. Ibid., p. 47.

31. Weckles, "Spanish Speaking People," pp. 81–82. Weckles explains:

In Chicago for example we have given grants-in-aid to two organizations. One is the Immigrants' Protective League which has received a grant enabling them to employ a Spanish speaking naturalization expert. We have also given a grant-in-aid to the Chicago Area Projects to enable them to establish two community houses in regions of heavy Mexican population. Resident directors will be installed in each of these community centers and will conduct such activities as adult education, Americanization courses, the teaching of leisure time activities to adolescents. . . .

In Texas we have given financial assistance to a project proposed by the University of Texas and the Hogg Foundation. The University plans to make use of its extension service and of its other connections throughout the State to help deal with local frictions and discriminations. . . .

In Albuquerque, New Mexico, we are helping to finance the Barelas Community Center which was built through the cooperative efforts of the City of Albuquerque, local citizens, and the WPA. This center is operating a nursery school, several clinics, a handicraft training program, playground activities, and other programs. A training course in social service work is also being given in cooperation with the University of New Mexico to several individuals of Spanish-American extraction. When they have been trained they will be available to work in other parts of New Mexico and the Southwest. (p. 82)

32. Davis, "Education Program for Spanish Speaking Americans," p. 44.

33. Rockefeller, "Education Is Removing Barriers"; Davis, "Education Program."

34. Holland Roberts, "What Is an American?" in *California Elementary Schools Principals Association Yearbook* 17 (1945): 15.

35. Helen Heffernan, "Inter-American Education in the War Effort," *California Journal of Elementary Education* 11, no. 1 (August 1942): 14–15.

36. Ibid.

37. Everett Ross Clinchy, Jr., *Equality of Opportunity for Latin Americans in Texas* (New York: The Arno Press, 1974), p. 140.

38. Thomas Sutherland, elected executive secretary of the commission in 1947, wrote:

The background of the Good Neighbor Commission must be traced to Hitler. Only the threat of German domination (of Latin America) brought U.S. leaders to the point of giving full attention to relations with Latin America. . . . At that point, 1938, a group of men in New York, using Nelson Rockefeller as a spokesman, submitted to President Roosevelt a memorandum recommending a special effort to improve relations with the Latin American countries. By 1940, this recommendation was undertaken by a Committee of the President, headed by Nelson Rockefeller, and called, finally, the Office of Inter-American Affairs. . . .

As quoted in Clinchy, Jr., *Equality of Opportunity,* pp. 140–41.

39. Hensley C. Woodbridge, "Mexico and U.S. Racism," *The Commonweal* 22 June 1945): 234–37.

40. See Alonso S. Perales, *Are We Good Neighbors?* (San Antonio, Texas: Artes Graficas, 1948).

41. Ibid., p. 145.

42. Ibid., p. 146.

43. Quoted in Clinchy, Jr., *Equality of Opportunity,* p. 147.

44. Ibid., p. 162.

45. Ibid., pp. 154–55.

46. Ibid., p. 164.

47. Ibid., p. 178.

48. Ibid., p. 2.

49. George I. Sanchez, *First Regional Conference on the Education of Spanish-Speaking People in the Southwest,* Inter-American Education Occasional Papers 1 (Austin: University of Texas Press, 1946).

50. Ibid., p. 16.

51. Sanchez, *Concerning the Segregation of Spanish-Speaking Children in the Public Schools,* Inter-American Education Occasional Papers 9 (Austin: University of Texas Press, 1951), p. 50.

52. Rockefeller, "Education Is Removing Barriers," pp. 49–50.

53. Ibid.

54. Davis, "Education Program," p. 48. In 1945 only fifteen such fellow-ships were awarded; thus the program proved minimal in its scope.

55. National Catholic Welfare Conference. Social Action Department, *The Spanish-Speaking of the Southwest and West* (Washington, D.C.: National Catholic Welfare Conference, 1944).

56. See Mary M. Peters, "The Segregation of Mexican Children in the Elementary Schools of California—Its Legal and Administrative Aspects" (Master's thesis, University of California, Los Angeles, 1948).

57. Los Angeles County Superintendent's *Bulletin* 3, no. 4 (May–June 1942): 6–7.

58. Los Angeles County, Office of the County Superintendent of Schools, *Monthly Bulletin* 2, no. 8 (May 1944): 9.

59. C. C. Trillingham and Marie M. Hughes, "A Good Neighbor Policy for Los Angeles County," *California Journal of Secondary Education* 18, no. 6 (October 1943): 344–45.

60. Ibid., p. 346.

61. Ethel Percy Andrus, "Workshop Studies Education of Mexican Americans," *California Journal of Secondary Education,* 18 (October 1943): 329.

62. Ibid., p. 330.

63. Byron England, "El Paso Develops Aids for Teachers of Bilinguals," *Texas Outlook* 29, no. 10 (October 1945): 42.

64. Ibid., p. 44.

65. See Davis, "Education Program."

66. Ellis M. Tipton, "The San Dimas Intercultural Program," *California Elementary School Principals Association Yearbook* 17 (1945): 94.

67. Ibid., p. 99.

68. *Education for Cultural Unity,* California Elementary Schools Principals Association Yearbook 17 (1945).

69. See, for example, "Hemispheric Solidarity," U.S. Office of Education, Education and National Defense Series, Pamphlet no. 13 (Washington: U.S. Government Printing Office), 1941.

70. See Charles Wollenberg, "Mendez vs. Westminster: Race, Nationality and Segregation in California Schools," *California Historical Quarterly* 53, no. 4 (1974): 317–22.

71. As quoted in Peters, "The Segregation of Mexican Children," p. 12.

72. McWilliams, *North From Mexico,* p. 279.

73. Seymour Martin Lipset and Aldo Solari, *Elites in Latin America* (New York: Oxford University Press, 1967), p. 5.

74. Ibid., p. 24.

75. Kibbe, *Latin Americans,* p. 273.

76. Florence Rockwood Kluckhohn, "Cultural Factors in Social Work Practice and Education," *Social Service Review* 25, no. 1 (March, 1951): 40.

77. Ibid.

78. Ibid., p. 44.

79. Sanchez, *Concerning the Segregation of Spanish-Speaking Children,* p. 16.

80. Kluckhohn, "Cultural Factors," p. 44.

CHAPTER 7. THE RISE AND FALL OF DE JURE SEGREGATION IN THE SOUTHWEST

1. Francisco Balderrama, *In Defense of La Raza: The Los Angeles Mexican Consulate and the Mexican Community, 1929 to 1936* (Tucson: University of Arizona Press, 1982), pp. 55–72.

2. Charles Wollenberg, *All Deliberate Speed* (Berkeley: University of California Press, 1976).

3. Thomas P. Carter and Robert D. Segura, *Mexican Americans in School: A History of Educational Neglect* (New York: College Entrance Examination Board, 1980).

4. Jessie Hayden, "The La Habra Experiment in Mexican Social Education" (Master's thesis, Claremont College, 1934), p. 1.

5. Simon L. Treff, "The Education of Mexican Children in Orange County" (Master's thesis, University of Southern California, 1934), pp. 23–24.

6. Annual Report of the Superintendent of Santa Ana School District, 8 July 1913, Santa Ana Board of Education, minutes, 8 July 1913.

7. A year later the superintendent recommended that "one room at each of the Lincoln, Roosevelt, and McKinley schools be set aside for Spanish [*sic*] children of the first and second grade, and that a room at Washington School be used for the older Spanish children. . . ." The recommendation was adopted. As quoted in Santa Ana Board of Education, minutes, 11 April 1914.

8. Ibid.

9. See Hazel Peck Bishop, "A Case Study of the Improvement of Mexican Homes Through Instruction in Homemaking" (Masters thesis, University of Southern California, 1937); also, Gonzalez, "The System of Public Education and Its Function in the Chicano Communities, 1910–1930" (Ph.D. diss., University of California, Los Angeles, 1974).

10. Gilbert G. Gonzalez, "Racism, Education and the Mexican Community in Los Angeles, 1920–1930," *Societas* 4 (Autumn 1974).

11. Santa Ana School District Board of Education, minutes, 8 November 1913.

12. Santa Ana Board of Education, minutes, 7 March 1916.

13. Ibid., 24 June 1918. On 15 July 1918 the minutes reported that the "Board looked over several locations for locating a Mexican School. It was agreed to lots #4 and #5 in Block 'B' of the Hawkins addition at $400, and also to offer $500 for the corner adjoining."

14. The text was included in ibid., 17 July 1918.

15. Ibid.

16. Ibid.

17. Ibid.

18. Ibid., 19 August 1918.

19. Ibid., 11 November 1918.

20. Ibid., 5 June 1919.

21. Ibid.

22. Ibid.

23. Ibid.

24. During the 1919–20 year, teachers at the Mexican School received an average of $960 per year, whereas teachers at three Anglo schools received an average of $1,040 per year. Ibid., 10 June 1919.

25. Ibid., 8 April 1924.

26. Osman R. Hull and Willard S. Ford, *Santa Ana School Housing Survey,* University of Southern California Studies, 2nd series, no. 6 (Los Angeles: University of Southern California, 1928), pp. 35, 36.

27. Santa Ana Board of Education, minutes, 13 March 1928.

28. Ibid., 27 March 1928.

29. Ibid., 10 April 1928.

30. Ibid., 8 May 1928.

31. Ibid., 22 May 1928.

32. Ibid.

33. Ibid., 29 January 1929.

34. Ibid., 26 April 1929.

35. Ibid.

36. From the foregoing discussion, the reader should now be aware that the Mexican schools were located within, as well as outside of, barrios. It is not quite clear why the Artesia school was situated in an Anglo area, although a few Mexican families lived in the district. The board seemed to use conflicting arguments when justifying Logan school in the Mexican barrio and Artesia school in the Anglo district. Apparently the principal reason was that it was less costly to bus Mexican children to Artesia, and Anglo children to outlying districts than to build a school in a Mexican area. In other words, the expense of a new Mexican or Anglo school was not justified, and thus, the Artesia school district was "burdened" with Mexican children. The Anglo community protested the action on several occasions but to no avail. Ibid., 30 April 1929.

37. Treff, "Education of Mexican Children," p. 34.

38. Santa Ana Board of Education, minutes, 13 September 1943. Ten years earlier, the superintendent reported to the Board: "... the Mexican

schools would be conducted on the basis of a minimum day, opening at 8:00 am and closing at 12:30 pm until the walnut picking season is over...." As quoted in Santa Ana Board of Education, minutes, 29 August 1933. See also Balderrama, *In Defense of La Raza.*

39. Santa Ana Board of Education, minutes, 12 February 1940.

40. *Mendez et al.* v. *Westminster School District of Orange County et al.,* 64 F. Supp. (San Diego, Calif.: 1946), p. 545.

41. Ibid.

42. Santa Ana Board of Education, minutes, 25 October 1943.

43. Ibid.

44. Ibid., 22 November 1943.

45. Ibid., 9 October 1944.

46. Much of the information relating to Gonzalo and Felicitas Mendez was obtained during a taped personal interview with Felicitas Mendez, 22 May 1986, in Fullerton, California.

47. As quoted in the *Westminster Herald,* 24 June 1972.

48. Charles Wollenberg, "Mendez vs. Westminster: Race, Nationality and Segregation in California Schools." *California Historical Quarterly* 53, no. 4 (1974): 325.

49. Gertrude Stoughton, "In California's Orange County Mexican-Americans Sue to End Bias in School Systems," *People's World,* 16 March 1945.

50. Ibid., p. 324.

51. Ibid., p. 326.

52. Wollenberg points out that the courts were swayed by the growing academic and professional trend opposing segregation. Segregation

limited the ability of the schools to assimilate Mexicans into the mainstream culture, that is, Americanization, the same goal as the segregationists. Wollenberg, "Mendez vs. Westminster," p. 324.

53. As quoted in Mary M. Peters, "The Segregation of Mexican-American Children in the Elementary Schools of California: Its Legal and Administrative Aspects" (Master's thesis, University of California, Los Angeles, 1948).

54. Ibid., p. 84.

55. Santa Ana Board of Education, minutes, 12 September 1946. "Mr. Ross" was Fred Ross, who was instrumental in community organizing in East Los Angeles during the forties and helped establish the Community Service Organization, an organization active in voter registration drives.

56. Ibid., 14 November 1946.

57. Ibid., 5 June 1947.

58. Ibid., 23 September 1947.

59. Guadalupe San Miguel, *Let Them All Take Heed: Mexican Americans and the Campaign for Educational Equality in Texas, 1910–1981* (Austin: University of Texas Press, 1987), p. 125.

60. Jorge C. Rangel and Carlos M. Alcala, "Project Report: De Jure Segregation of Chicanos in Texas Schools," *Harvard Civil Rights-Civil Liberties Review* 7 no. 2 (1972): 348–59. See also Guadalupe Salinas, "Mexican-Americans and the Desegregation of Schools in the Southwest: A Supplement," *El Grito* 4 (Summer 1971).

61. As was pointed out in chap. 6, cold war political developments influenced these movements and desegregationist efforts. This chapter also points out the importance of recognizing the impact of the international situation and of U.S. foreign policy upon domestic policy affecting the Chicano people. Whereas continental expansionist policy set the tone for Anglo-Mexican social relations in the nineteenth and the early

decades of the twentieth century, the expansionist international struggle for power at midcentury had the effect of highlighting antidemocracy within the United States, thus creating a need to reform and democratize (albeit in a limited way) minority/nonminority relations. However, that reformist trend did not consistently follow a path toward full equality. Instead, it deviated as reforms in the interests of minorities have been reduced or eliminated in the interests of an economic policy favoring the wealthy, corporations, and the military. Again, as in the past, international policy has deeply affected domestic policy toward the Chicano community, although not in the reformist sense as in the previous several decades.

CONCLUSION: CONTINUITY AND CHANGE IN THE EDUCATION OF CHICANO CHILDREN

1. "Unassimilated Illegal Immigrants Imperil Society, Lamm Tells Panel," *Los Angeles Times,* 30 May 1986.

BIBLIOGRAPHY

GOVERNMENT PUBLICATIONS, DOCUMENTS, AND REPORTS

Arizona. State Department of Education. "Instruction of Bilingual Children," *Course of Study for Elementary Schools of Arizona, Bulletin No. 13.* Phoenix, Ariz.: State Department of Education, 1939.

Bobbit, J. F. *The San Antonio Public School System.* San Antonio, Tex.: The San Antonio School Board, 1915.

Davis, Edward Everett. *A Report on Illiteracy in Texas.* Austin, Tex.: University of Texas Bulletin No. 2328, 22 July 1923.

Fitzgerald, N. E. *Texas Educational Survey Report,* vol. 7. Vocational Education. Austin, Tex.: Texas Educational Survey Commission, 1924.

Hemispheric Solidarity. *Education and National Defense Series Pamphlet No. 13.* Washington, D.C.: U.S. Office of Education, Federal Security Agency, 1941.

Hoard, Lucy Claire. "Teaching English to the Spanish Speaking Child in the Primary Grades." El Paso, Tex.: Board of Education, 1936.

Los Angeles City School District, Department of Psychology and Educational Research. *A Handbook for Teachers of Opportunity "B" and Adjustment "B" Rooms,* School Publication No. 132. Los Angeles, Calif.: Los Angeles City School District, 1 September 1926.

Los Angeles City Schools. *Background Information Related to the Mexican-American Child In-Service Training Manual, Los Angeles City Schools.* Revision of Instructional Services. Curriculum Branch, 1966.

———. *English for "Z" Pupils.* Course of Study Monographs no. 32, School Publication no. 99, Los Angeles City Schools, June 1924.

———. *First Annual Report.* Division of Psychology, Los Angeles City School District, 1919.

———. *Manual For Development Schools and Rooms.* Los Angeles City School District, September 1924.

Los Angeles City School District. *First Annual Report,* Department of Immigrant Education and Elementary Evening Schools, "Elementary Adult Education." School Publication no. 27, Los Angeles City School District, October 1919.

———. *Schools and Classes for Exceptional Children: The Child With a Problem,* School Publication no. 373, Los Angeles City School District, 1941.

———. *Third Yearbook of the Psychology and Educational Research,* School Publication no. 185, 1929.

Los Angeles County. Office of the Superintendent of Schools. *Monthly Bulletin.* Los Angeles County.

McGill, Nettie P. *Children in Agriculture,* U.S. Department of Labor, Children's Bureau, Bulletin, no. 187. Washington, D.C.: U.S. Government Printing Office, 1929.

Meriam, Junius. *Learning English Incidentally: A Study of Bilingual Children,* Bulletin no. 15, 1937. U.S. Office of Education.

National Unity Through Intercultural Education, Pamphlet no. 10. Education and National Defense Series. Washington, D.C.: U.S. Office of Education, 1942.

161 Federal Reporter, 2nd Series. "Westminster School District of Orange County et al. vs. Mendez et al., no. 11310. Circuit Court of Appeals, Ninth Circuit.

Report of the Survey of the Schools of Port Arthur, Texas. Institute of Educational Research. Teachers College, Columbia University. New York: Teachers College, Columbia University, 1926.

Reynolds, Annie S. "The Education of Spanish Speaking Children in Five Southwestern States," U.S. Office of Education, Bulletin no. 11. Washington, D.C.: U.S. Government Printing Office, 1933.

Southwest Texas State Teachers College. *First Report. Inter-American Teacher Education in the Southwest. School and Community Cooperation.* San Marcos: Southwest Texas State Teachers College, June 1945.

State of California, Department of Education. *A Guide for Teachers of Beginning Non-English Speaking Children,* Bulletin no. 8. San Francisco, Calif.: State Department of Education, 1932.

State of California, *31st, 32nd Bienial Report of the Superintendent of Public Instruction.* Sacramento: California State Printing Office, 1924, 1927.

State of California, Department of Education. "Vocational Education in California," *Bulletin of the California State Department of Education* 4, no. 4, October 1945. Sacramento: State Department of Education.

State of California. "Occupational Trends in California with Implications for Vocational Education," *Department of Education Bulletin,* no. 10, 15 May 1937.

Texas Department of Education. "A Course on English for Non-English Speaking Pupils," *Bulletin* 8, no. 3. Austin: The Department of Education, 1932.

Texas Education Agency. *Instructions and Regulations to All School Officers of County, City, Town and School Districts: Concerning Segregation of Pupils of Mexican or Other Latin American Descent.* Austin: Texas Education Agency, 1948.

———. *Statement, Discussion and Decision on the Segregation in the Del Rio Public Schools,* by the Texas State Superintendent of Public Instruction. Austin: Education Agency, 1949.

———. *State-Wide Survey of Enumeration, Enrollment, Attendance and Progress of Latin American Children in Texas Public Schools, 1945–1944.* Austin: Texas Education Agency, 1944.

Underhill, Bertha. "A Study of 132 Families in California Cotton Camps." Sacramento: California Department of Social Welfare, 1937.

U.S. Department of Health, Education, and Welfare. Office of Education. *Report of Regional Conferences on the Education of Migrant Children, 1952.* Washington, D.C.: Government Printing Office, 1952.

Warburton, Amber A., Helen Wood, and Marian M. Crane, M.D. "The Work and Welfare of Children of Agricultural Laborers in Hidalgo County, Texas." U.S. Department of Labor, Children's Bureau Publication no. 298. Washington, D.C.: Government Printing Office, 1943.

Weble, John N., and Malcolm Brown. *Migrant Families.* WPA Research Monograph no. 18, 1938.

Works, George A. *Texas Educational Survey Report* 8. General Report. Austin: Texas Educational Survey Commission, 1925.

UNPUBLISHED MASTER'S THESES AND DISSERTATIONS

Bishop, Hazel Peck Campbell (Mrs.). "A Case Study of the Improvements of Mexican Homes Through Instruction in Homemaking." Master's thesis, University of Southern California, 1937.

Broom, Perry M. "An Interpretative Analysis of Latin Americans in Texas." Ph.D. diss., University of Texas, 1942.

Buckner, Herman A. "A Study of Pupil Elimination and Failure Among Mexicans." Master's thesis, University of Southern California, 1935.

Calderon, Carlos I. "The Education of Spanish-Speaking Children in Edcouch-Elsa, Texas." Master's thesis, University of Texas, 1950.

Cameron, John William. "The History of Mexican Public Education in Los Angeles, 1910–1930." Ph.D. diss., University of California, Los Angeles, 1976.

Carpenter, C. C. "Mexicans in California: A Case Study of Segregation Versus Non-Segregation of Mexican Children." Master's thesis, University of Southern California, 1935.

Clinchy, Everett Ross. "Equality of Opportunity for Latin-Americans in Texas: A Study of the Economic, Social, and Educational Discrimination Against Latin-Americans in Texas, and the Efforts of the State Government on Their Behalf." Ph.D. diss., Columbia University, 1954.

Cobb, Wilbur K. "Retardation in Elementary Schools of Children of Migratory Laborers in Ventura County, California." Master's thesis, University of Southern California, 1932.

Cornelius, John Scott. "The Effects of Certain Changes of Curriculum and Methods on the Achievement of Mexican Children in a Segregated School." Master's thesis, University of Southern California, 1941.

Cox, L. M. "Analysis of the Intelligence of Sub-Normal Negro, Mexican and White Children." Master's thesis, University of Southern California, 1939.

Cromack, Isabel Work. "Latin Americans: A Minority in the Austin Public Schools." Master's thesis, University of Texas, Austin, 1949.

Doerr, Marvin Ferdinand. "The Problem of the Elimination of the Mexican Pupils from School." Master's thesis, University of Texas, Austin, 1938.

Farmer, William Andrew. "The Influence of Segregation of Mexican and American Children Upon the Development of Social Attitudes." Master's thesis, University of Southern California, 1937.

Gilbert, Ennis Hall. "Some Legal Aspects of the Education of Spanish-Speaking Children in Texas." Master's thesis, University of Texas, 1947.

Gillette, George Curtiss. "A Diagnostic Study of the Factors Affecting the Low Scores of Spanish-Speaking Children in Standardized Tests." Master's thesis, University of Southern California, 1941.

Gonzalez, Gilbert G. "The System of Public Education and Its Function Within the Chicano Communities, 1910–1930." Ph.D. diss., University of California, Los Angeles, 1974.

Gould, Betty. "Methods of Teaching Mexicans." Master's thesis, University of Southern California, 1931.

Harris, James K. "A Sociological Study of a Mexican School in San Antonio, Texas." Master's thesis, University of Texas, Austin, 1927.

Hayden, Jessie. "The La Habra Experiment." Master's thesis, Claremont College, 1934.

Hill, Marguerite W. "A Proposed Guidance Program for Mexican Youth in the Junior High School." Master's thesis, Claremont College, 1945.

Hogan, Milo Arthur. "A Study of the School Progress of Mexican Children of the Imperial Valley." Master's thesis, University of Southern California, 1934.

Holliday, J. N. "Segregated Schools." Master's thesis, University of Southern California, 1936.

Jensen, James M. "The Mexican-American in an Orange County Community." Master's thesis, Claremont Graduate School, 1947.

Kaderli, Albert Turner. "The Educational Problem in Americanization of the Spanish Speaking Pupils of Sugarland, Texas." Master's thesis, University of Texas, Austin, 1940.

Kaderli, James Nicholas. "A Study of Mexican Education in Atascosa County with Special Reference to Pleasanton Elementary School." Master's thesis, University of Texas, Austin, 1938.

Kienle, John E. "Housing Conditions Among the Mexican Population of Los Angeles." Master's thesis, University of Southern California, 1912.

King, John Randle. "An Inquiry into the Status of Mexican Segregation in Metropolitan Bakersfield." Master's thesis, Claremont Colleges, 1946.

Knox, William J. "The Economic Status of the Mexican Immigrant in San Antonio, Texas." Master's thesis, University of Texas, Austin, 1927.

Leis, Ward W. "The Status of Education for Mexican Children in Four Border States." Master's thesis, University of Southern California, 1931.

Lofstedt, Anna L. "A Study of the Mexican Population in Pasadena, California." Master's thesis, University of Southern California, 1922.

Lyon, Laura Lucille. "Investigation of the Program for the Adjustment of Mexican Girls to the High Schools of the San Fernando Valley." Master's thesis, University of Southern California, 1933.

McEwen, William W. "A Survey of the Mexican in Los Angeles." Master's thesis, University of Southern California, 1914.

Meguire, Katherine. "Educating the Mexican Child in Elementary Schools." Master's thesis, University of Southern California, 1939.

Mendenhall, W. C. "A Comparative Study of Achievement and Ability of the Children in Two Segregated Mexican Schools." Master's thesis, University of Southern California, 1937.

Merryweather, Rose. "A Study of the Comparative Ability of the Mexican and American Children in the Upper Elementary Grades." Master's thesis, University of Southern California, 1937.

Parsons, Jr., Theodore Williams. "Ethnic Cleavage in a California School." Ph.D. diss., Stanford University, 1965.

Peters, Mary. "The Segregation of Mexican American Children in the Elementary Schools of California: Its Legal and Administrative Aspects." Master's thesis, University of California, Los Angeles, 1948.

Randalls, Edwyna H. "A Comparative Study of the Intelligence Test Results of Mexican and Negro Children in Two Elementary Schools." Master's thesis, University of Southern California, 1929.

Reeves, Grace Elizabeth. "Adult Mexican Education in the United States." Master's thesis, Claremont College, 1929.

Reynolds, Evelyn Dolores. "A Study of Migratory Factors Affecting Education in North Kern County." Master's thesis, University of Southern California, 1932.

Sauter, Mary C. "Arbol Verde: Cultural Conflict and Accommodation in a California Mexican Community." Master's thesis, Claremont College, 1933.

Trautwein, Mary C. "A History of the Development of the Schools for Foreign-Born Adults in Los Angeles." Master's thesis, University of Southern California, n.d.

Treff, Simon L. "The Education of Mexican Children in Orange County." Master's thesis, University of Southern California, 1934.

Walker, Helen. "The Conflict of Culture in First Generation Mexicans in Santa Ana, California." Master's thesis, University of Southern California, 1928.

Wright, Frank M. "Survey of the El Monte School District." Master's thesis, University of Southern California, 1930.

Wueste, Gladys Riskind. "A Survey of Factors Relating to the Education of the Children of Migratory Parents of Eagle Pass, Texas." Master's thesis, University of Texas, August, 1950.

BOOKS AND MONOGRAPHS

Arizona Council for Civil Unity. *Close the Breach: A Study of School Segregation in Arizona.* Phoenix: Arizona Council for Civic Unity, 1949.

Balderrama, Francisco E. *In Defense of La Raza.* Tucson: University of Arizona Press, 1982.

Boas, F. *Race, Language, and Culture.* New York: Macmillan Publishing Co., 1940.

Bobbit, Franklin. *Curriculum-Making in Los Angeles.* Chicago: University of Chicago Press, 1922.

Bogardus, Emory S. *Essentials of Americanization.* Los Angeles: University of Southern California Press, 1919.

Bremeld, Theodore. *Minority Problems in the Public Schools—A Study of Administrative Policies and Practices in Seven School Systems.* New York: Harper and Brothers, 1946.

Brown, Francis J., and Joseph S. Roucels. *One America.* New York: Prentice-Hall, Inc., 1948.

Brown, Sara A., Robie O. Sargent, and Clara B. Armentrout. "Children Working in the Sugar-Beet Fields of Certain Districts of the South Platte Valley." *Colorado National Child Labor Committee.* New York: National Child Labor Committee, 1925.

Bryson, Lyman, Louis Finkelstein, and Robert M. McIver, eds. *Approaches to National Unity: Fifth Symposium of the Conference on Science, Philosophy and Religion.* New York: Harper and Brothers, 1945.

Carter, Thomas P., and Robert D. Segura. *Mexican Americans in School: A History of Educational Neglect.* New York: College Entrance Examination Board, 1970.

Cooke, Henry W. "The Teaching of International and Intercultural Understanding in the Public Schools of California." San Francisco: The International Center, 1946.

Coombs, Philip H. *The Fourth Dimension of Foreign Policy: Educational and Cultural Affairs.* New York: Harper & Row, Publishers 1964.

Davis, Edward Everett, and C. T. Gray. "A Study of Rural Schools in Karnes County." Austin: University of Texas, Austin, Bulletin no. 2246 (December 1922).

Ellis, Pearl I. *Americanization Through Homemaking*. Los Angeles, Calif.: Wetzel Publishing Co., 1929.

Frankel, Charles. *The Neglected Aspect of Foreign Affairs*. Washington, D.C.: The Brookings Institution, 1965.

Garcia, Mario. *Desert Immigrants: The Mexicans of El Paso, 1880–1930*. New Haven, Conn.: Yale University Press, 1981.

Garth, T. R. *Race Psychology*. New York: McGraw-Hill, 1931.

Gibbons, Charles E., and Howard M. Bell. "Children Working on Farms in Certain Sections of the Western Slope of Colorado." *National Child Labor Committee*. New York, 1925.

Gonzalez, Gilbert. *Progressive Education: A Marxist Interpretation*. Minneapolis: Marxist Educational Press, 1981.

Henrick, Irving G. *The Education of Non-Whites in California, 1849–1970*. San Francisco: R. and E. Research Associates, 1977.

Hill, Merton E. *Development of An Americanization Program*. Ontario, Calif.: Union High School District, 1928.

Kibbe, Pauline. *Latin Americans in Texas*. Albuquerque: University of New Mexico Press, 1946.

Kilpatrick, William Heard, and William Van Tel. *Intercultural Attitudes in the Making*. New York: Harper and Brothers, 1947.

Koch, H. L., and R. Simmons. "A Study of Test Performance of American, Mexican and Negro Children." *Psychological Monographs*, 35, no. 5 (1928).

Leyburn, James G. "World Minority Problems." *Public Affairs Pamphlet*, no. 132. New York: Public Affairs Committee Incorporated, 1947.

Linton, Ralph, ed. *The Science of Man on the World Crisis*. New York: Columbia University Press, 1945.

Little, Wilson. *Spanish Speaking Children in Texas*. Austin: University of Texas Press, 1944.

Locke, Alain. *When Peoples Meet: A Study in Race and Culture Contacts.* New York: Progressive Education Association, 1942.

MacIver, Robert M. *Discrimination and National Welfare.* New York: Harper and Brothers, 1949.

———, ed. *Group Relations and Group Antagonisms.* New York: Peter Smith, 1951.

Manuel, Herschel T. *The Education of Mexican and Spanish-Speaking Children in Texas.* Austin: University of Texas Press, 1930.

Manuel, Herschel T. "Spanish and English Editions of the Stanford-Binet in Relation to the Abilities of Mexican Children." *Bulletin No. 3532.* Austin: University of Texas, 1935.

Mautner, Bertram, and W. Lewis Abbott. "Child Labor in Agriculture and Farm Life in the Arkansas Valley of Colorado." *Colorado College Publication General Series,* no. 164 (1929).

McWilliams, Carey. *Ill Fares the Land: Migrants and Migratory Labor in California.* Boston: Little, 1942.

Myrdal, Gunnar. *An American Dilemma.* New York: Harper & Row, Publishers, 1962.

National Catholic Welfare Conference Social Action Department. *The Spanish-Speaking of the Southwest and West.* Washington, D.C.: National Catholic Welfare Conference, 1944.

Olmsted, Roger, and Charles Wollenberg, eds. *Neither Separate Nor Equal: Race and Racism in California.* San Francisco: California Historical Society, 1971.

Park, Robert E. *On Social Control and Collective Behavior.* Edited and with an introduction by Ralph H. Turner. Chicago: University of Chicago Press, 1967.

Pastore, Nicholas. *The Nature-Nurture Controversy.* New York: Kings Crown Press, 1949.

Perales, Alonso. *Are We Good Neighbors?* San Antonio: Artes Graficas, 1948.

Romo, Ricardo. *East Los Angeles: History of a Barrio.* Austin: University of Texas Press, 1983.

Sanchez, George I. "Concerning Segregation of Spanish-Speaking Children in the Public Schools." *Inter-American Occasional Papers IX.* Austin: Study of Spanish-Speaking People, University of Texas.

———. "The Equalization of Educational Opportunity—Some Issues and Problems." *University of New Mexico Bulletin Educational Series* 10, no. 1 (1 December 1939).

———. "First Regional Conference on the Education of Spanish-Speaking Children in the Southwest—A Report." *Inter-American Education Occasional Papers I.* Austin: University of Texas Press, March 1946.

Spring, Joel. *The Sorting Machine.* New York: David McKay Co., Inc., 1976.

Terman, Louis. *Intelligence Tests and School Reorganization.* Yonkers-on-the-Hudson, N.Y.: World Book Co., 1922.

Thompson, Wallace. *The Mexican Mind: A Study of the National Psychology.* Boston: Little, Brown and Company, 1922.

Tireman, Loyd Spencer. *A Community School in a Spanish-Speaking Village.* Albuquerque: University of New Mexico Press, 1948.

Tuck, Ruth D. *Not with the First, Mexican Americans in a Southwest City.* New York: Harcourt, Brace, 1946.

Vickery, William E., and Stewart G. Cole. *Intercultural Education in American Schools.* New York: Harper and Brothers, 1943.

Wacker, R. Fred. *Ethnicity, Pluralism, and Race Relations Theory in America before Myrdal.* Westport, Conn.: Greenwood Press, 1983.

Wiggins, James W, and Helmut Schoek, eds. *Foreign Aid Re-examined. A Critical Reappraisal.* Washington, D.C.: Public Affairs Press, 1958.

Williams, Robin M. "The Reduction of Intergroup Tensions: A Survey of Research on Problems of Ethnic, Racial and Religious Group Relations." *Bulletin No. 57.* New York: Social Science Research Council, 1947.

Winters, Jet C. "Report on the Health and Nutrition of Mexicans Living in Texas." *University of Texas Bulletin No 3127,* 15 July, 1931.

Wollenberg, Charles. *All Deliberate Speed: School Segregation and Exclusion in California Public Schools.* Berkeley: University of California Press, 1976.

Young, Kimball. "Mental Differences in Certain Immigrant Groups." *University of Oregon Publication* 1, no. 11 (July 1922).

Journal Articles

Albig, W. "Opinions Concerning Unskilled Mexican Immigrants." *Sociology and Social Research* 15 (September-October 1930): 62–72.

Altus, William D. "The American Mexican: The Survival of a Culture." *Journal of Social Psychology* 29, no. 2 (May 1949): 211–20.

Amidon, Beaulah. "Home Teachers in the City." *Survey Graphic* 56 (June 1926): 304.

Andrus, Ethel Percy. "Social Living Classes for the Underprivileged." *California Journal of Secondary Education* 14 (November 1939): 414–17.

———. "Workshop Studies—Education of Mexican-Americans." *California Journal of Secondary Education* 18, no. 6 (October 1943): 328–30.

Armour, D. T. "Problems in the Education of the Mexican Child." *Texas Outlook* 16 (December 1932): 29–31.

Austin, Mary. "Education in New Mexico." *New Mexico Quarterly* 3 (1933): 217–31.

Baughman, Ruby. "Elementary Education for Adults." *Annals of the American Academy* 97 (January 1920): 161–68.

Bogardus, Emory S. "Second Generation Mexicans." *Sociology and Social Research* 13 (January-February 1929): 276–83.

———. "The Mexican Immigrant and Segregation." *American Journal of Sociology* 36 (July 1930): 74–80.

Borrego, Eva R. "American Child with a Two Language Heritage." *National Elementary Principal* 25, no. 6 (June 1946): 32–5.

Bowers, Gladine. "Mexican Education in East Donna." *Texas Outlook* 15, no. 3 (March 1931): 29–30.

Bradford, H. Frank. "The Mexican Child in Our American Schools." *Arizona Teacher Parent* 27 (March 1939): 198–99.

Branigan, J. "Education of Over Age Mexican Children." *Sierra Educational News* 25 or 29 (December 1929): 25–29.

Brigham, Carl C. "Intelligence Tests of Immigrant Groups." *Psychology Review* 37 (1930): 158–65.

Broom, M. E. "Sex and Race Differences Discovered by Mental Tests." *El Paso School Standard* 16 (November 1938): 29–32.

Brown, Gilbert L. "Intelligence as Related to Nationality." *Journal of Educational Research* 5 (1922): 324–27.

Brown, Sara A. "Neglected Children of Migrant Workers." *Missionary Review of the World* 36 (23 July 1923): 515–20.

Burbeck, E. "Problems Presented to Teachers of Bilingual Pupils." *California Journal of Elementary Education* 8 (August 1939): 49–54.

Carlson, Hilding, and Norman Henderson. "Intelligence of American Children of Mexican Parentage." *Journal of Abnormal and Social Psychology* 45 (April 1950): 544–51.

Cattell, Raymond B. "A Culture Free Intelligence Test I." *Journal of Educational Psychology* 31 (March 1940): 161–79.

Clark, Adelle. "Fiesta in the Patio." *Texas Outlook* 27, no. 39 (October 1943): 39.

Coers, Walter C. "Comparative Achievement of White and Mexican Junior High Pupils." *Peabody Journal of Education* 12 (1934): 157–62.

Coindreau, Josephine. "Teaching English to Spanish-Speaking Children." *National Elementary Principal* 25, no. 6 (June 1946): 40–44.

Cole, Stewart G. "Towards Better Intercultural Education." *California Elementary School Principals' Association Yearbook,* 17 (1945): 110–41.

Cooke, Henry W. "The Segregation of Mexican American School Children in Southern California." *School and Society* 67 (5 June 1948): 417–21.

Coronel, Paul. "Underlying Philosophy of a Bi-Lingual Program." *Claremont College Reading Conference Yearbook* 10 (1945): 51–57.

Cox, Phillip W. L. "Pan American Solidarity: Challenge and Opportunity." *The Educational Forum* 8 (May 1944): 415–32.

Davis, Harold E. "Education Program for Spanish-Speaking Americans." *World Affairs* 108 (March 1945): 43–48.

Delmet, Don T. "A Study of the Mental and Scholastic Abilities of Mexican Children in the Elementary School." *Journal of Juvenile Research* 14 (October 1934): 267–79.

Deutsch, Martin E. "California's Part in Race Relations," *Education for Cultural Unity.* Seventeenth Yearbook, California Elementary School Principals' Association, Los Angeles, 1945, 11–13.

Dickerson, Roy E. "Some Suggestive Problems in the Americanization of Mexicans." *Pedagogical Seminary* (September 1919): 288–97.

"Education for Spanish American Children in San Antonio, Texas." *School and Society* 50 (23 December 1939): 824.

Edwards, N. "Segregation of Spanish-Speaking Children in Public Schools." *Elementary School Journal* 52, no. 6 (February 1952): 318.

England, Byron. "El Paso Develops Aids for Teachers of Bilinguals." *Texas Outlook* 29, no. 10 (October 1945): 42, 44.

Eyring, E. "Spanish for the Spanish Speaking Pupil in the United States." *Modern Language Forum* 22 (May 1937): 138–45.

Faltis, Joseph. "Understanding Our Students of Mexican Extraction." *California Teachers Association Journal* 47, no. 2 (February 1951): 11.

Freeman, Frank G. "Sorting the Students." *Educational Review* 68 (November 1924): 169–74.

Galarza, Ernesto. "The Mexican Ethnic Group." *California Elementary School Principals' Association Yearbook* 17 (1945): 34–35.

———. "Program for Action." *Common Ground* 9, no. 4 (Summer 1949: 27–38.

Gamble, Leo M. (Mrs.). "The Mexican, An Educational Asset or Educational Liability." *Los Angeles Educational Research Bulletin* 10, no. 4 (December 1925): 9–12.

Garcia, Mario. "Americanization and the Mexican Immigrant, 1880–1930." *Journal of Ethnic Studies* 6, no. 2 (1978): 19–34.

Garth, Thomas R. "A Comparison of the Intelligence of Mexican and Mixed and Full Blood Indian Children." *Psychological Review* 30 (1923): 388–401.

———. "The Industrial Psychology of the Immigrant Mexican." *Industrial Psychology Monthly* 1 (March 1926): 183–87.

———. "The Intelligence of Mexican School Children." *School and Society* 27 (30 June 1928): 791–94.

———. "The Problem of Racial Psychology." *Journal of Abnormal and Social Psychology* 17 (1922–23): 215–19.

Garth, Thomas R. and E. Candor. "Musical Talent of Mexicans." *American Journal of Psychology* 49 (1937): 298–301.

Garth, Thomas R., Thomas Elson, and Margaret Morton. "The Administration of Non-Language Intelligence Tests to Mexicans." *Journal of Abnormal and Social Psychology* 31 (1936–37): 53–58.

Garth, Thomas R., Walter M. Holcomb, and Irma Gesche. "Mental Fatigue of Mexican School Children." *Journal of Applied Psychology* 16, no. 6 (1932): 675–80.

Garth, Thomas R. and H. D. Johnson. "The Intelligence and Achievement of Mexican Children in the United States." *Journal of Abnormal and Social Psychology* 29 (1934): 222–39.

Gibson, Mary S. "Schools for the Whole Family." *Survey Graphic* 56 (June 1926): 301.

Glicksberg, Charles L. "Intercultural Education: Utopia or Reality." *Common Ground* 6, no. 4 (1946): 61–68.

Gonzalez, Gilbert. "Racial Intelligence and Mexican Children." *Explorations in Ethnic Studies* 5 (July 1982):

———. "Racism, Education and the Mexican Community in Los Angeles, 1920–1930." *Societas* 4 (Autumn 1974): 287–301.

Grant, Jettye Fern. "Educational Achievement and Needs of Migratory Children in California." *California Journal of Elementary Education* 12 (November 1943): 22–30.

Hamill, Mary Henson. "Teaching the Foreign Beginner." *Texas Outlook* 21 (June 1937): 38–39.

Hanson, Rita M. "Educating the Children of Seasonally Migrant Agricultural Workers in the San Joaquin Valley." *California Journal of Elementary Education* 18 (May 1950): 244–51.

Haught, B. F. "The Language Difficulty of Spanish American Children." *Journal of Applied Psychology* 15 (February 1931): 92–95.

Heffernan, Helen. "Inter-Cultural Education in the War Effort." *California Journal of Elementary Education* 11, no. 1 (August 1942): 13–21.

———. "Migrant Children in California Schools." *California Journal of Elementary Education* 30 (May 1962): 228–36.

Hill, Lillian B. "A Study of Migratory Schools in California." *Western Journal of Education* 37 (January 1931): 9, 11.

Hines, Harlan C. "What Los Angeles is Doing with the Results of Testing." *Journal of Educational Research*, 6, no. 1 (January 1922): 45–57.

Hodgkin, George. "Making the Labor Camp Pay." *California Citrograph* (August 1921): 354.

Hoijer, Harry (Dr.). "Racial and Cultural Differences." *California Elementary School Principals' Association Yearbook,* 17 (1945): 36–40.

Humphrey, Norman D. "The Education and Language of Detroit Mexicans." *Journal of Educational Sociology* 17, no. 9 (May 1944): 534–42.

Hunter, W. S., and N. E. Sommermier. "The Relation of the Degree of Indian Blood to the Scores on the Otis Intelligence Test." *Journal of Comparative Psychology* 2 (1922): 257–77.

Jeidy, Pauline. "First Generation Mexican-American Children in Ventura County." *Journal of Elementary Education* 15, nos. 3–4 (February-May 1947): 200–208.

Johnson, H. M., and J. Patterson. "Informal Textbook Method for Mexican Children." *Sierra Educational News* 32 (September 1937): 12.

Johnson, Loaz W. "A Comparison of the Vocabularies of Anglo-American and Spanish-American High-School Pupils." *Journal of Educational Psychology* 29, no. 2 (February 1938): 135–144.

Johnston, Edgar G. "The Education of Children of Spanish-Speaking Migrants in Michigan." *The Papers of the Michigan Academy of Science, Arts, and Letters* 32 (1946): 509–20.

Jones, Harold J. "All-Mexican School." *Sierra Educational News* 36 (1940): 17.

Jones, Robert C. "Mexican American Youth." *Sociology and Social Research* 32, no. 4 (March-April 1948): 793–97.

———. "Mexican Youth in the United States." *Texas Outlook* 29, no. 8 (August 1945): 11–13.

"The Junior Schools Organization and Administration." *San Antonio Public Schools Bulletin* 1, no. 1 (February 1924): 53–68.

KeFauver, Grayson N. "Education an Important Factor in Achieving and Enduring Peace." *The School Review* 52 (January 1944): 16–25.

Kelley, Victor H. "The Reading Abilities of Spanish and English Speaking Public School Pupils." *Journal of Educational Research* 29 (November 1935): 209–11.

Kluckhohn, Florence Rockwood. "Cultural Factors in Social Work Practice and Education [Mexican Culture as an Example of Diversity in Cultural Orientations]." *Social Science Review* 25, no. 1 (March 1951): 38–45.

Kress, D. M. "Spanish-Speaking School Child in Texas." *The Texas Outlook* 18, no. 24 (December 1934): 24.

Kuhns, L. "Music With Mexican Children, The Basis of an All School Activity." *Arizona Teacher Parent,* 27 (April 1939): 237–39.

Lamb, E. "Racial Differences in Bi-Manual Dexterity of Latin and American Children." *Child Development* 1 (1930): 201–31.

Locke, Alain (Dr.). "The Minority Side of Intercultural Education." *California Elementary School Principals' Association Yearbook* 17 (1945): 60–64.

Longmore, T. Wilson, and Homer L. Hitt. "A Demographic Analysis of First and Second Generation Mexican Population." *Southwestern Social Science Quarterly* 24 (September 1943): 138–49.

Mangold, G. B., and Lillian B. Hill. "Migratory Child Workers in California and Elsewhere." *Monthly Labor Review* 29 (September 1929): 557–58.

Manuel, Herschel T. "Comparison of Spanish-Speaking and English-Speaking Children in Reading and Arithmetic." *Journal of Applied Psychology* 19 (April 1935): 189–202.

———. "The Mexican Child in Texas." *Southwest Review* 17, no. 3 (Spring 1932): 290–302

———. "The Mexican Population of Texas." *Southwestern Social Science Quarterly* 15 (June 1934): 29–51.

———. "Spanish Speaking Child." *Texas Outlook* 14 (January 1930): 21, 47.

Martinez, P. G. "Teaching English to Spanish-Speaking Americans." *New Mexico School Review* 13 (September 1933): 22–23.

Martingale, G. "Teaching English to Mexican Boys." *Elementary English* 6 (December 1929): 276–78.

McAnulty, Ellen Alice. "A Comparison of the Responses of American and Mexican Sub-Normals on the Stanford Binet Examination." *Los Angeles Educational Research Bulletin* 11, no. 3 (November 1931): 40–42.

McGorray, W. E. "Needs of a Mexican Community." *California Journal of Secondary Education* 18, no. 6 (October 1943): 349–50.

McKenna, Alice Osborne. "Americanizing the Foreign Home." *Los Angeles School Journal* 9, no. 4 (28 September 1925): 13–14.

McRae, Edna, and W. F. Cobb. "Education of Migrant Children in Ventura County." *Western Journal of Education* 35, no. 12 (December 1929): 8–9.

McWilliams, Carey. "America's Disadvantaged Minorities: Mexican Americans." *Journal of Negro Education* 20, no. 3 (Summer 1951): 301–9.

———. "California and the Wetback." *Common Ground* 9, no. 4 (Summer 1949): 15–20.

———. "Los Angeles: An Emerging Pattern." *Common Ground* 9, no. 3 (Spring 1949): 3–10.

———. "Mexicans to Michigan." *Common Ground,* 2, no. 1 (Autumn 1941): 5–18.

———. "Spectrum of Segregation." *Survey Graphic* (January 1947): 22–25, 106–7.

Meriam, Junius L. "An Activity Curriculum in a School of Mexican Children." *Journal of Experimental Education* 1 (June 1933): 304–8.

"Mexicans in Los Angeles." *The Survey* 44 (15 September 1920): 715–16.

Milor, J. H. "Problems of a Junior High for Mexicans." *California Journal of Secondary Education* (December 1941): 482–84.

Mitchell, A. J. "The Effect of Bilingualism on the Measurement of Intelligence." *Elementary School Journal* 38 (September-June 1937–38): 29–37.

Morril, D. B. "The Spanish Language Problem." *New Mexico Journal of Education* 14 (May 1918): 6–7.

———. "Teaching the Spanish American Child." *New Mexico Journal of Education* 13 (April 1917): 8, 10–11.

Murphy, Laura F. "Experiment in Americanization." *Texas Outlook* 23, no. 11 (November 1939): 23–24.

Neal, Elma A. "The Teaching of English to Foreign Children." *College of Education Record* (University of Washington) 2 (January 1936): 53–57.

Neff, Walter S. "Socio-Economic Status and Intelligence." *Psychological Bulletin* 35 (December 1938): 727–57.

Netzer, Helen E. "Teaching Mexican Children in the First Grade." *Modern Language Forum* 25 (January 1941): 322–25.

Newcomb, W. Fred. "Caring for Children of Seasonal Workers in Ventura County Schools." *California Journal of Elementary Education* 6 (August 1937): 54–59.

Palomares, Uvaldo Hill, and Laverne C. Johnson. "Evaluation of Mexican American Pupils for Educable Mentally Retarded Classes." *California Education* 3, no. 8 (April 1966): 27–29.

Paschal, F. C, and C. R. Sullivan. "Racial Differences in the Mental and Physical Development of Mexican Children." *Comparative Psychology Monographs* 314 (1925): 1–76.

Patterson, John C. "Our Schools Promote Inter-Americanism." *Journal of Education* 127 (February 1944): 43–45.

Patterson, I., and E. M. Johnson. "Informal Methods vs. Textbook Method for Mexican Children." *Sierra Educational News,* 33 (September 1937): 12.

Phillips, H. "The School Follows the Child." *The Survey,* 66, no. 2 (September 1931): 493, 525.

Phillips, Lester H. "Segregation of Spanish-Speaking Children in the Public Schools." *Phylon* 10 (1949): 407–13.

Pinter, Rudolf. "The Influence of Language Background on Intelligence Tests." *Journal of Social Psychology* 3 (May 1932): 235–40.

Potter, Gladys L. "Adapting Curriculum to the Needs of Foreign Language Groups." *California Journal of Elementary Education* 6 (November 1937): 105–14.

"The Public Schools of San Antonio." *San Antonio Public Schools Bulletin* 2, no. 1 (1924): 69–73.

Rangel, Jorge C, and Carlos M. Alcala. "Project Report: De Jure Segregation of Chicanos in Texas Schools." *Harvard Civil Rights-Civil Liberties Law Review* 7 (March 1972): 307–91.

Richardson, Ethel. "Doing the Things that Couldn't Be Done." *Survey Graphic* 56 (June 1926): 297–99, 333–36.

Rockefeller, Nelson A. "Education Is Removing Barriers." *Journal of Education* 127 (February 1944): 49–50.

Roden, Fuller. "Occupation of the Mexican Born Population of Texas, New Mexico, and Arizona." *American Statistical Association Journal* 23 (March 1928): 64–67.

Rogde, Margaret. "Learning to Speak English in First Grade." *Texas Outlook* 22, no. 9 (September 1938): 40–41.

Ross, J. C. "Industrial Education for Spanish Speaking People." *New Mexico Journal of Education* 7 (February 1911): 19–21.

Russell, Daniel. "Problems of Mexican Children in the Southwest." *Journal of Educational Sociology* 17, no. 4 (December 1943): 216–22.

Russell, Edward Lee, and Thomas Frederic Humiston. "Mental Ability in Children of White and Mexican Parentage." *California Journal of Elementary Education* 2, no. 4 (May 1934): 239–42.

Salinas, Guadalupe. "Mexican Americans and the Desegregation of Schools in the Southwest: A Supplement." *El Grito* 4, no. 4 (Summer 1971): 59–69.

Sanchez, George I. "Bilingualism and Mental Measures." *Journal of Applied Psychology* 18 (December 1934): 765–72.

———. "Group Differences and Spanish-Speaking Children: A Critical Review." *Journal of Applied Psychology,* 16 (October 1932): 549–58.

———. "The Implications of a Basal Vocabulary to the Measurement of the Abilities of Bilingual Children." *Journal of Social Psychology* 5 (August 1934): 395–402.

———. "Spanish Speaking People in the Southwest—A Brief Historical Review." *California Journal of Elementary Education* 22 (November 1953): 106–11.

Seeling, Martha (Dr.). "Segregation in Our Public Schools." *California Elementary School Principals' Association Yearbook,* 17 (1945): 69–71.

Senter, Donovan, and Florence Hawley. "The Grammar School as the Basic Acculturating Influence for Native New Mexicans." *Social Forces* 24, no. 4 (May 1946): 398–407.

Shafer, Harry M. "Americanization in the Los Angeles Schools." *Los Angeles School Journal* 7, no. 34 (17 May 1924): 31–33.

―――. "Tendencies in Immigrant Education." *Los Angeles School Journal* 9, no. 8 (5 October 1925): 9–10.

Sheldon, W. H. "The Intelligence of Mexican Children." *School and Society* 19 (February 1924): 139–42.

Sisk, William O. "The Mexican in Texas Schools." *The Texas Outlook* 14 (December 1930): 10–12, 61.

Stanley, Grace. "Special Schools for Mexicans." *The Survey* 44 (15 September 1920): 714–15.

Steuber, Josephine. "Racial Differences in Reading Achievement." *Texas Outlook* 24 (January 1940): 32.

Strickland, V. E., and G. I. Sanchez. "Spanish Name Spells Discrimination." *The Nation's Schools* 41 (January 1948): 22–24.

Sturges, Vera L. "The Progress of Adjustment in Mexican/U.S. Life." *National Conference on Social Welfare Proceedings* (1939): 481–86.

―――. "Home Standards Among Our Mexican Residents." *Los Angeles School Journal* 9, no. 4 (28 September 1925): 15–16.

Taylor, J. T. "The Americanization of Harlingen's Mexican School Population." *Texas Outlook* 18 (September 1934): 37–8.

Taylor, Paul S. ". . . An End to the Beginnings. . . ." *California Elementary School Principals' Association Yearbook* 17 (1945): 46–50.

―――. "Migratory Agricultural Workers on the Pacific Coast." *American Sociological Review* 3, no. 2 (April 1938): 225–32.

Teel, Dwight. "Preventing Prejudice Against Spanish-Speaking Children." *Educational Leadership* 12, no. 2 (November 1954): 94–98.

Tetreau, E. D. "Social Aspects of Arizona's Farm Labor Problem." *Sociology and Social Research* 26, no. 6 (July-August 1940): 550–57.

Tipton, Ellis M. "The San Dimas Intercultural Program." *California Elementary School Principals' Association Yearbook* 17 (1945): 93–99.

Trillingham, C. C, and Marie M. Hughes. "Good-Neighbor Policy for Los Angeles County." *California Journal of Secondary Education* 18, no. 6 (October 1943): 342–46.

Tuck, Ruth. "Sprinkling the Grass Roots." *Common Ground* 7 (Spring 1947): 80–83.

———. "Mexican Americans: A Contributory Culture." *California Elementary School Principals' Association Yearbook* 17 (1945): 106–9.

Tupper, C. R. "The Use of Intelligence Tests in the Schools of a Small City." In *Intelligence Tests and School Reorganization,* edited by Lewis Terman, 92–111. Yonkers-on-the-Hudson, N.Y.: World Book Co., 1922.

Uribe, Oscar, Jr. "The Impact of 25 Years of School Desegregation on Hispanic Students." *Agenda: A Journal of Hispanic Issues* 4, no. 5 (September–October 1980): 18–19, 30.

Walker, Helen. "Mexican Immigrants as Laborers." *Sociology and Social Research* 13 (September 1928): 55–62.

Walker, Helen W. "Mexican Immigrants and American Citizenship." *Sociology and Social Research* 13, no. 1 (September–October 1928): 59.

Waxman, Frances Sheafer. "How Mexican Children Learn to Draw." *The School Arts Magazine* 30 (June 1931): 649–53.

Wilder, L. A. (Mrs.). "Problems in the Teaching of Mexican Children." *Texas Outlook* 20 (August 1936): 9–10.

Williams, J. Harold. "Educational Retardation of Children of Migratory Families." *Elementary School Journal,* 30 (October 1929): 88–89.

Wollenberg, Charles. "Mendez vs. Westminster: Race, Nationality and Segregation in California Schools." *California Historical Quarterly* 53, no. 4 (1974): 317–22.

Wooten, Flaud C. (Dr.). "Cultural Pluralism—A Challenge to Permanent Peace." *California Elementary School Principals' Association Yearbook* 17 (1945): 17–18.

Works, G. A. "The Non-English Speaking Children and the Public Schools." *Texas Educational Survey Commission* 8 (1925): 207–26.

Wright, C. E., and H. T. Manuel. "The Language Difficulty of Mexican Children." *Journal of Genetic Psychology* 38 (1929): 458–66.

INDEX